MASONIC RITES
AND WRONGS

MASONIC RITES AND WRONGS

AN EXAMINATION OF FREEMASONRY

Steven Tsoukalas

PUBLISHING
P.O. BOX 817 • PHILLIPSBURG • NEW JERSEY 08865-0817

Scripture quotations are from the King James Version or the author's own translation.

Printed in the United States of America

Library of Congress Cataloging-in-Publication Data

Tsoukalas, Steven, 1956—
    Masonic rites and wrongs : an examination of Freemasonry / Steven Tsoukalas.
       p. cm.
    Includes bibliographical references.
    ISBN 0-87552-457-5 (pbk.)
    1. Freemasonry—Religious aspects—Christianity. I. Title.
HS495.T77 1995
366'.12—dc20   95-8219

IN LOVING MEMORY OF MY FATHER,

❧

Christos Tsoukalas

CONTENTS

PREFACE

In 1985, one and a half years after becoming a Christian, I heard on the radio something that alarmed my young Christian heart—Freemasonry stood in opposition to Christian doctrine. My father was a Christian and a Mason. Sitting in my kitchen, I listened intently as the radio show host explained that Freemasonry was a religion because it taught about God and the afterlife, and that it claimed that men may go to heaven apart from faith in Jesus Christ. Having just lost my wife to leukemia, and thankful to Christ for bringing us both to faith before her death, I was convinced that Jesus was the only way, the only truth, and the only life. So I was greatly concerned for my father.

After the program ended, I immediately called my dad, but he resisted everything the radio host had to say. I loved my father dearly, so the last thing I wanted was for him to be involved in something that might hinder his relationship with the Lord. I decided to research the subject on my own. After all, I needed to give my father *reasons* why he should not be a Mason. (Talk shows are wonderful but often give little documentation of views expressed.) So I developed a library of resources: Masonic encyclopedias, rituals, monitors (which contain portions of ritual, as well as ceremonies, rules, and regulations), and other texts. The more I read, the more convinced I became that Masonry was neither Christian nor compatible with Christianity as some Masons argue.

I have written this book in the hope that it will be useful both to Christians and to Masons. I have attempted to demonstrate to both groups that

Freemasonry is indeed a religion and, by its religious nature, is contrary to the claims of Christ and the theology of the Christian church. I hope that Masons and Masonic scholars will understand why Christianity is opposed to Freemasonry and be challenged to give a reasonable defense against the position argued here. I do not ask the Mason to agree blindly with the Christian position, but to consider the arguments presented. Too often critics of Freemasonry have been prone to make sweeping and unfounded statements. Masonic apologists are justified in rejecting such careless criticism based on poor research. One of the goals of this book is to model a sounder methodology for theological criticism of Freemasonry.

Freemasons may want to respond to this book. I not only welcome but encourage that. I only ask that such responses concern my exegesis (drawing out the intended meaning of a text) of ritual and the resulting conclusions. In responding, Masons should be aware that they also enter into the realm of interpretation of the biblical text, and that is no easy task. Exegeting any document involves numerous careful considerations. Cultural background, immediate and larger contexts, grammatical analysis, the reason the document was written, the overall theological themes of the Bible, etc., all may play a necessary part in the proper understanding of any biblical verse or passage.

Ignoring such considerations has produced inaccurate, misleading, and unjustified interpretations. For example, the phrase "God is love" is often thought to exclude the doctrine of eternal judgment from the Bible. Such a view, however, does not take into account the context in which we read that God is love. In 1 John 4:8, which was written to Christians, the statement "God is love" appears as a reason why Christians ought to love one another. As John proceeds to define this love, the justice of God comes to the forefront: God demonstrated His love by sending Christ to die for our sins. Thus, the way people escape God's wrath (Rom. 1:18) is through Christ's atonement on the cross. Moreover, the larger context of the Bible warns of the wrath of God (Rom. 1:18) and the reality of eternal damnation (Matt. 25:46).[1]

So, while I invite Freemasons to respond to my arguments, I would urge that that be done in a careful, logical way that focuses on whether my theological conclusions are based on sound exegesis of the biblical text, Old and New Testaments. In asking that, I am merely calling upon Masons to do what I have attempted to do in my criticism of Freemasonry.

In this book I will use the terms *Lodge* and *Masonic Lodge* in four ways: (1) an actual building called a "Lodge" or a "Masonic Lodge"; (2) the worldwide institution known as "the Lodge" or "the Masonic Lodge"; (3) a ritual performance or any other activity inside a Masonic Lodge, for example, "Masons who attend Lodge"; and (4) a group of Masons, for example, "the Lodge came and performed a funeral service."

An additional note on the methodology of this book may be helpful: The most authoritative Masonic sources one can draw from are Masonic rituals and monitors. These are produced by Freemasonry's highest authorities—the individual Grand Lodges for each state, province, or geographic area. Rituals tell us what goes on behind the closed doors of a Masonic Lodge and can be in code, thus keeping secret from non-Masons various spoken portions and ritualistic actions performed by participants. Monitors contain the symbolic teaching already found in the ritual and are not in code, but go beyond the ritual by adding various other ceremonies (dedication of a Lodge, burial services, etc.), Lodge rules, etc. My approach will be: (1) to cite various rituals and monitors from Grand Lodges, (2) to support the conclusions of Masonic scholars by these sources, so as to avoid the allegation that these are the opinions of particular Masonic scholars, (3) to draw similar conclusions, and (4) to show how they conflict with Christianity.

For the sake of the lay reader, I have tried to define any unfamiliar terms as they arise. I have also placed the more technical and scholarly data in the notes at the end of each chapter. Those with knowledge of the biblical languages may consult the notes for references to these. Hebrew and Greek terms have been transliterated according to the basic system of transliteration used in *The New American Standard Exhaustive Concordance of the Bible: Hebrew-Aramaic and Greek Dictionaries* (Nashville, Tenn.: Holman, 1981).

Anyone wishing to respond to this book, and anyone interested in contacting me for other concerns, may write to me at Sound Doctrine Ministries, P.O. Box 1962, Exeter, NH 03833.

My deepest appreciation extends to the following people, without whom this book would not have been published: my loving wife, Sandy, for her support, encouragement, and scholarly input; Barbara Lerch of Presbyterian and Reformed Publishing Company, for her continuous support and encouragement throughout the evaluation process; Thom Notaro and all at Presbyterian and Reformed, for their decision to publish this book; Bob Allen of Coral Ridge Ministries, and Larry Kunk of Ephesians 5:11, Inc., for their evaluations, comments, and kind words; my colleague, John Dennis, for his many theological insights throughout the years; my associate, Barbara Sander, for her help and friendship; and my mother, Olga, for her constant love throughout my life.

This book is the fruit of nine years of research—research born out of my love for my father and a desire to share with others the love and mercy of Christ. It is therefore with all praise and honor to Jesus Christ that I dedicate this book to the memory of my father, who, in case you are wondering, did renounce Masonry a few months before his death in 1989.

Notes

1. See, for example, the faulty interpretation of the phrase "God is Love" by John Robinson, a more recent Masonic apologist who, in his book *A Pilgrim's Path* (New York: M. Evans and Company, 1993), interprets the phrase as teaching "religious tolerance" (p. 175).

INTRODUCTION

"I believe that in all men's lives at certain periods, and in many men's lives at all periods between infancy and extreme old age, one of the most dominant elements is the desire to be inside the local Ring and the terror of being left outside."—C. S. Lewis, The Inner Ring

The Christian who endeavors to hold dialogue with Freemasons faces two possible roadblocks.

First, as is well known among Masonic writers, the average Mason is largely ignorant of Masonic teachings. That ignorance of basic teachings is coupled with a general apathy, as well as low attendance at Lodge meetings,[1] leading Masonic leaders to constantly exhort their brothers to further their knowledge of Freemasonry. The following statement from a leading authority on Freemasonry illustrates what an informed Christian faces when dialoguing with the average Mason:

> Receiving the degrees in the Craft [i.e., Freemasonry] makes one a member, but he does not become a Mason until he has learned the meaning of the degrees, the moral lessons taught in the degrees, and how to make them a part of his life. Engaging in the reading of Masonic books is designed to help make a member a Mason. . . . Most

1

Masons are surprised when they learn for the first time that there are Masonic books. This is probably due to the wording of the Obligation [promises made by Masons during ritual] which indicates there can be no Masonic books and also because rarely are new Masons told that there are good Masonic books available for them to read so they can learn more about Freemasonry.[2]

The fact is that the overwhelming majority of Masons hardly ever attend Lodge and are ignorant of the availability of Masonic books.

Why, then, have so many men been attracted to Freemasonry? If many Masons are largely ignorant of the teaching of the Lodge, what keeps them there? One of the dominant reasons concerns C. S. Lewis's observation quoted at the beginning of this chapter: all of us feel a need to belong, to join the "inner ring." Inner rings of all kinds and sizes exist. We seem as desperately to need them as to want them. Throughout our lives there are temptations to join with "the people in the know."

I can sympathize with men who see the Lodge as an inner ring they can belong to. And for the majority of Masons, theology is the last thing on their minds when they first consider becoming Masons. But sadly, theology is also the last thing on their minds once they are in the inner ring of Freemasonry.

A second possible roadblock to dialogue is that the Mason may or may not be a Christian. He may not claim any adherence to Christianity, since Masons are only required to profess belief in *a* Supreme Being; it is possible for Masons to be Muslims, Buddhists, Hindus,[3] Jews, Unitarians, or members of any other religion that affirms belief in a Supreme Being. A Mason may claim to be a Christian but not actually prove to be one when asked to affirm essential Christian doctrines.[4] Or he may indeed be a Christian, but because of the element of surprise in the ritual[5] and the possibility that he has not attended Lodge meetings since receiving his degrees, he may remain in the dark with regard to the spiritual and theological nature of the rituals. In the first and second cases I suggest explaining to the Mason the gospel of Christ—such people are not likely to benefit from a comparison of Masonic teachings with the Bible.[6] If a Mason falls into the third category, he should have no quarrel with a concerned Christian brother or sister wanting to discuss the teachings of the Lodge.[7]

The Mason also may face roadblocks in his dialogue with Christians. The Christian may have gathered information from poorly researched sources and drawn unsubstantiated conclusions. An example widely known by Masons is the statement allegedly made by Masonic scholar Albert Pike that Lucifer is the god of Freemasonry. This spurious statement actually came from a Masonic dissenter named Leo Taxil.[8] Also, the Christian may not be educated in the teachings of Freemasonry. If the Mason is similarly uninformed of the basics of the Craft, that can lead to fruitless argumentation that leaves both parties frustrated.

For genuine and fruitful dialogue to occur, both Masons and Christians must strive to educate themselves in the doctrines of Christianity *and* Freemasonry. Freemasons should do so because of the ever-increasing debate between Masonic Lodges and Christian denominations (such as in the Southern Baptist Convention in June 1993). And Christians should do so because they will most likely be confronted with the issue somewhere along the road, whether by a fellow church member, a pastor, a family member, or a friend who is a Mason.

What Is Freemasonry?

How one views Freemasonry obviously determines how one defines the Craft. Most Masons see it as a fraternal organization dedicated to furthering the good of society. For example, the Massachusetts Grand Lodge describes Freemasonry in part as a "society for the joint effort of its members towards individual self-improvement, a fraternity for learning and cultivating the art of living and the building of character."[9] Many Masonic publications claim that Freemasonry is dedicated to the principles of brotherly love, relief, and truth. "Its ethical principles can be accepted by all good men, and tolerance toward all mankind is embraced by the entire membership."[10] These are some reasons why Masons the world over call Freemasonry a "Way of Life." Perhaps the most popular definition is taken from the *English Lectures,* which states that "Freemasonry is a peculiar system of morality veiled in allegory and illustrated by symbols."[11]

Theories of Origin

Though the origin of the term *Freemason* is not exactly known, there have been attempts to locate the origin of Freemasonry. One of the most widely accepted theories is that Freemasonry stems from the time when medieval stonemasons, who cut stones for walls, edifices, etc. (also known as "operative masons," in contrast to the "Speculative Masons" of Freemasonry—see below) accepted into their guilds men who were not operative masons. Another theory is propagated by some esoteric Masonic scholars in their attempt to trace Masonry's origin to the ancient Mystery Religions of Egypt, Rome, and Greece. Yet another theory, at least as popular as the first, fixes the origin at the building of King Solomon's Temple, the key Masonic figure at that time being Hiram Abif, who is mentioned in the Old Testament.

Whatever theory one might choose, it would be just that—theory. Since there is no hard evidence for any of these explanations, it is a "pay your nickel and take your choice" situation. Perhaps the most interesting of the theories of origin was put forth by John Robinson in his book *Born in Blood.* Here Robinson asserts that Freemasonry may have stemmed from the persecution of the crusading order of the Knights Templar by Pope Clement V. Excommunicated by papal decree in the early part of the fourteenth century, the Templars who escaped arrest fled and went underground. This may explain many of the secret recognition signs.[12]

Types of Masons

Regarding what Freemasonry *is,* Masonic scholar Henry Wilson Coil cautions,

> Nobody knows what Freemasonry is. Let those who deem this statement extravagant or absurd attempt, for themselves, to answer the question, not by mere aphorism or pithy phrase, but with considerable precision and completeness, and they will, at once, find themselves in difficulty and in conflict with others pretending to be expert on the subject. The more there are who attempt to explain what Freemasonry comprises or teaches or stands for, the more their disagreements seem to multiply and clash.[13]

Coil's observation implies that there are different "types" of Masons. The first and most popular type is the one already described: one who is content to obtain the degrees, not attend Lodge, pay his dues, and be called a Mason. Though this Mason has been told that Freemasonry is a "Way of Life," he has not given much thought to the implications of this phrase, but will use it at certain times in casual conversation to deflect the argument that it is a religion. He denies that Masonry is a religion, though, again, without giving much thought to the issues. He sees Masonry as enhancing his particular religion and not conflicting with it. Masons who do not attend religious services are also in this group.

The second type, though far less in number, is the Mason who sees the Craft as a religion but still practices his own religion, believing that Masonry adds greater depth to his religious convictions. Some Masonic scholars fit into this group.

Third is the Mason who views the Craft as his religion, and all the religion he will ever need. There is no religion for him outside of the Lodge. Here we may also find Masonic scholars.

A fourth type is the Mason who does not see the Lodge as a religion and attends meetings regularly. It is in this group that we are most likely to find clergy, the Grand Master (the chief officer of a Grand Lodge in a jurisdiction or state) and Past Grand Masters (former Grand Masters), the Worshipful Master (the chief officer of a Masonic Lodge), and other Lodge officers. They may or may not have a religion outside the Lodge.

A Way of Life

Despite Coil's caution, and the different types of Masons, it is still safe to say that most in the Craft view it as a way of life. This way of life is brought about by the great lessons of the first three degrees of Masonry, which are intended to impress upon the candidate's mind a system of morality, veiled in allegory and illustrated by symbols.[14]

Morality may be defined as "the doctrine of moral duties; morals; ethics; the practice of the moral duties; virtue; moral character or quality; the quality of an action, as estimated by a standard of right and wrong."[15] *Mackey's Encyclopedia* states that "in the American system it [morality] is one of the three precious jewels of a Master Mason."[16] Coil writes that "morality runs like a silver thread through the dogma of Freemasonry. . . . No tenet of Freemasonry has been more consistently maintained and free from question."[17]

Allegory conveys a message by means of a story that on the surface seems to have another meaning. It comes from the Greek word *allegoria,* meaning "the description of one thing under the image of another."[18] A classic case of allegory in Freemasonry is the legend of the third degree, called the legend of Hiram Abif. *Mackey's Encyclopedia* not only admits this, but it goes on to say that the third degree is "evidently to be interpreted as teaching a restoration to life."[19] In fact, "All the legends of Freemasonry are more or less allegorical."[20]

Symbols are things that put forth meaning and represent (and take part in) what is to be learned and represented by the symbols. Coil is correct in distinguishing symbols from allegory, noting that the two are sometimes confused.

An allegory explains itself to the reader who has the necessary perspective penetrating sight, and it needs no previous explanation or agreement about its significance. But that is not true of a symbol, which has no secondary meaning at all, except by usage, association, or agreement attaching it to some other thing, event, or idea. Thus, light is said to symbolize learning, truth, instruction, or knowledge.[21]

Sometimes Masons try to avoid discussing the religious character of Masonic symbols by stating that "they are symbolic." That, however, should not satisfy the Mason or the person pressing the issues. Saying that something is symbolic does not reduce its significance. For example, the American flag symbolizes life, liberty, and the pursuit of happiness, as well as the courage of those who gave their lives that we might enjoy these freedoms. One could never justifiably dismiss the meaning of this symbol by stating that it is only symbolic. The meaning is real and is to be conveyed, comprehended, and integrated into one's life. So it is with all worthwhile symbols. The Grand Lodge of Alberta, Canada, cautions,

> When, therefore, you encounter a Masonic symbol, such as the Square, the Compasses, the letter G, etc., you are not to suppose that it is a hazy, vague thing that may mean anything or nothing and that you can be indifferent to it; on the contrary, its meaning is perfectly clear and definite, and that meaning is quite as binding on you as a Mason as if it had been expressed in a written statement.[22]

Masonic symbolism, especially within the first three degrees, utilizes the actual working tools of operative masons (stone cutters and builders) and gives to them meanings that inculcate moral lessons.[23] For this reason Freemasonry is called at times "Speculative Masonry" or "Symbolic Masonry," meaning the science of consecrating the tools of the trade of operative masonry to a system of religious ethics. Thus we find in Masonic rituals the Common Gavel, Plumb Line, Square, and Level. Even the first three degrees of Freemasonry are named after the different levels of expertise and accomplishments of operative masonry—Entered Apprentice, Fellow Craft (Journeyman), and Master Mason.

Do the rituals of Freemasonry teach a system of morality to its adherents that is veiled in allegory and illustrated by symbols? Let us examine a few of the definitions given for the "working tools" of Freemasonry.

> The Plumb is an instrument made use of by operative Masons to try perpendiculars; the Square, to square their work; and the Level, to prove horizontals; but we, as Free and Accepted Masons, are taught to make use of them for more noble and glorious purposes. The Plumb

admonishes us to walk uprightly in our several stations before God and Man, squaring our actions by the Square of virtue, ever remembering that we are travelling upon the Level of time "to that undiscovered country, from whose bourne no traveller returns."[24]

In some European degrees the wording is different but the gist is similar.

The Sq[uare] teaches us to regulate our lives and actions according to the Masonic line and rule. . . . The L[evel] demonstrates that we are all sprung from the same stock, partakers of the same nature and sharers in the same hope. . . . The infallible P[lumb] R[ule], which, like Jacob's ladder, connects heaven and earth, is the criterion of rectitude and truth. It teaches us to walk justly and uprightly before God and man, neither turning to the right nor left from the paths of virtue.[25]

Clearly, Masons are exhorted to a morality that is illustrated by the symbols of the Plumb, Square, and Level, and couched in the allegorical teaching of Jacob's Ladder.

As stated earlier, *Mackey's Encyclopedia* mentions the allegorical lesson of the third (Master Mason) degree. Here the candidate is blindfolded and is led around the Lodge room, playing the Masonic legendary hero Hiram Abif. The allegory is seen in the story line of Hiram, who is met by three ruffians who ask him (the candidate) to give them the secrets of a Master Mason. The candidate (or conductor of the candidate) answers in the negative and consequently is killed (symbolically). The lesson of the third degree, in part, is that the candidate, just as the great Grand Master Hiram, can overcome the great trials of life that lie ahead if he is true to the exhortations of the degree and if he puts into practice the lessons learned in the degree. Moral lessons illustrated by the symbolism of the Skirret, the Pencil and Compasses[26] or the Trowel, the Three Steps, the Pot of Incense, the Scythe, and the All-Seeing Eye[27] are featured in the third degree. There can be no doubt then that ritual in Freemasonry is the foundation for the statement that the Craft is a system of morality, veiled in allegory and illustrated by symbols.

Early Developments in Freemasonry

Though debate still rages as to the historical roots of Freemasonry, all Masonic scholars agree that the Craft began in 1717 when the Grand Lodge of

London was formed. But to say that modern Freemasonry (as we know it today) began in England in 1717 is not precise. For example, the third degree (Master Mason) was not even part of Masonry until several years later, and, according to John Robinson, the symbolism of the Square and the Compass surfaced a generation later.[28] There is no doubt that degrees were added *after* 1717. The popular York and Scottish Rites came into existence several decades later, and both of these, like Blue Lodge Freemasonry,[29] developed over many years.[30]

It is also difficult to speak generally of Freemasonry because it includes several factions that arose from disagreements. The Grand Lodge of England and the Grand Orient of France separated in 1773.[31] Today, French Freemasonry does not require its initiates to profess belief in Deity. It is atheistic and is not recognized by numerous Grand Lodges.[32]

Finally, there is the opinion that when Freemasonry began in London in 1717, it was viewed as Christian and that until the second half of the nineteenth century the degrees and their symbolism were interpreted in a Christian way.[33]

Masonic Degrees

The vast majority of Masons throughout the world are Blue Lodge (or Symbolic Lodge) Masons only. The Blue Lodge confers the first three (and most important, as they are foundational) degrees of Entered Apprentice, Fellow Craft, and Master Mason. Every Mason must begin with Blue Lodge and either remain or move on to other Rites[34] (as mentioned earlier, the majority do not). Two of the most popular of Rites are the York and the Scottish. The York Rite consists of thirteen degrees, *including* the three degrees of Blue Lodge.[35]

4. Mark Master
5. Past Master
6. Most Excellent Master
7. Royal Arch
8. Royal Master
9. Select Master
10. Super Excellent Master
11. Order of Red Cross
12. Order of Malta
13. Order of the Temple

The Scottish Rite contains thirty-three degrees, again including those of Blue Lodge.[36]

4. Secret Master
5. Perfect Master
6. Intimate Master
7. Provost and Judge
8. Intendent of the Building
9. Elu of the Nine
10. Elu of the Fifteen
11. Elu of the Twelve or Prince Ameth
12. Master Architect
13. Royal Arch of Solomon
14. Perfect Elu or Grand Elect, Perfect and Sublime Mason
15. Knight of the East or Sword
16. Prince of Jerusalem
17. Knight of the East and West
18. Knight Rose Croix
19. Grand Pontiff
20. Grand Master of all Symbolic Lodges
21. Noachite or Prussian Knight
22. Knight of the Royal Axe or Prince Libanus
23. Chief of the Tabernacle
24. Prince of the Tabernacle
25. Knight of the Brazen Serpent
26. Prince of Mercy or Scottish Trinitarian
27. Knight Commander of the Temple
28. Knight of the Sun or Prince Adept
29. Grand Scottish Knight of St. Andrew
30. Knight Kadosh
31. Grand Inspector Inquisitor Commander
32. Sublime Prince of the Royal Secret
33. Sovereign Grand Inspector General

In addition to these two Rites, there are a great many bodies (organizations) either related to or connected in some way to Freemasonry. Sometimes membership in these organizations is limited to Master Masons or spouses and relatives of Master Masons. Groups such as the Tall Cedars of Lebanon, the Square and Compass Clubs, the Order of the Amaranth, the Daughters of Osiris, the Daughters of the Nile, the Order of DeMolay (boys), the Order of the Rainbow or Rainbow Girls, Job's Daughters, the Order of the Eastern Star, and the Ancient Arabic Order Nobles of the Mystic Shrine (called Shriners, limited to full York and Scottish Rite Masons) are just a few of the scores of groups that are allied with Freemasonry.[37]

Summary

I have presented here a basic definition of Freemasonry, mentioned the various theories of origin, and listed the many possible degrees. What ultimately concerns us, however, is Freemasonry today, and what it is about Freemasonry that causes Christians and some Christian denominations to view the Craft not only as a fraternal organization, but as a religion opposed to the foundational teachings of Christianity.[38] In the next chapter I will demonstrate why the Craft is a religion.

Notes

1. See Robert C. Singer, "How Do Non-Masons and Masons View Freemasonry?" *The Scottish Rite Journal* (Washington, D.C.: The Supreme Council, 33rd, Ancient and Accepted Scottish Rite of Freemasonry of the Southern Jurisdiction, USA, November 1990): 50–55. Singer reports on the Masonic Renewal Task Force's project of a survey of one thousand Masons from 21 Grand Lodges in the United States. He notes that "18% attended nearly every Blue Lodge meeting, and another 25% attended three or four times a year." Surprisingly, Singer admits that "this would seem to be in conflict with actual experience, and may indicate a lack of pride in the member's not supporting the Fraternity. . . . It is more likely that 10% is active, 90% inactive." Singer observes, and I concur from actual experience, that "it would appear that most Masons are content to take their degrees, identify themselves as a Mason, not attend Lodge, but continue to pay dues." It seems logical to conclude that these inactive Masons do little or no reading about the Craft. Moreover, we must not assume that all the remaining "active" Masons engage in deep study.

   In the *Review of Religious Research,* 22, no. 2 (December 1980): 125–36, Professor John Wilson (Department of Sociology at Duke University) wrote an article entitled "Voluntary Associations and Civil Religion: The Case of Freemasonry." Professor Wilson reported on a survey of Masons from a Midwestern state: "The data report a largely inactive membership (81.4%) which, at the same time, is staunchly loyal to the principles of Freemasonry and convinced of its value as a means of moral education and training for citizenship." Wilson further states that "added to these signs of apathy is a rather extensive ignorance about some of the more basic teachings of the order."

2. Alphonse Cerza, *A Masonic Reader's Guide* (Missouri: Missouri Lodge of Research, 1980), ix.

3. For Hindus and Buddhists it is possible during Lodge questioning to affirm belief in a Supreme Being while still technically remaining polytheistic or pantheistic, since all they may be asked is, "Do you believe in the existence of a Supreme Being?" This is also true of the Mormons, who are polytheists.

4. The most frequent denial concerns Jesus Christ's being the only way for a reconciling relationship with the Father (see John 14:6).

5. In the Blue Lodge (or Symbolic Lodge), for example, which confers the first three degrees, the candidate is blindfolded throughout portions and not told beforehand what is to transpire.

6. In countries where the prevailing religion is Christianity, the Bible is on the altar of the Lodge. Since the Bible is on the altar it clearly carries some weight of authority. The Christian may want to use this authoritative revelation to contrast the teachings of the Bible with Masonic teachings.

7. Note, however, that Masons in any of the above-described categories may be influenced by their Lodges' particular Charges or Landmarks, which are basically the principles of any particular Grand Lodge. Some Grand Lodges issue a Charge concerning behavior in the presence of strangers who are not Masons. For example, the *Standard Manual* for the Grand Lodge of A.F. & A.M. of Oregon (1991) states, "You shall be cautious in your words and carriage, that the most penetrating stranger shall not be able to discover or find out what is not proper to be intimated, and sometimes you shall divert a discourse, and manage it prudently for the honor of the Worshipful Fraternity" (p. 72).

8. For information, see *Coil's Masonic Encyclopedia* (New York: Macoy Publishing and Masonic Supply Co., 1961), 649, and *Mackey's Revised Encyclopedia of Freemasonry,* 3 vols. (Richmond: Macoy Publishing and Masonic Supply Co., 1946), 2:1013–17.

9. *Freemasonry: A Way of Life.* Published by the Most Worshipful Grand Lodge of Ancient Free and Accepted Masons of the Commonwealth of Massachusetts.

10. Ibid.

11. Taken from *Mackey's Revised Encyclopedia of Freemasonry,* 1:269.

12. See John Robinson, *Born in Blood* (New York: M. Evans & Co., 1989), and *Pilgrim's Path* (New York: M. Evans & Co., 1993), 113–19, for the different origin theories.

13. Henry W. Coil, *Conversations on Freemasonry* (Richmond: Macoy Publishing and Masonic Supply Co., n.d.), 3. For numerous definitions of Freemasonry, consult Robert Macoy's *A Dictionary of Freemasonry* (New York: Bell Publishing, 1989), 147–49.

14. After completing the first three degrees of Blue Lodge (or Symbolic Lodge—Blue Lodge Masonry concerns itself with the first three degrees of Freemasonry: Entered Apprentice, Fellow Craft, and Master Mason) Masonry, the Mason is free to proceed to complete degrees in the York and/or Scottish Rites. The

third degree (Master Mason) of Blue Lodge Masonry, however, is viewed as the "Pinnacle of Freemasonry." See Allen Roberts, *The Craft and Its Symbols* (Richmond: Macoy Publishing and Masonic Supply Co., 1974), 61. *Mackey's Encyclopedia,* 2:651–52, lists it as "the Sublime Degree." It is so mentioned in the ritual of the third degree of various Masonic Lodges (Massachusetts, Minnesota, New Brunswick, Oxford and Emulation Rituals of England, the Irish Workings of Craft Masonry, etc.). The reason this degree is the pinnacle, or the sublime degree, is no doubt because of the moral lessons contained in ritual, and because of the "dying and raising" of the candidate in an acted-out drama play. See chap. 3.

15. *Webster's Encyclopedic Dictionary* (Chicago: Consolidated Book Publishers, 1944), 469. For Freemasonry, the standard of right and wrong is the VSL (Volume of the Sacred Law), which can be the Bible, the Koran, various Hindu or Buddhist Scriptures, etc., since Freemasonry, as a worldwide Brotherhood, does not hold to the Bible as the only authoritative VSL.

16. 2:680.

17. Coil, *Encyclopedia,* 422.

18. *Webster's New Twentieth Century Dictionary: Unabridged,* 2d ed. (New York: The Publisher's Guild, 1965), 48–49.

19. 1:51.

20. Ibid.

21. Coil, *Encyclopedia,* 27.

22. *Lodge Plan for Masonic Education: Mentor's Guide* (The Grand Lodge of Alberta, Canada, A.F. & A.M., 1993), 38.

23. We shall see that there are also religious and very definite theological meanings given to the working tools.

24. *Official Cipher* (Boston: Grand Lodge of Masons in Massachusetts, 1978), 93. The same content can be found in rituals from Grand Lodges in New York, Minnesota, New Hampshire, and New Brunswick, as well as others.

25. *Emulation Ritual* ("As demonstrated at the Emulation Lodge of Improvement, London and with whose approval this ritual has been compiled and published"— London: Lewis Masonic, 1986), 252–53. The same content is seen in the Oxford Ritual, the Revised Ritual of Craft Freemasonry, the Irish Workings of Craft Masonry, and the Scottish Workings of Craft Masonry.

26. European rituals such as the *Emulation Ritual* use these working tools.

27. *Ancient Craft Masonry* (New York: Grand Lodge of Free and Accepted Masons of the State of New York), 234–40. See later chapters for the symbolic meanings of many of these working tools.

28. Robinson, *A Pilgrim's Path,* 114.

29. Or Symbolic Lodge Freemasonry (dealing with the first three degrees). No one knows the origin of the term "Blue" Lodge. Some have suggested that blue denotes the canopy of heaven, which is the symbolism of the "Covering of a Lodge" in ritual.

30. See Coil, *Conversations on Freemasonry,* 133–62.
31. Ibid., 25.
32. See Oliver D. Street, *Freemasonry in Foreign Lands,* 5 vols. (Richmond: Macoy Publishing and Masonic Supply Co., 1977), 1:123–40, for this information and a contrary opinion that the Grand Orient in France *should* be recognized by Masonic Lodges throughout the world.
33. See Robert A. Morey, *The Origins and Teachings of Freemasonry* (Southbridge, Mass.: Crowne Publishers, 1990), 17–26. Dr. Morey states, "The Christian interpretation of Freemasonry was the accepted norm until the latter half of the 19th century. All of the early writers were committed Christians and many of them were clergymen of conservative churches" (p. 17). I see that as possible but raise some observations: (1) In 1805 Thomas Smith Webb, listed by Morey as having given "a Christian view of the origin of the Lodge," wrote his famous *Freemason's Monitor* (printed for Henry Cushing and Thomas S. Webb, Providence, 1805). Many Lodges in various countries make use of the Webb form of Blue Lodge ritual (see Kent Henderson, *Masonic World Guide* [Richmond: Macoy Publishing and Masonic Supply Co., 1984]). It contains the symbolism of various "working tools" of Freemasonry that could be interpreted in a non-Christian way. An example is the Lambskin Apron (pp. 38–39), by which a Mason—whether he be (even at the time Webb wrote this) Unitarian, Muslim, Jew, Buddhist, Hindu, or Christian—is "reminded of that purity of life and conduct, which is essentially necessary to his gaining admission into the Celestial Lodge above, where the Supreme Architect of the Universe presides." (2) In 1723 Anderson's *Constitutions,* which contains *The Charges of a Free-Mason,* lists as the first charge that "in ancient Times Masons were charged in every Country to be of the Religion of that Country or Nation, whatever it was, yet 'tis now thought more expedient only to oblige them to that Religion in which all Men agree, leaving their particular Opinions to themselves, that is, to be good Men and true, or Men of Honour and Honesty, by whatever Denomination or Persuasion they may be distinguished; whereby Masonry becomes the Center of Union, and the Means of conciliating true Friendship among Persons that must have remained at a perpetual Distance." A charge such as this leaves the door wide open for non-Christians to be made Masons (the Charge does not condone atheism). On p. 21 of his book, Morey states, "As we commenced our research, we decided to read all the masonic literature in its chronological order beginning with Anderson's *Constitutions* written in 1723. This procedure made it crystal clear that Freemasonry was understood to be a Christian institution until the anti-masonic movement of 1826." However, Masonic scholar Lionel Vibert conveys at least the potential of some viewing the Craft as non-Christian: "Of the six Charges themselves the first caused trouble immediately on its appearance. It replaced the old invocation of the Trinity and whatever else there may have been of statements of religious and Christian belief in the practice of the lodges, by a vague statement that we are only to be obliged to

that religion in which all men agree" (Lionel Vibert, *Anderson's Constitutions of 1723*, in the *Little Masonic Library,* 5 vols. [Richmond: Macoy Publishing and Masonic Supply Co., 1977], 1:172). Other samples of early addresses made by Masons seem to coincide with what Vibert states. For example, *The Pocket Companion and History of Free-Masons,* published in 1764, contains "An Apology for the Free and Accepted Masons." On p. 268 we read, "The Free and Accepted Masons, so famous in our Times, are a Society of Men of all Ages, Conditions, Religions and Countries . . . united by the most indissoluble Ties of Brotherly Affection."

34. I use the term "Rite" to refer to certain Masonic bodies. This is the most popular and broadest use of the term. For a thorough discussion, and a caution against using the term in this manner, see Coil's *Conversations on Freemasonry,* 133–36.

35. The following list is in the order that one would generally find in America.

36. The following list is from the Southern Jurisdiction of the U.S.A. There is also a Northern Jurisdiction. Although the Northern Jurisdiction also confers thirty-three degrees, as Coil states, "the names are not identical" (Ibid., 138).

37. For a hefty though not exhaustive list of organizations affiliated or influenced by Freemasonry, see ibid., 31–33.

38. A few churches that have written statements regarding the incompatibility of Freemasonry with Christianity are the Russian Orthodox Church, the Church of Scotland, the Free Church of Scotland, the Orthodox Presbyterian Church, the Lutheran Church—Missouri Synod, the Church of England, the Baptist Unions of Scotland and Great Britain and Ireland, the British Methodist Church, the Eastern Orthodox Church, and the Reformed Presbyterian Church.

PART ONE

THE BLUE LODGE

CHAPTER 1

IS FREEMASONRY A RELIGION?

"The fact that so many clergymen of different denominations can be Masons and find no conflict in carrying on their duties is proof enough that Freemasonry is not a religion." —Alphonse Cerza, "Let There Be Light": A Study in Anti-Masonry

It is the proverbial sixty-four-thousand–dollar question: Is Freemasonry a religion or isn't it? Though a few Masons believe that Freemasonry is a religion, the overwhelming majority of Masons do not. This chapter demonstrates that Freemasonry is indeed a religion. To do so we must define *religion,* note the essential characteristics of a religion, and then, using Blue Lodge rituals from the United States, Canada, and Europe, show how Freemasonry meets these criteria for being a religion. Blue Lodge (or Symbolic Lodge) rituals will be cited because every Mason, whether he later proceeds to Scottish Rite or York Rite[1], must pass through Blue Lodge.[2] The first section, however, will feature the opinions of various Masons.[3]

What Do Masons Say?

Most Masons say that their Craft is not a religion but simply a fraternal order dedicated to performing good deeds of service and to making good men better. For example, the Grand Lodge of Massachusetts states,

Though religious in character, Masonry is not a religion, nor a substitute for one. It fosters belief in a Supreme Being—this being a prerequisite for membership. Freemasonry accepts good men who are found to be worthy, regardless of their religious convictions, and strives to make better men of them by emphasizing a firm belief in the Fatherhood of God, the Brotherhood of Man, and the immortality of the Soul.[4]

Jim Tresner, a Masonic apologist and a thirty-third–degree Mason with a Ph.D. in business communications, argues that it all depends on how you define *religion*.

No, not by the definitions most people use. Religion, as the term is commonly used, implies several things: a plan of salvation or path by which one reaches the afterlife; a theology which attempts to define the nature of God; and the description of ways or practices by which a man or woman may need to communicate with God. Masonry does none of those things. . . . **Have some Masonic writers said that Masonry is a religion?** Yes, and again, it's a matter of definition. If, as some writers have, you define religion as "man's urge to venerate the beautiful, serve the good and see God in everything," you can say that Masonry subscribes to a religion. But that, surely, is not in conflict with Christianity or any other faith.[5]

Note that Tresner admits that some Masonic writers have called Freemasonry a religion when *religion* is defined a certain way.

Masonic apologist John Robinson asserts,

Usually, the allegation that Masonry is a separate religion is helped along by one or more blatant falsehoods—for example, the charge that Masonry has its own path to salvation, through the performance of good works. I never met a Mason who believed that, or who would be able to understand how anyone could ever draw such a conclusion. . . . Clearly, one can easily assert that Freemasonry is not a separate religion. It promotes no heaven, no hell, and no means of salvation.[6]

Robinson's logic, however, is flawed. Whether Freemasonry is a religion depends not on what Masons consciously believe, but on what Masonic ritual actually means. The proof lies in the ritual itself, concerning which—

remember—many Masons are uninformed. Moreover, although it is true that Freemasonry promotes no hell, it most surely promotes heaven and a means of salvation.

Another method of Masonic defense is the evidence from its membership. U.S. presidents and other popular figures who were Masons are typically cited. The *Scottish Rite Journal* dedicated its May 1993 issue to Freemasonry's compatibility with Christianity, in response to the Southern Baptist Convention's investigation into the subject.[7] The issue had a portrait of Harry S. Truman on the front cover and a picture of Jimmy Carter on the back. In an article titled "Closing Ranks: The Buck Stops Here," Grand Commander Francis G. Paul said of Truman: "He was a Baptist. He was a Mason. He was the President of the United States. And He was proud of all three."[8] Some Masons conclude that because certain presidents were members of both the Craft and a church, that validates membership in the organization.

Clergy who are Masons are also cited as evidence that Freemasonry is not a religion. Paul Harasim quotes Norman Vincent Peale as saying that "Freemasonry has no dogma or theology.... It teaches that it is important for every man to have a religion of his choice and to be faithful to it.... A good Mason is made even more faithful to the tenets of his faith by membership."[9] One of the more popular addresses on this issue was made by Thomas S. Roy, D.D., Grand Master of the Grand Lodge of Massachusetts in 1952.

> We have none of the marks of a religion. We have no creed, and no confession of faith in a doctrinal statement. We have no theology. We have no ritual of worship. We have no symbols that are religious in the sense of the symbols found in church and synagogue. Our symbols are related to the development of the character of the relationship of man to man. They are working tools to be used in the building of a life. Our purpose is not that of a religion. We are not primarily interested in the redemption of man. We seek no converts. We solicit no new members. We raise no money for religious purposes. By any definition of religion accepted by our critics, we cannot qualify as a religion.... And there is nothing in Freemasonry that is opposed to the religion he brings with him into the lodge.[10]

Though the majority of Masons worldwide believe that the Craft is not a religion, there are exceptions. Albert G. Mackey (1807–81) was a Masonic historian, ritualist, and symbologist.[11] A thirty-third–degree Mason and prolific Masonic writer, he has been surpassed by few, if any, with regard to his research and scholarship in Craft studies, and his *Encyclopedia of Freemasonry* is a landmark work for the institution. Concerning the "Religion of Freemasonry" Mackey writes,

> There has been a needless expenditure of ingenuity and talent, by a
> large number of Masonic orators and essayists, in the endeavor to
> prove that Freemasonry is not a religion. . . . On the contrary, we
> contend, without any sort of hesitation, that Freemasonry is, in every
> sense of the word, except one, and that its least philosophical, an
> eminently religious institution—that it is indebted solely to the reli-
> gious element it contains for its origin as well as its continued exist-
> ence, and that without this religious element it would scarcely be
> worthy of cultivation by the wise and good. . . . We open and close
> our Lodges with prayer; we invoke the blessing of the Most High
> upon all our labors; we demand of our neophytes a profession of
> trusting belief in the existence and the superintending care of God;
> and we teach them to bow with humility and reverence at His awful
> name, while His Holy Law is widely opened upon our altars. Free-
> masonry is thus identified with religion.[12]

Mackey goes on to list *Webster's* definitions of religion, arguing that, "closely and accurately examined, it [Freemasonry] will be found to answer to any one of the requirements of either of these three definitions."[13] It is worth noting that Mackey was a student of religion, especially the ancient Mystery Religions[14] of Egypt, Greece, and Rome. Since he was a premier Masonic ritualist, he was in a good position to see how Freemasonry lived up to the designation of a religion.

Masonic scholar Henry W. Coil, 33rd, also considered Freemasonry a religion. Born in 1885 and eventually a holder of many high Masonic offices, Coil is best known for his *Masonic Encyclopedia,* another must for the serious student of the Craft. In it he states,

> Some attempt to avoid the issue by saying that Freemasonry is not
> a religion but is religious,[15] seeming to believe that the substitution
> of an adjective for a noun makes a fundamental difference. . . . The
> oft repeated aphorism: "Freemasonry is not a religion, but is most
> emphatically religion's handmaid," has been challenged as mean-
> ingless, which it seems to be. . . . Freemasonry certainly requires a
> belief in the existence of, and man's dependence upon, a Supreme
> Being to whom he is responsible. What can a church add to that,

except to bring into one fellowship those who have like feelings? That is exactly what the lodge does. . . . Does Freemasonry have a *creed* (I believe) or *tenet* (he holds) or *dogma* (I think) to which all members must adhere? Does Freemasonry continually teach and insist upon a creed, tenet, and dogma? Does it have meetings characterized by the practice of rites and ceremonies in and by which its creed, tenet, and dogma are illustrated by myths, symbols, and allegories? If Freemasonry were not religion, what would have to be done to make it such? . . . The difference between a lodge and a church is one of degree and not of kind. . . . Freemasonry has a religious service to commit the body of a deceased brother to the dust whence it came and to speed the liberated spirit back to the Great Source of Light.[16] . . . Many Freemasons make this flight with no other guarantee of a safe landing than their belief in the religion of Freemasonry. If that is a false hope, the Fraternity should abandon funeral services and devote its attention to activities where it is sure of its ground and its authority.[17]

Masonic scholar Robert Macoy (1815–95) was another prolific Masonic writer and ritualist. He is well known for his contribution to the Order of the Eastern Star, supervising the formation of the Supreme Grand Chapter in New York City in 1868.[18] Macoy begins his entry under "Religion" in his *Dictionary of Freemasonry* with a quotation from Blue Lodge ritual.

"Speculative Masonry is so far interwoven with religion as to lay us under obligations to pay that rational homage to the Deity which at once constitutes our duty and our happiness. It leads the contemplative mind to view with reverence and admiration the glorious works of creation, and inspires him with the most exalted ideas of the perfection of his divine Creator." That Freemasonry should be spoken of as a religious institution, or as imparting religious instruction, undoubtedly sounds strange to those who think religion must necessarily be confined to a particular set of theological dogmas, or, in other words, be sectarian. But why should it be thought necessary to make religion traverse simply the narrow circle of sectarian ideas? Is it not a degradation to confine it to so limited a sphere?[19]

Macoy goes on to cite Masonic lectures and lessons in ritual that speak of the Deity and describe His infinite and mighty power and His glorious creation.[20]

Mackey and Coil do the same, appealing to the most authoritative sources of Freemasonry, the rituals, to build their case that Freemasonry is religion.

Other well-known Masonic writers assert that Freemasonry is religion. Joseph Fort Newton, 33rd (1880–1950), Past Grand Chaplain of the Grand Lodge of Iowa, states that "it is true that Masonry is not *a* religion, but it is Religion, a worship in which all good men may unite, that each may share the faith of all."[21] Newton offers much food for thought by distinguishing between *a* religion and Religion. By "Religion" Newton means that Freemasonry provides the framework in which men of differing religious persuasions may meet under the canopy of an eclectic institution and worship the "God" who is known by various definitions.[22] And yet, I would argue that there is still every reason to call Freemasonry *a* religion. One religion that has this eclectic theme is Sufism, which teaches that the true God is known by different names and designations.[23] While I agree that religion can demonstrate the eclectic traits that Freemasonry exhibits, I will show why I believe that Freemasonry can be called *a* religion. Nevertheless, Newton was most likely referring to *Anderson's Constitutions,* which lists six "Charges" of a Freemason. Under the charge "Concerning God and Religion" we read,

> A Mason is obliged, by his Tenure, to obey the moral Law; and if he rightly understands the Art, he will never be a stupid atheist, nor an irreligious Libertine. But though in ancient Times Masons were charged in every Country to be of the Religion of that Country or Nation, whatever it was, yet 'tis now thought more expedient only to oblige them to that Religion in which all Men agree, leaving their particular Opinions to themselves; that is, to be good Men and true, or Men of Honour and Honesty, by whatever Denominations or Persuasions they may be distinguished; whereby Masonry becomes the Center of Union, and the Means of conciliating true Friendship among Persons that must have remained at a perpetual Distance.[24]

This is the prevailing opinion among Masons today. Interestingly enough, when we compare the previous quotation by Roy with the following from Melvin M. Johnson, Past Grand Master of the Grand Lodge of Massachusetts, we see a tension between these two men. I believe that Johnson is more on the mark concerning our question of whether Freemasonry is a religion, and more in keeping with the spirit of Anderson and his *Constitutions.* Before the Grand Lodge of Indiana in May 1948, Johnson addressed the Masonic prohibition against discussing religion in the Lodge.

Those things about which we can differ in religion were forbidden to be discussed within the Lodge but there is nothing in Anderson's Constitutions, if you consult the dictionaries of that day and the oldest one is the dictionary of Samuel Johnson, which was being prepared at about the time that Anderson's Constitutions were written—if you consult that, you will find the definition of general religion, which is a thing we not only may discuss within the Lodge but you never attended a Masonic Lodge where it wasn't discussed. You never attended a Masonic Lodge, which wasn't either opened by a declaration to the glory of the Grand Architect of the Universe, or by prayer to Him that He would guide us in our deliberations, or both. There isn't a degree in symbolic Freemasonry that isn't based upon belief in one single, powerful, dominating, loving Father, who is the Creator and God of us all. We certainly are not forbidden by Anderson's Constitutions to discuss that kind of religion and if we omit that there will be no ritual left.[25]

The Reverend Forrest D. Haggard, D.D., seems to agree with Newton's thesis, saying that Freemasonry "is man's grasp towards Divinity both internal and external" and that "Masonry is a basic religion but it is not, nor has it been at least since 1717, in any sense of the word an 'organized religion.'"[26]

Having seen a sampling of Masonic opinion concerning the relationship between Freemasonry and religion, let us now define what religion is.[27]

What Is Religion?

The word *religion* comes from the Latin *religare,* which means "to bind back."[28] The question now arises as to the subject and the object of the phrase. In one sense the Deity (or deities) is the subject, taking the initiative of drawing the object, which is humanity, to Him-/Her-/Itself. In another sense humanity may be the subject, which, through various means, attempts to bind itself back to the Deity (or deities). We may say that through a belief system a group of "believers" are bound together, since without this common faith they would remain spiritually estranged from one another. Thus, the binding together takes place horizontally (person to person) and vertically (person/people to God, or gods).[29] The horizontal expression of religion also takes place from believer to unbeliever, according to the dictates of the particular religious worldview. In addition, usually religions are concerned with a belief in God (or gods or power[s]), moral behavior that stems from divine sanction, and some form of an afterlife.

Webster's Dictionary gives a rather extensive definition of religion.

> 1. belief in a divine or superhuman power or powers to be obeyed and worshipped as the creator(s) and ruler(s) of the universe. 2. expression of this belief in conduct and ritual. 3. (a) any specific system of belief, worship, conduct, etc., often involving a code of ethics and a philosophy; as, the Christian religion, the Buddhist religion, etc.; (b) loosely, any system of beliefs, practices, ethical values, etc. resembling, suggestive of, or likened to such a system; as, humanism is his religion. 4. a state of mind or way of life expressing love for and trust in God, and one's will and effort to act according to the will of God, especially within a monastic order or community; as, he achieved religion. 5. any object of conscientious regard and pursuit; as, cleanliness was a religion to him. 6. (a) the practice of religious observances or rites; (b) [pl.] religious rites [Obs.] 7. a religious order or state; a monastery [Obs.][30]

Though cautious in their definitions of religion, scholars are willing to suggest a number of essential characteristics. Stanley A. Cook states, "The term 'religion' whatever its best definition, clearly refers to certain characteristic types of data (beliefs, practices, feelings, moods, attitudes, etc.)."[31] Vergilius Ferm says, "A religion is a set of meanings and behaviors having reference to individuals who are or were or could be religious."[32] The word *religious,* in Ferm's use, means "effect[ing] in some way and in some measure a vital adjustment (however tentative and incomplete) to whatever is reacted to or regarded implicitly or explicitly as worthy of serious and ulterior concern."[33]

Our Working Definition

We will work from the following definition of religion, noting how Masonic ritual fulfills the criteria of a religion. Keep in mind, however, that even the above definitions may be fulfilled in this same way.

In *The Encyclopedia of Philosophy,* William P. Alston lists nine "religion-making characteristics."

> 1. Belief in supernatural beings (gods).
> 2. A distinction between sacred and profane objects.

3. Ritual acts focused on sacred objects.
4. A moral code believed to be sanctioned by the gods.
5. Characteristically religious feelings (awe, sense of mystery, sense of guilt, adoration), which tend to be aroused in the presence of sacred objects and during the practice of ritual, and which are connected in idea with the gods.
6. Prayer and other forms of communication with gods.
7. A world view, or a general picture of the world as a whole and the place of the individual therein. This picture contains some specification of an over-all purpose or point of the world and an indication of how the individual fits into it.
8. A more or less total organization of one's life based on the world view.
9. A social group bound together by the above.[34]

Alston later states that "when enough of these characteristics are present to a sufficient degree, we have a religion."[35] I will show how Freemasonry sufficiently manifests all nine characteristics.

If Masons suspect that I have selected only those definitions that describe Freemasonry, I offer this simple challenge: Find another definition of religion, or create one, that meets with scholarly consensus, and see whether you come to a different conclusion.

With our working definition in mind, we now turn to Blue Lodge rituals to demonstrate our point.

The Religious Character of Blue Lodge Ritual

(Note: In this chapter, only teachings common to the greatest number of Grand Lodges are cited, so as to make the scope of the demonstration as broad as possible. This will also eliminate numerous note citations of Blue Lodge ritual sources, since what may be found in, let us say, New Hampshire, may also be found in England, Ireland, etc.)

1. *Belief in a supernatural being.* The most basic requirement of Freemasonry is that each candidate believe in the existence of a Supreme Being. A man may be accepted as a candidate regardless of whether he is a Muslim, a Jew, a Buddhist, a Hindu, a Christian, a Unitarian, etc.

The first degree (Entered Apprentice) involves a question and answer period. The following questions and answers are cited as they appear in the

Massachusetts Blue Lodge ritual so that the reader can get a feel for the secrecy of Masonic ritual. They are then decoded:

> Q: Af re th be of pr, wh we yo as?
> A: In wh I pu my tr. Q: Yor an? A: In Go.[36]

> [Decoded]
> Q: After receiving the benefit of prayer, what were you asked?
> A: In whom I put my trust. Q: Your answer? A: In God.

This portion of ritual suggests that Freemasonry *as an institution* mandates that candidates for the Craft put their trust in God. Theologically, trust is synonymous with faith, which is a required component of religion. Although Freemasonry does not ask its candidates to name or define their God, as elaborated upon earlier, that does not exclude Masonry from being a religion (see n. 23). Like some religions, Freemasonry provides a canopy under which men of differing religious persuasions may bring their particular conceptions of God. Thus, corporately Freemasonry believes in God, and individual Masons do as well. To illustrate this corporate aspect, Masonic scholars Coil and Mackey note how Lodge meetings are opened and closed with prayer. Masons the world over will recognize the following prayer from Entered Apprentice Blue Lodge ritual:

> Vouchsafe Thine aid, Almighty Father of the Universe, to this our present convention, and grant that this candidate for Freemasonry may dedicate and devote his life to Thy service, and become a true and faithful brother among us. Endue him with a competency of Thy Divine Wisdom, that he may be the better enabled to display the beauties of holiness, to the honour of Thy Holy Name. Amen.[37]

Here Freemasonry provides the candidate with a prayer that covers both the vertical and the horizontal dimensions of faith: dedication and service unto God and to his brethren. And all this is to bring honor to God's holy name. The closing of a Lodge features a statement offered by the Worshipful Master.[38]

> ad nw ma th bl o hv rs up u, ad al rg Mn! Ma br lv pr, ad ev mo ad so vt cm u.[39]

> [Decoded]
> and now may the blessing of heaven rest upon us, and all regular

Masons! May brotherly love prevail, and every moral and social virtue cement us.

The *Emulation Ritual* of London has different wording, though the
meaning is essentially the same.

> Brethren, before we close the Lodge, let us with all reverence and
> humility express our gratitude to the Great Architect of the Universe[40]
> for favors already received; may He continue to preserve the Order
> by cementing and adorning it with every moral and social virtue.[41]

The most basic and essential characteristic of most religions is a belief
in a Deity or deities or power(s). As has been stated, it is possible for a religion to provide only a canopy designation for God—the Absolute, the Almighty, the One, God, the Supreme (or Great) Architect of the Universe, etc.
Freemasonry clearly fulfills this first characteristic in the way of a canopy
designation. It may even be argued, that when one reads Masonic ritual, with
its frequent allusions and prayers to the Deity, the designation "Great Architect of the Universe" can become more than a canopy term to a Mason who
has no religion outside the Lodge.[42]

2. *A distinction between sacred and profane objects.* "Sacred" means
holy, as with an object set apart for religious use. The object may even be
said to be set apart for God (or gods) and/or to be venerated (or worshiped).
"Profane" means connected with the secular, or nonreligious. It may also
denote an object in direct contrast to a sacred object. In Christianity a sacred
object would be the cross, as it symbolizes the crucifixion of Christ and
reminds Christians of the price Jesus paid on the cross for their sins. A
profane object would be a pornographic magazine, which depicts fornication, a sin that separates humankind from Christ and thus stands in direct
opposition to the cross. Profane objects remind religious people of the state
they once were in: they were unenlightened, immoral, concerned with the
things of the world, etc.

Freemasonry also distinguishes between sacred and profane objects.
The Rough Ashlar and the Perfect Ashlar are two examples. "By the Rough
Ashlar we are reminded of our rude and imperfect state by nature; by the
Perfect Ashlar, of that state of perfection at which we hope to arrive, by a
virtuous education, our own endeavors, and the blessing of God."[43] The "Hoodwink," or Blindfold, is another profane object. In the Entered Apprentice
degree the candidate begins his initiation by being led blindfolded into the

Lodge room. The candidate's conductor (who guides the candidate around the Lodge) is asked, "Who comes here?" He answers, "[The candidate's name], who is in darkness and wishes for light, to have and receive a part of the rights and benefits of this Worshipful Lodge, erected to God and dedicated to the holy Saints John [the Baptist and the apostle]."[44]

What does the blindfold symbolize? The answer is not difficult—darkness. But what *kind* of darkness is it? As the initiation ceremony continues, the candidate is led around the Lodge room to the Masonic altar, which has upon it the "Three Great Lights" of Freemasonry: the VSL (Volume of the Sacred Law), the Square, and the Compass (or Compasses).[45] The symbolism and lessons given on the Three Great Lights help us to determine what "darkness" symbolizes. The candidate is asked, "What do you most desire?" He answers, "Light." Once the Hoodwink is removed, the Three Great Lights are introduced: "The Bible [or other sacred writings; see n. 45] we take to be the rule and guide of our faith; the Square to square our actions; and the Compass to circumscribe our desires and keep our passions within due bounds with all mankind, more especially with our Brethren in Freemasonry."[46]

So, the darkness that the candidate was in is both moral and spiritual: moral because of the squaring of actions and the circumscribing of passions; spiritual because, upon answering that he desires light, the candidate is led to the VSL, "the rule and guide of our faith."

Soon the candidate is presented with a white leather, or Lambskin, Apron. This is an important symbol to the Craft.

> I now invest you with the distinguishing Badge of a Mason. It is more ancient than the Roman Eagle or any other ancient Badge or ensign. It is more honourable than the Garter, the Golden Fleece, or any other Noble Order which has ever existed. It is the Badge of Innocence and Friendship, and I strongly exhort you ever to wear and value it as such.[47]

Further elaboration on this symbol indicates that it is viewed as a sacred object of the Craft.

> The Lamb has in all ages been deemed an emblem of innocence; he, therefore, who wears the Lamb Skin as a badge of Masonry is thereby continually reminded of that purity of life and conduct which is essentially necessary to his gaining admission into the Celestial Lodge above, where the Supreme Architect of the Universe presides.[48]

In light of the symbolism of the Rough and Perfect Ashlars, the Hoodwink, and the Lambskin Apron, we may conclude that Freemasonry distinguishes between sacred and profane objects. This symbolism is filled with allusions to the present state of humanity and a hope of perfection in an afterlife.

3. *Ritual acts focused on sacred objects.* As we have seen in the distinction between sacred and profane objects, some ritual acts illustrate this distinction. The Rough and Perfect Ashlars, the Hoodwink, and the Lambskin Apron are all introduced in ritual. Thus, with these we have ritual acts focused on sacred objects.

In Freemasonry, the VSL is a sacred object upon which ritual acts are focused. In all three degrees of Blue Lodge Masonry—Entered Apprentice, Fellow Craft, and Master Mason—the candidates approach the Masonic altar, on which are laid the VSL, the Square, and the Compass. They then place their hands (using different positions for different degrees) on and/or under the VSL and swear an oath of secrecy.

> I, [name], in the presence of The Great Architect of the Universe,[49] and of this worthy and Worshipful Lodge of Ancient, Free, and accepted Masons, regularly held, assembled, and properly dedicated, of my own free will and accord, do hereby, and hereon most solemnly and sincerely swear, that I will always hele,[50] conceal and never willfully reveal any part or parts, point or points, of the secrets or mysteries of or belonging to Ancient Freemasonry, which may heretofore have been known by, shall now, or may at any future time be communicated to me, to any one in the world, unless it be a true and lawful Brother or Brethren. . . . So help me God, and keep me steadfast in this my great and solemn Oath, being that of an Entered Apprentice Freemason.[51]

Upon swearing the oath, the candidate is instructed to kiss the VSL. This is a distinctly ritualistic act focused on a sacred object.

Blue Lodge ritual includes a lesson on the letter "G." The insignia of a "G" enclosed between a level and a compass is usually on the outside of a Masonic Lodge and can also be seen on car bumpers and license plates. Ritual teaches that the Level (the Compass has already been treated) is to remind the Mason "that we are travelling upon the Level of time 'to that undiscovered country, from whose bourne no traveller returns.'"[52] The candidate is given a lecture on the letter G and is told that it refers to the noble science of Geometry. Moments later the Worshipful Master relates,

> But, my Brother, the letter G has a still further and more solemn
> allusion. It alludes to the sacred name of God,[53] to whom should we
> all, from the youngest Entered Apprentice who stands in the north-
> east corner of the Lodge to the Worshipful Master who presides in
> the East, most humbly and reverently bow.[54] [Here the Brethren per-
> form some ritualistic procedure such as bowing, crossing the arms—
> another ritualistic act focused on a sacred object.]

The Common Gavel is another spiritual and sacred object of the Craft.
During the initiation ceremony of the first degree the candidate is taught,

> The Common Gavel is an instrument used by operative Masons,
> to break off the rough and superfluous parts of stones, the better
> to fit them for the builder's use. But we, as Free and Accepted
> Masons, are taught to use it for the more noble and glorious
> purpose of divesting our hearts and consciences of the vices and
> superfluities of life, thereby fitting our minds as living stones for
> that spiritual building, that house not made with hands, eternal in
> the heavens.[55]

Freemasonry can thus be said to fulfill our third characteristic.

4. *A moral code sanctioned by God.* Since Freemasonry is a system of
morality, it should not be difficult to document whether it fulfills our fourth
characteristic. Is this system of morality sanctioned by God? Again, Freemasonry provides the canopy framework for each of its initiates to study and
apply the Craft's moral lessons in the light of their particular VSL. This is not
uncommon for an eclectic, or syncretistic, religion such as Freemasonry, just
as it is not uncommon for the religion of Sufism or the pluralistic religious
framework of the New Age Movement.

Third degree (Master Mason) ritual features several objects that portray
certain moral traits. If these are fulfilled by the Mason, a reward from the
Deity follows. We see this in the symbolism of the Sword and the All-Seeing
Eye:

> The Sword Pointing to a Naked Heart demonstrates that justice will
> sooner or later overtake us, and although our thoughts, words, and
> actions may be hidden from the eyes of man, yet that All-seeing Eye,

whom the Sun, Moon, and Stars obey, and under whose watchful care even comets perform their stupendous revolutions, pervades the inmost recesses of the human heart, and will reward us according to our merits.[56]

In this symbolism a moral lesson is put forth, and the teaching implies strongly a sanctioning by the Deity with a reward for individual merit.

The importance of the VSL in Freemasonry should not be minimized. It is considered sacred because it is, in the Lodge's view, inspired by God. This charge is given to the new Entered Apprentice:

> As a Freemason, I would first recommend to your most serious contemplation the volume of the Sacred Law, charging you to consider it as the unerring standard of Truth and Justice, and to regulate your actions by the Divine precepts it contains; as therein you will be taught the important duties you owe to God, to your neighbor, and to yourself.[57]

Obviously, if a VSL contains "Divine precepts," then it comes from Deity. And Freemasonry provides the authoritative charge to regulate the vertical and the horizontal aspects (which characterize religions) contained in any particular VSL; the vertical is the duty we owe to Deity; the horizontal the duty we owe to humanity. Thus, Freemasonry fulfills our fourth characteristic of a religion.

5. *Religious feelings (awe, guilt, etc.).* Here we enter into the realm of the subjective. That is to say, the feelings experienced during ritual or in the presence of sacred objects are personal, depending on multiple reasons as to why one person may have feelings aroused, and why another person, in the same service, may not have any feelings aroused. Obviously, because we are dealing with feelings that are by nature personal, we are not likely to find, in a religious service or ritual, commands or suggestions to feel awe or guilt or adoration. Rather, we should examine certain religious services or rituals to see if they have the *potential* to arouse characteristically religious feelings or if they *express* religious feelings through certain prayers or language.

Emotions such as awe, guilt, and adoration are aroused in ritual. Think of your experience in watching television documentaries or observing certain kinds of religious services. These same feelings are aroused in connection with the Deity, or deities, of any religion. Is this the case with the Lodge? In the following example from Blue Lodge ritual, characteristically religious feelings are described:

> By Speculative Masonry [Freemasonry] we learn to subdue the passions, act upon the square, keep a tongue of good report, maintain secrecy, and practice charity. It is so far interwoven with religion as to lay us under obligations to pay that rational homage to Deity which at once constitutes our duty and our happiness. It leads the contemplative to view with reverence and admiration the glorious works of creation, and inspires him with the most exalted ideas of the perfections of his Divine Creator.[58]

This lesson to the initiate of the Fellow Craft teaches that Freemasonry leads and inspires a man to experience reverence, admiration, and other exalted ideas of his Creator. These are characteristically religious feelings.

Religious feelings have the great potential to be aroused during Masonic prayers. The following prayer is offered in the Master Mason degree:

> Thou, O God, knowest our down-sitting and our up-rising, and understandest our thoughts afar off. Shield and defend us from the evil intentions of our enemies, and support us under the trials and afflictions we are destined to endure, while travelling through this vale of tears. . . . For there is hope of a tree, if it be cut down, that it will sprout again, and that the tender branch thereof will not cease. But man dieth and wasteth away; yea, man giveth up the ghost, and where is he? . . . Yet, O Lord! have compassion on the children of Thy creation; administer them comfort in time of trouble, and save them with an everlasting salvation. Amen.[59]

The Worshipful Master also utters this prayer at the beginning of the Master Mason degree:

> Almighty and Eternal God, great Architect and Ruler of the Universe, at whose creative fiat all things first were made, we, the frail creatures of Thy providence, humbly implore Thee to pour down on this Convocation, assembled in Thy Holy Name, the continual dew of Thy blessing. More especially we beseech Thee to impart Thy grace to this Thy servant, who now seeks to participate with us in the mysterious Secrets of a Master Mason. Endue him with such fortitude, that in the hour of trial he fail not, but passing safely under Thy

protection through the valley of the shadow of death, he may finally arise from the tomb of transgression to shine as the stars for ever and ever.[60]

Thus is our fifth characteristic fulfilled.

6. *Prayer and other forms of communication with God.* For examples, see those already cited for the previous characteristics.

7. *A worldview and how the individual fits into it.* As defined above, a worldview is a general understanding of the world as a whole. It is usually accompanied by a view of the universe and its way of coming into existence and by some view of an afterlife. Since a worldview includes an understanding of the place of individuals, it is not surprising that religions help to define what *type* of afterlife the individual receives. One form of Hinduism, for example, stresses that the material world is an illusion, and that attachment to the seeming material world keeps one's soul from being liberated. A person must see the world as an illusion and be enlightened to the fact that Brahman is the only reality. Thus, detachment from the world means liberation. Upon the person's seeming death the soul is absorbed into Brahman. This school of thought is known as nondualism.

Christianity teaches a completely different worldview. God is absolutely good and holy, but there is also evil in the world. Evil is a reality, as is the material world. Salvation occurs through faith in Jesus Christ, whose Spirit indwells those who believe in Him. The Holy Spirit then brings to fruition the Christian's lifestyle, thereby glorifying God, and at death the individual enjoys God's presence forever.

Worldviews determine how we interpret events, the people and things around us, and our part in the world. Every religion, including Freemasonry, has a worldview, which it teaches to its initiates. Since it promotes belief in a Supreme Being, Freemasonry's worldview resembles those of Christianity, Islam, and Judaism (among others) insofar as it subscribes to belief in a Creator, some sort of moral law that is sanctioned by the Creator, and an afterlife based on one's experience in the world and one's relationship to the Deity. We may observe the first two components in the symbolism of the Master Mason emblem, The Pot of Incense.

The Pot of Incense is an emblem of a pure heart, which is always an acceptable sacrifice to the Deity; and as this glows with fervent heat, so should our hearts continually glow with gratitude to the great and beneficent Author of our existence, for the manifold blessings and comforts we enjoy.[61]

In the *Emulation Ritual* of England, the symbolism of the Covering of the Lodge teaches belief in a Deity, moral precepts laid out by the Deity, and an afterlife based on a moral life.

> The Covering of a Freemasons' Lodge is a celestial canopy of diverse colours even the Heavens. The way by which we, as Masons, hope to arrive there is by the assistance of a ladder, in Scripture called Jacob's ladder. It is composed of many staves or rounds, which point out as many moral virtues, but three principle ones, which are Faith, Hope and Charity: Faith in the Great Architect of the Universe, Hope in Salvation, and to be in charity with all men. It reaches to the Heavens, and rests on the VSL, because, by the doctrines contained in that Holy Book, we are taught to believe in the dispensations of Divine Providence, which belief strengthens our Faith, and enables us to ascend the first step; this Faith naturally creates in us a Hope of becoming partakers of the blessed promises therein recorded, which Hope enables us to ascend the second step; but the third and last, being Charity, comprehends the whole, and the Mason who is possessed of this virtue in its most ample sense may justly be deemed to have attained the summit of his profession; figuratively speaking, an Ethereal Mansion veiled from mortal eyes by the starry firmament.[62]

Similar content is found in the symbolism of the Three Steps of the Master Mason degree. Here we find how the individual is to fit into the world, with the ultimate purpose of dying in the hope of a glorious immortality.

> The Three Steps delineated on the Master's Carpet are emblematical of the three principal stages of human life,—Youth, Manhood, and Age. They also allude to the three degrees in Freemasonry,—Entered Apprentice, Fellow Craft, and Master Mason. In Youth, as Entered Apprentices, we ought industriously to occupy our minds in the attainment of useful knowledge; in Manhood, as Fellow Crafts, we should apply that knowledge to the discharge of our respective duties to God, our neighbor, and ourselves; so that in Age, as Master Masons, we may enjoy the happy reflection consequent on a well-spent life, and die in the hope of a glorious immortality.[63]

From the preceding examples we must conclude that Freemasonry provides Masons with a general perspective on the world as a whole and the place of the individual therein. Within the Craft's rituals we also find an overall purpose for the world and lessons on how the Mason is to fit into the world.[64]

Worldviews are vital to understanding people, their religions, and their actions. A worldview is the springboard for both the collective actions of a particular religious sect and the individual actions of its followers. Many Masons defend Freemasonry by pointing to the good works that the institution accomplishes. These good deeds, I submit, are the outgrowth of Freemasonry's worldview, in which good works merit the reward of a glorious afterlife.[65] The Sovereign Grand Commander of the Southern Jurisdiction of the Scottish Rite, C. Fred Kleinknecht, agrees. "The performance of the Ritual, the conferring of Degrees, is the only real business of Masonry. All the rest—the charities, the educational programs, the fun and fellowship—are *outgrowths* of the lessons taught in those Rituals."[66]

If Masonic good deeds are motivated by the "real business of Masonry"—the rituals—and the rituals can be shown to be incompatible with Christianity, we must not be hasty in praising the Lodge for its good works. Motives, after all, are extremely important. When the Freemason points to the good things Masons do for society, we would do well to ask *why* members of the Lodge perform those good works.

8. *A more or less total organization of one's life based on the worldview.* Because our worldview determines how we view the world and how we should fit into it, the natural outcome of this is to organize our lives according to that view. Freemasonry establishes through its lessons and symbols a definite scheme of moral behavior that stems from divine sanction and promises the hope of immortality. This is best illustrated in the concluding address of the Master Mason degree in a Scottish Blue Lodge ritual:

> I now present you with the working tools of a Master Mason, which are, the Skirret, the Pencil, and the Compasses. [Ritual then defines the use of these three in an operative sense—as by actual stone masons.] . . . Not meeting as Operative Masons, but as Brethren engaged in speculative or symbolic Freemasonry, we apply these tools to our Morals. In this sense—the Skirret points out to us that straight and undeviating line of conduct laid down for our pursuit in the V. of the S.L. The Pencil teaches us that all our words and actions are observed and recorded by the Most High, to whom we must give an account of our conduct through life. And the Compasses remind us

of His unerring and impartial justice in having accurately defined for our instruction the limits of good and evil,[67] and that He will either reward or punish us according as we have obeyed or disregarded His divine commands. Thus the working tools of a Master Mason teach us to bear in mind, and to act according to, the Laws of the Divine Creator, so that, when we shall be summoned from this sublunary abode, we may hope to ascend to that Grand Lodge above, where the World's great Architect lives and reigns forever.[68]

The lesson of the Trestle-Board (where, in operative masonry, building plans are laid out) is to organize one's life according to the Masonic worldview.

By the Trestle-Board, we are reminded, that as the operative workman erects his temporal building agreeably to the rules and designs laid down by the Master on his Trestle-Board, so should we, both Operative and Speculative, endeavor to erect our spiritual building agreeably to the rules and designs laid down by the Supreme Architect of the Universe in the Book of Life,[69] which is our Spiritual Trestle-Board.[70]

Note that the organization of one's life is based upon divinely sanctioned precepts, a fulfillment of characteristic number 4 above.

Finally, let us consider the symbolism of the twenty-four–inch Gauge, which stresses how the Entered Apprentice is to spend each of his twenty-four–hour days on earth, and the Common Gavel, which stresses that he restrain his thoughts in order to please the Deity.

In this sense [that is, applying these working tools of an Operative Mason in a speculative or symbolic sense to morals], the twenty-four–inch gauge represents the twenty-four hours of the day; part to be spent in prayer to Almighty God; part in labor and refreshment; and part in serving a friend or Brother in time of need, without detriment to ourselves or connections. The common gavel represents the force of conscience, which should keep down all vain and unbecoming thoughts which might obtrude during any of the aforementioned periods, so that our words and actions may ascend unpolluted to the Throne of Grace.[71]

The examples noted demonstrate that Freemasonry manifests the eighth characteristic of a religion.

9. *A social group bound together by the above.* Freemasonry prides itself in being a fraternal organization and having social interactions. It prides itself in that men of different religious persuasions may unite as brethren under the Four Cardinal Virtues of Temperance, Fortitude, Prudence, and Justice.[72] If it were not for Freemasonry, these men would have remained separated. Freemasonry is a social group, as Masons themselves will admit.[73] And we have seen that the Lodge is bound together by the characteristics that make up the essence of religion.

The symbolism of the Trowel officially portrays the Masonic Lodge as a social group with a glorious purpose.

> The *Trowel* is an instrument used by Operative Masons to spread the cement which unites the building into one common mass; but we, as Free and Accepted Masons, are taught to use it for the more noble and glorious purpose of spreading the cement of brotherly love and affection,—that cement which unites us into one sacred band, or society of friends and brothers, among whom no contention should ever exist, save that noble contention, or rather emulation, of who can best work and best agree.[74]

Thus, ritual shows that Freemasonry is a "sacred band, or society of friends" united in a glorious purpose. Our final characteristic has been met.

Conclusion

Freemasonry is not only a religious institution, but a religion. Its Blue Lodge ritual fulfills the essential characteristics of a religion. What remains for us is to examine the theological tenets of the Craft to see if they are compatible with the essentials of the Christian faith. If they are not, then it is imperative that Christians who are Masons exit the Lodge, for there can be no allegiance with a non-Christian religion. Denominations proclaiming that Jesus is Lord need to study the Craft to understand why members of their churches should not be joined with the religion of Freemasonry.

Notes

1. After receiving the first three degrees of Blue Lodge Masonry (Entered Apprentice, Fellow Craft, and Master Mason), the Mason may enter either or both of these rites. The Scottish Rite offers an additional twenty-nine degrees, with an additional honorary degree. The York Rite offers an additional ten degrees.

2. The third degree (Master Mason) is said to be the pinnacle of Freemasonry. It is the Sublime Degree of the Craft because of the great lessons it inculcates. All later degrees are to be taken not as higher but as concentric circles branching out from the pinnacle degree.

3. Masons often state that no one person can speak for Freemasonry. See Jim Tresner, "Riding the Semantic Merry-Go-Round," *The Scottish Rite Journal* (Washington, D.C.: The Supreme Council, 33rd, Ancient and Accepted Scottish Rite of Freemasonry of the Southern Jurisdiction, USA, May 1993): 14. Does Tresner speak for Freemasonry when he makes this statement?

4. *Freemasonry: A Way of Life* (The Most Worshipful Grand Lodge of Ancient Free and Accepted Masons of the Commonwealth of Massachusetts, 1983), 6.

5. *Conscience and the Craft* (Masonic Grand Lodge of New Mexico, 1992), 2–3.

6. John J. Robinson, *A Pilgrim's Path* (New York: M. Evans and Co., 1993), 34–35.

7. In 1992 James Holly, M.D., spearheaded the fight to have the Southern Baptist Convention take a denominational stand against Freemasonry. He is the author of *The Southern Baptist Convention and Freemasonry,* 3 vols. (Beaumont, Tex.: Mission and Ministry to Men, n.d.).

8. Francis G. Paul, "The Buck Stops Here," *Scottish Rite Journal* (May 1993): 4. This form of argumentation begs the question. Additionally, one might offer the example of a former president who was an outspoken anti-Mason: John Quincy Adams published letters debunking the Craft. See *Letters on the Masonic Institution, by John Quincy Adams* (1831–33).

9. Paul Harasim, "Calling Masons Satanic Is Folly," *The Scottish Rite Journal* (May 1993): 24.

10. Cited in Alphonse Cerza, *Let There Be Light: A Study in Anti-Masonry* (Silver Spring, Md.: The Masonic Service Association, 1983), 41. Roy's further remarks are most alarming in light of orthodox Christian doctrine: "It is the glory of Masonry that a man who believes implicitly in the deity of Christ, and a man who says he cannot go that far, can meet as brothers in their acknowledgement of the sovereignty of the Supreme Being, the Maker of Heaven and earth, and in acknowledgment of their duty to love Him with heart and mind and soul and strength. . . . Freemasonry rightfully conceived and practised will enhance every worthy loyalty in man's life. It will not weaken a man's loyalty to his church, but will strengthen it by the increased sense of responsibility to God and dependence on God taught in our ritual" (pp. 43–44).

First, this statement is alarming because anyone who rejects the deity of Christ cannot be a Christian (John 8:24 states, "If you should deny that I am, you will die in your sins." Here the "I am" saying of Jesus is seen in light of the Septuagint's rendering of Deut. 32:39; Isa. 41:4; 43:10, where Yahweh states, *"Egō eimi,"* as does Christ in John's gospel). Consequently, anyone denying Jesus Christ as having come in the flesh (this phrase in 1 John 4:2–3 should be interpreted with John's gospel prologue in view, where the eternal Son of God is shown to have united Himself with perfect humanity and thus to be fully God and fully human) is not of God and in reality is denying both the Father and the Son (1 John 2:22–23). Thus a person "who says he cannot go that far" denies the Father. How, then, can this person and a Christian "meet as brothers in their acknowledgment of the Sovereignty of the Supreme Being"?

Second, if, as Roy says, the Lodge has no theology, then what is this "dependence on God" that is taught in ritual? Dependence is "faith," which is a necessary component of all theological systems.

Simply because a man possesses the title of "Reverend," this does not automatically qualify him to be a Christian. A person making a statement such as Roy's is either sincerely ignorant of Christian theology or not a Christian. Sadly, it is possible to be ordained in many Christian denominations while denying the essentials of Christian theology.

11. Henry W. Coil, *Coil's Masonic Encyclopedia* (New York: Macoy Publishing and Masonic Supply Co., 1961), 389.

12. Albert G. Mackey, *Mackey's Revised Encyclopedia of Freemasonry,* rev. ed., 2 vols. (Richmond, Va.: Macoy Publishing and Masonic Supply Co., 1966), 2:846–47.

13. Ibid., 847. Webster actually lists four definitions, three of which Mackey says Freemasonry fulfills.

14. These will be treated in chap. 3.

15. The idea that Freemasonry is religious but is not a religion was established by John A. Mirt in an article for the Masonic *Temple Topics* (cited in Cerza, *Let There Be Light,* 41). This is a very popular notion among those in the Craft.

16. The Masonic Funeral Service will be examined in chap. 4.

17. *Coil's Masonic Encyclopedia,* 512. Coil does a good and thorough job in his entry (s.v., "Religion," 511–22).

18. Ibid., 391.

19. Robert Macoy, *A Dictionary of Freemasonry* (New York: Bell Publishing Co., 1989), 324.

20. Ibid., 325.

21. Joseph Fort Newton, *The Builders* (Lexington, Mass.: The Supreme Council, 33rd, Ancient Accepted Scottish Rite of Freemasonry, Northern Masonic Jurisdiction, 1973), 233.

22. Ibid., 236–39. It appears that Newton knew well the *Secret Doctrine* revealed in Scottish Rite ritual. See chap. 9.

23. See Hazrat Inayat Khan, *The Unity of Religious Ideals* (New Lebanon, N.Y.: Sufi Order Publications, 1979), 90–91: "It is true, too, that as many conceptions there are, so many gods are there. And yet many gods mean many conceptions of the One Only God. . . . If one could only see how marvellously, in the diversity of the conception of the Divine Ideal, wisdom has played its part, guiding the souls of all grades of evolution towards the same goal, which in the end becomes spiritual attainment!"

24. *Anderson's Constitutions of 1723,* in *Little Masonic Library,* 5 vols. (Richmond, Va.: Macoy Publishing and Masonic Supply Co., 1977), 1:233.

25. Taken from the *Standard Manual* (Grand Lodge of A.F. & A.M. of Oregon, revised April 13, 1991), 93. This manual is quite correct in stating that "the charges [in *Anderson's Constitutions*] say '. . . and if he rightly understands the Art, he will never be a stupid atheist nor an irreligious libertine.' How is he to attain this true understanding of the Art that he may avoid these pitfalls if nothing of a religious character can be mentioned?" (p. 94).

26. Forrest D. Haggard, *The Clergy and the Craft* (Missouri: Missouri Lodge of Research, 1970), 18–19. These statements were made in response to Joseph Fort Newton's argument.

27. It is debatable whether or not *early* Freemasonry was a religion, or, if it was, whether it rivaled Christianity. For a treatment on this subject, see Henry W. Coil, *Conversations on Freemasonry* (Richmond, Va.: Macoy Publishing and Masonic Supply Co., 1976), 163–83. Though this is debated, for our purposes we are concerned with *current* Freemasonry.

28. *Webster's New Twentieth-Century Dictionary, Unabridged* (New York: The Publisher's Guild, 1965), 1527.

29. I am aware that some religions do not fit the definition. For example, Hinayana Buddhism offers no belief in a god or gods and is chiefly concerned with a system of ethical behavior. The same may be said of humanism. This, however, does not excuse Freemasonry. If Hinayana is said to be a religion, how much more should that be said of Masonry, which most certainly requires of its initiates a trusting belief in a Deity?

30. *Webster's New Twentieth-Century Dictionary,* 1527. "Obs." means obsolete or no longer in use.

31. James Hastings, ed., *Encyclopedia of Religion and Ethics* (New York: Charles Scribner's Sons, 1919), 10:662.

32. Vergilius Ferm, *Encyclopedia of Religion* (New York: The Philosophical Library, 1945), 647. See Ferm's caution concerning the etymological approach (which I use) of citing the Latin *religare* and working from its meaning (p. 646).

33. Ibid., 646.

34. William P. Alston, "Religion," *The Encyclopedia of Philosophy,* 8 vols. (New York: Macmillan, 1967), 7:141–42.

35. Ibid., 142.

36. *Official Cipher* (Boston: Grand Lodge of Masons in Massachusetts, 1978), 55–56.

37. *The Ceremonies of Craft Masonry,* rev. ed. (New Brunswick, Canada: The Grand Lodge of New Brunswick, 1954), 8.

38. The term "Worshipful Master" should not be construed as bestowing to a man that which should only be said of God. The term comes from old English tradition and is simply a term of respect.

39. *Official Cipher* (The Grand Lodge of Minnesota, n.d.), 39.

40. This is Freemasonry's designation for the Deity. I see *the Great Architect of the Universe* as a "Canopy Deity," because it covers all the different candidates' individual ideas of Deity and includes these ideas within it.
41. *Emulation Ritual* (London: Lewis Masonic Publishers, 1986), 58.
42. Coil makes the assertion that, for some Masons, the Craft is all the religion they have (*Encyclopedia*, 512).
43. *Official Cipher* (1960; reprint, New Hampshire: Grand Lodge of New Hampshire, F. & A.M., 1975), 24.
44. *Official Cipher*, Massachusetts, 26, decoded.
45. Though some Grand Lodges use the Bible as their VSL, it is only because the predominant religion in their part of the world is Christianity. In a Muslim country we find the Koran (or Qur'an) on the altar; in India, perhaps the Bhagavad Gita; in a Jewish Lodge, the Pentateuch; etc. Freemasonry as an institution does not recognize the Bible to the exclusion of other holy books; if a Muslim candidate wishes to be initiated in a Lodge that usually has the Bible on its altar, it is replaced by (or joined with) the Koran. This is why some Grand Lodges use the term "VSL," instead of "The Holy Bible." Technically, such Lodges are more in keeping with the spirit of Masonry.
46. *Official Cipher*, Massachusetts, 30, decoded.
47. *The Irish Workings of Craft Masonry in the Three Symbolic Degrees* (London: Lewis Masonic Publishers, 1957), 62.
48. *Official Cipher*, Minnesota, 28, decoded.
49. Rituals differ in the designation used. Some read "Supreme Architect of the Universe," others read "Almighty God," etc.
50. This word is old Saxon, meaning to cover or hide.
51. *The Oxford Ritual of Craft Freemasonry* (London: Lewis Masonic, 1988), 39–41. Many (not all) Blue Lodge ritual workings have removed the penalties of having the throat cut, the heart torn out, and the bowels ripped open. Therefore, these penalties will not be mentioned in the text of this work.
52. *Official Cipher*, Massachusetts, 111.
53. One wonders just what this "sacred name" is. Christians who write against the teachings of Freemasonry have been criticized by John Robinson for stating that Freemasonry's name for God is T.G.A.O.T.U. (the Great Architect of the Universe). Robinson says that it is not a name but a designation (*A Pilgrim's Path*, 35–36). If we take "of" in the phrase "name of God" to be appellative (and thus "of" means "which is"), ritual here disagrees with Robinson. There is the possibility, however, that "name" means "authority."
54. *Official Cipher*, Massachusetts, 104, decoded.
55. *Official Cipher*, New Brunswick, 19.
56. *Official Cipher*, Minnesota, 126, decoded.
57. Viscount Valentia, *Ritus Oxoniensis: Being the Ritual of Craft Freemasonry as Antiently Practised in the Province of Oxfordshire and Elsewhere* (London: Lewis Masonic, 1988), 55–56.

58. *Official Cipher,* Massachusetts, 94–95.
59. Ibid., 163–64.
60. *The Standard Ceremonies of Craft Masonry: As Taught in the Stability Lodge of Instruction* (sometimes known as the *Muggeridge Working*) (London: Lewis Masonic Publishers, n.d.), 124–25.
61. *The Ceremonies of Craft Masonry,* New Brunswick, 106–7.
62. *Emulation Ritual,* 243–44.
63. *Official Cipher,* Massachusetts, 169.
64. The *Indiana Monitor and Freemason's Guide* (The Most Worshipful Grand Lodge of Free and Accepted Masons of the State of Indiana, 1975) perhaps recognizes this conclusion. It states that "behind the ceremonies of all Masonic degrees lies a fundamental conception of this world in which we live and man's place in it" (p. 40).
65. Note the symbolism of the Lambskin Apron, where "purity of life and conduct are essentially necessary to gaining admission to the Celestial Lodge above," the All-Seeing Eye, which "will reward us according to our merits," the Three Steps, the Common Gavel, and the Rough Ashlar.
66. C. Fred Kleinknecht, "Reality and Ritual," *Scottish Rite Journal* (February 1995): 6, emphasis added.
67. This is another ingredient in the worldview of Freemasonry.
68. *The Scottish Workings of Craft Masonry* (London: Lewis Masonic, 1982), 124–25. Recall also the various citations from rituals that fulfill the previous characteristics of a religion. Take the Square, Level, Common Gavel, etc., and apply them to this characteristic.
69. Some rituals have "great books of Nature and Revelation" instead of "Book of Life."
70. *Official Cipher,* Minnesota, 32, decoded. Some rituals end with "which is our spiritual, moral, and Masonic Trestle-Board."
71. *The Sussex Ritual of Craft Freemasonry* (London: Lewis Masonic, 1989), 67–68.
72. See the *Official Cipher,* Massachusetts, 48–50.
73. "It is an Institution having for its foundation the practice of the moral and social virtues" (*Official Cipher,* New Brunswick, 34).
74. Ibid., 83–84.

Chapter 2

The Entered Apprentice Degree

"You have entered a new world. Symbolically and spiritually you have been reborn. This started the moment you were prepared to become a Freemason." —Allen E. Roberts, The Craft and Its Symbols

In this chapter we will examine certain portions of the first degree of Freemasonry and hold them up to the teachings of Christianity. As always, in the task of Christian critique, one must strive to represent fairly others' views, quoting accurately and in context the various sources. Once this is done, one must then apply sound exegesis of the biblical text in the effort to show how an opponent's views are incompatible with Christianity.[1]

Freemasonry's Concept of Deity

As we begin our critique of Masonic theology, there is a fundamental principle that needs to be understood. Common among Grand Lodges throughout the world[2] is the practice that initiates state a trusting belief in a Supreme Being.[3] Masonic Grand Lodges and Masonic literature claim that it is not the institution's purpose to dictate to any man *which* God he must believe in. That is left up to the individual Mason. He may believe in Allah, Jehovah,

God [generically], Jesus, Krishna, Brahman, or another Deity. As Henry Wilson Coil states, "The Masonic Doctrine of the petitioner's declaration as generally recognized is that he must declare in writing his belief in a Supreme Being but need not qualify that in any way. In some jurisdictions, qualifications and additions are required, as has been indicated."[4]

Albert Mackey writes that "the religion of Freemasonry is cosmopolitan, universal; but the required belief in God is not incompatible with its universality."[5] He adds, "There never was a time when the dogma [belief in God] did not form an essential part of the Masonic system."[6] The *Blue Lodge Text-Book,* an "Official Publication of the Grand Lodge of Mississippi," requires every Entered Apprentice candidate to declare his belief in the existence of God.[7] The following interchange between the Worshipful Master and the candidate for Entered Apprentice is common among many Grand Lodges: "[Question:] In whom do you put your trust? [Answer:] In God."[8]

Blue Lodge rituals throughout the world feature a prayer in the Entered Apprentice degree.

> Vouchsafe Thine aid, Almighty Father and Supreme Governor of the Universe, to our present convention, and grant that this Candidate for Freemasonry may so dedicate and devote his life to Thy service as to become a true and faithful brother among us. Endue him with a competency of Thy divine wisdom, that, assisted by the secrets of our Masonic art, he may the better be enabled to unfold the beauties of true godliness, to the honour and glory of Thy Holy Name.[9]

Here Freemasonry is clearly providing initiates with a prayer that petitions God in order to consecrate one's life to Him in devotion and service. But who is this God?

The Masonic name (or "designation"[10]) for God is T.G.A.O.T.U., "the Great Architect of the Universe."[11] The Masonic designation for God is a canopy designation, since, as will be shown, T.G.A.O.T.U. is able to contain in Himself all the various deities of different Masons. If Freemasonry requires of its initiates belief in *a* Supreme Being, then it is possible for men who believe in either Krishna or Jesus, Brahman or Vishnu, Allah or Jehovah to be Masons. Now what happens when a Muslim, a Hindu, a Unitarian,[12] and a Christian attend the same Lodge meeting and bow their heads to the preceding prayer? The Mason may answer that each is praying to the God of his own religious persuasion. If this is so, why is this not specified in the prayer? Why not ask the initiate *who* his God is and pray accordingly? Furthermore, why must Masonic lectures or lessons specifically mention "the Great Architect of the Universe," or "The Grand Artificer of the Universe," or "The Supreme Architect of the Universe"? Distinctly Masonic themes (Architect, Artificer) are being employed here. If the Masonic rebuttal is correct, why not replace these phrases with "the God of your understanding"?

The fact is that these options are conspicuously missing in Masonic rituals. We now observe why. Albert G. Mackey writes that

> the religion of Freemasonry is not sectarian. It admits men of every creed within its hospitable bosom, rejecting none and approving none for his peculiar faith. It is not Judaism, though there is nothing in it to offend the Jew; it is not Christianity, but there is nothing in it repugnant to the faith of a Christian.[13]

Henry W. Coil agrees: "The Masonic test is *a Supreme Being,* and any qualification added is an innovation and distortion."[14] Freemasonry seems to present to its initiates a generic God. It does so to avoid any offense. For example, to specifically name God "Allah" would offend an initiate who does not worship Allah. Thus, on the surface, Freemasonry seems to remain neutral.

But is it neutral? To answer this question, as well as "What happens when a Muslim, Hindu, Unitarian, and Christian find themselves bowing their heads in prayer in Lodge meetings?" we can state on the authority of ritual that the canopy designation (T.G.A.O.T.U.) serves to accommodate all the deities of Masonic initiates. Masonic scholar Carl H. Claudy adds,

> It is the Masonic way of setting forth that simplest and most profound of truths which Masonry has made so peculiarly her own: that there *is* a way, there *does* run a road on which men "of all creeds and of every race" may travel happily together, be their differences of religious faith what they may. In his private devotions a man may petition God or Jehovah, Allah or Buddha, Mohammed or Jesus; he may call upon the God of Israel or the Great First Cause. In the Masonic Lodge he hears the humble petition to the Great Architect of the Universe, *finding his own deity under that name.*[15]

Claudy is not alone. He is joined by Masonic scholar Allen E. Roberts. But first, an introductory word.

The latest and perhaps most popular Masonic apologist is John Robinson.[16] In his book *A Pilgrim's Path,* Robinson takes James Holly (a Christian who opposed the Lodge in writing[17]) to task.

One must wonder why Dr. Holly dwells so much on Masonic writers of generations ago and does not seek information from current Masonic writers who *are* universally recognized as authorities: the prolific Masonic author, Allen Roberts; the Masonic scholar, Professor Wallace McLeod; or the librarian of the United Grand Lodge of England, John Hamill, for example. Why doesn't Dr. Holly contact such men, or quote their writings? Because they won't provide what he wants to hear.[18]

Robinson endorses Allen Roberts as a universally recognized authority on Freemasonry. Though I cannot speak for Dr. Holly, I am certain that *any* Christian[19] writing on the subject of Freemasonry would take issue with this statement from Roberts:

> You have learned that Freemasonry calls God "The Great Architect of the Universe." This is the Freemason's special name[20] for God, because He is universal. He belongs to all men regardless of their religious persuasion. All wise men acknowledge His authority. In his private devotions a Mason will pray to Jehovah, Mohammed, Allah, Jesus, or the Deity of his choice. In a Masonic Lodge, however, the Mason will find the name of his Deity within the Great Architect of the Universe.[21]

Though a previous quotation by Coil (near the beginning of this chapter) stated that the candidate's belief in a Supreme Being need not be qualified in any way—and it seems that Masonic scholars state this over and over again—in Blue Lodge ritual a designation (if not a name) is indeed given to the Deity. This strongly implies that ritual seeks, at the very least, to take up all the various possible deities of Masons in any one particular Lodge room and bring them under the canopy designation T.G.A.O.T.U. Thus, *Blue Lodge Freemasonry does define God!* It does so in a most subtle way by not initially obligating the candidate to define *which* God he believes in, but then *in practice* placing all candidates' gods under its canopy designation. By doing this the Craft defines who God is.

Freemasonry's God *is* universal. "Universal" qualifies and thus defines the term "God." With (1) the possibility of any man who believes in a Supreme Being joining the ranks of Freemasonry, and (2) the usage in Blue Lodge ritual of such terms as "God," "Grand Artificer," and "the Great Architect of the Universe," the Lodge makes it possible for its initiates to read any of their particular gods into T.G.A.O.T.U.[22]

From a Christian perspective, the pluralistic conception that the true and living God is worshiped, prayed to, or sought by many people using different designations cannot hold, either exegetically (from the Bible) or logically. In other words, the statement that "God is God and it doesn't matter what you call Him" is useless and fallacious.

From an exegetical standpoint, the exclusiveness of Christ's claims about Himself, and those from the apostles,[23] cannot be true and at the same time coincide with the pluralistic framework of Freemasonry. In John 14:6, Jesus confronts such beliefs by stating, "I am the way, the truth, and the life; no one comes to the Father except through me." Jesus claims to be the only one who can reconcile sinful humanity with God the Father.

Two observations follow: (1) Other beliefs of the candidates of Freemasonry have no place for Jesus Christ (as He is defined in Scripture) as God the Father's only way for people to be saved. Neither do they have a place for the biblical Jesus as *exclusively* and *uniquely* fully God and fully human (John 1:14, 18).[24] Thus they end up denying Christ's deity and uniqueness as Savior. If they deny His deity, it logically follows that they in turn deny the God of the Bible, who is triune.[25] The point is that you cannot reject Christ as God, call God by some other name, and still believe in and worship the God of the universe, who is the God of the Bible (Isa. 44:6; 45:5; Heb. 1:1–2). (2) Since the biblical record shows that the God of the universe is the God of the Bible, the claim in John 14:6 cannot be taken to be *only* for a certain people. If He is the God of the universe, He is God over all, and consequently all must be saved in the way that He and He alone ordains.

Logically, if there is only one God and it does not matter what someone calls or defines as God, then it is possible to call a tree in Colorado "God." If that is true—and I admit that it is an extreme example—then is that person really worshiping Allah, or Jehovah? No, because worship must be *directed* in some way *toward* something. And if it is directed toward something or someone, it must therefore be cognitively defined.[26] The tree in Colorado is *not* Allah or Jehovah; and, for reasons given above, neither is Allah Jehovah!

Turning back to exegesis, in the Old Testament one continuously finds God condemning nations that worship other gods (Deut. 7:1–5, 9; 13:1–3; 1 Chron. 16:26). Nowhere does the Bible teach that God can be called by various names when the content, character, and attributes of the gods known by those various names clash with Yahweh. God does not tolerate worship of Him that differs from what He has revealed in Scripture (see Deut. 13:1–2, 6, and esp. 12–14).

Second, if (as I will show later in this chapter) Freemasonry offers a hope of salvation in its ritual, and any man who believes in a Supreme Being (regardless of what he calls that Supreme Being) may be a Mason, then what would the Muslim say? The Muslim would certainly hold that Christians, Jews, and Unitarians are guilty of not worshiping the true God, since in his view all must turn to Allah. It is theologically naive to maintain that an all-encompassing Deity like T.G.A.O.T.U. would not offend the Muslim. If in ritual the hope or reminder of being in the presence of God is provided for a man who does not believe in Allah and rejects Mohammed as a prophet of God, then this hope or reminder is purely blasphemous. According to Islamic beliefs, these infidels will never enter into the presence of Allah. Thus, Christians should not be the only people who have theological difficulty with Freemasonry. Anyone of an exclusive monotheistic faith should have such difficulty.[27]

Third, carried to its logical conclusion, T.G.A.O.T.U. is guilty of providing several written revelations (the Koran, the Bible, the Bhagavad Gita, etc.) that contradict each other.[28] Masonry recognizes as equally valid any sacred writing a particular candidate considers binding unto himself; thus, Freemasonry as an institution does not hold the Bible to be God's only written revelation to humankind. If all the various deities such as Jehovah, Allah, Krishna, and others are subsumed under the Masonic canopy designation of the Great Architect of the Universe, and sacred writings (VSLs) may come from these deities,[29] then T.G.A.O.T.U. has given us these revelations. And yet they contradict each other.[30] For example, the Bible teaches that Jesus is the Son of God and that He died on the cross. The Koran, however, teaches that He is not the Son of God (Sura 4:171) and that He did not die on the cross (Sura 4:157). Therefore the view that God has given to humanity both the Bible and the Koran cannot be sustained, since God cannot change, lie, or contradict Himself. Moreover, with all the contradictions that can be found when comparing the Koran to the Bible, the Bhagavad Gita to the Koran, the Bible to the Bhagavad Gita, the Upanishads to the Koran, etc., one is forced to one of two possible conclusions: either they are all wrong, or one of them is right. They cannot all be right.

In the following critique, the most important thing to remember is that Freemasonry will initiate any man who believes in *a* Supreme Being.[31] At the outset, Freemasonry is not concerned with *which* God the candidate puts his faith in. A candidate may reject Jesus Christ as Savior and Lord, deny His deity (see John 8:24 for the ramifications of such a denial) and still be made a Mason. Having demonstrated this, it remains to be shown whether Freemasonry teaches that its initiates may obtain salvation. If it does, we must then determine whether the Bible contradicts Freemasonry on this issue.

Masonic Apron

Perhaps the most distinguished article of Masonic regalia is the Lambskin Apron. In the ritual of the first degree the initiate is presented with the Apron and is told that "it is an emblem of innocence and the badge of a Mason, more ancient than the Golden Fleece or Roman Eagle, more honorable than the Star and Garter,[32] or any other order that can be conferred upon you."[33]

Later in the ritual the Apron is mentioned again, this time hinting at the afterlife.

> The Lamb has in all ages been deemed an emblem of innocence. He, therefore, who wears the Lambskin as the Badge of a Mason is constantly reminded of that purity of life and rectitude of conduct so essentially necessary to his gaining admission into the Celestial Lodge above, where the Supreme Architect of the Universe presides.[34]

The following segment from a European ritual shows that the *content* of rituals is essentially the same worldwide, though the *wording* may differ.[35]

> You will observe that this Apron is made from the skin of a Lamb, and as the Lamb has been from time immemorial the universally acknowledged[36] emblem of Purity and Innocence, you will be thereby reminded of that purity of life and actions which should at all times distinguish a Freemason, and which is most essential to your gaining admission to that Grand Lodge above, where the blessed ever rest in eternal peace.[37]

Biblical Response

A critique of the symbolism and lesson of the Masonic Lambskin Apron must begin with Freemasonry's most commonly held requirement: candidates must believe in *a* Supreme Being. We can logically assume therefore that Unitarians, Muslims, Jews, and others who believe in a Supreme Being may enter the portals of Freemasonry.

Let us take Unitarians, who deny that Jesus Christ is God's only Savior, is divine, was born of a virgin, made atonement for sin, and was bodily resurrected. According to the Bible, Christ's atonement and resurrection are *necessary* components of the gospel, by which one is saved (1 Cor. 15:1–4; Rom. 1:16). Christ's deity must also be believed in if one is to be saved (Rom.

10:9–10; John 8:24). According to the Bible then, Unitarians cannot be Christians.

For the reader who is a Mason but not a Christian, please understand the theological dilemma that the Christian church[38] has at this point. The main question here is this: When the Unitarian is given the lecture on the Masonic Apron and is told that he is reminded of that purity of life and conduct that is essential to his gaining admission into the Celestial Lodge above, is that a *false* reminder? Is it a false reminder according to the Bible?[39] Yes, for the Craft in its ritual tells the Unitarian, who denies who Christ is and what He did on the cross, that he is reminded of purity of life and conduct so essentially necessary to gaining admission into the Celestial Lodge above. This is diametrically opposed to the teachings of Christ and the apostles. Jesus stated, "I am the way, the truth, and the life; no one comes to the Father except through me" (John 14:6). Peter also preached the exclusivity of Christ as the only way for all humanity to be saved (Acts 4:12). For the Christian who is a Mason[40] (or for the Mason who claims to be a Christian), this theological incompatibility should be clear.

The Mason might respond at this point by saying that "the ritual is merely reminding the Unitarian of what *he* believes to be true *for himself.*" But that is not the point I am contesting. The question I asked above ("Is that a false reminder?") calls for an answer concerning objective realities (spelled out in the Bible), not subjective personal feelings. In other words, "Is it ultimately, in reality, a false reminder?" Here we are distinguishing between "what is true *for him*" and "what is *true* for him." The first focuses on the subjective sense, such as someone's believing with all his strength and mind that the Cleveland Indians won the 1993 World Series; it is true *for him*. The second focuses on the objective reality. Though someone believes that the Cleveland Indians won the World Series, it is not really true.

Now let us apply this to our theological question. If ontologically (as to His real nature) Christ is the only way, and the Unitarian denies who Christ is and what He did, should a Christian be involved in this ritualistic teaching in which the Apron reminds the Unitarian of that purity of life and conduct that is essential to his gaining admission into the Celestial Lodge above?

Christ's claim in John 14:6 must be interpreted in light of the opening of John's gospel, which states that "the Word [Christ in His preincarnate existence] was God." With the Bible's affirmation that God is the God of the universe, Christ's claim in John 14:6 cannot be limited to His culture or to His followers only. The Unitarian will not enter heaven if he rejects the person and the claims of Christ (John 8:24). Ontologically the Apron *is* a false reminder. It does not square with the real nature of Christ as God.

The Hoodwink

When the candidate for Entered Apprentice enters the Lodge room, he wears a "Hoodwink" (blindfold). Every Mason knows that the Hoodwink symbolizes "darkness." The question that concerns us is what *kind* of darkness. Is it moral darkness? Is it spiritual darkness? Or does it simply mean ignorance of the teachings of Freemasonry? Our answer must come from ritual. As we shall see, what occurs *after* the Hoodwink is taken off the candidate's eyes is vital to understanding its symbolism. But first some introductory observations are necessary.

The ritual contains a question-and-answer segment in which the candidate's conductor is asked, "Who comes here?" He answers, "[The candidate's name], who is in darkness and wishes for light, to have and receive a part of the rights and benefits of this Worshipful Lodge, erected to God and dedicated to the holy Saints John [the Baptist and the apostle]."[41] After another short series of questions the candidate is led to the Masonic Altar, upon which rest the "Three Great Lights in Freemasonry"—the Volume of the Sacred Law (VSL), the Square, and the Compass. He is then asked to kneel, still blindfolded, before the altar on his naked left knee, and swear an oath of secrecy that he will never reveal the secrets of Freemasonry.[42] Upon completion of this obligation the candidate is asked, "What do you now most desire?" He answers, "Light."[43] Genesis 1:1–3 is then recited (this particular reading occurs only if the candidate wishes to take his obligation on the Bible; for those of other faiths, passages from the appropriate VSL are read). The Hoodwink is removed from the candidate. He finds himself kneeling before the Three Great Lights in Freemasonry. He is told the following: "The Bible we take to be the rule and guide of our faith; the Square to square our actions; and the Compass to circumscribe our desires and keep our passions within due bounds with all mankind, most especially with our Brothers in Freemasonry."[44]

We must therefore interpret the "darkness" to be both spiritual and moral because of what immediately follows—a lecture on the symbolism of the Three Great Lights. The VSL (first Great Light) is said to be the rule and guide of the Mason's faith (spiritual); the Square and Compass are said to symbolize the squaring of actions and the circumscribing of desires (moral). If, after the Hoodwink (which symbolizes darkness) is removed, the candidate finds himself before the Three Great *Lights,* and one of those Lights is the rule and guide of faith, does not this "darkness" mean spiritual darkness? Some Masons may argue that the Hoodwink represents darkness with respect to the teachings of Freemasonry. This statement actually ends up affirming our interpretation, for Blue Lodge Freemasonry's symbolism is laden with spiritual and moral teachings designed to be impressed upon the candidate's mind![45]

The science of hermeneutics (principles of interpretation) provides solid ground upon which to conclude that the Hoodwink's symbolic meaning is spiritual and moral darkness. Whenever we interpret a text or a speech, we must listen to what precedes it as well as what follows it. (This is one of the basic principles of interpretation.) Having done this, we can find no other option for interpretation of the Hoodwink.[46]

Biblical Response

The Mason enters the Lodge room with a Hoodwink on, symbolizing that he is in spiritual and moral darkness and in need of "Light." But the Christian, redeemed and justified by God through faith in Christ, is not in spiritual and moral darkness. Christ calls His followers the "light of the world," because they are to be beacons of light to a dark and unredeemed world (Matt. 5:14–16). It was probably for this reason that Paul wrote, "Ye were sometimes darkness, but now are ye light in the Lord: walk as children of light" (Eph. 5:8, KJV). Christians are "light in the Lord" because they have been born again by grace through faith in Christ, who is *the* Light of the World, and following Him means not walking in darkness (John 8:12). For this reason (and others), one cannot be a Christian and an informed Mason at the same time.

The Common Gavel

Assigning religious meanings to the working tools of stone masons is part and parcel of Freemasonry (Speculative Masonry).[47] That is illustrated in the symbolism of the "Common Gavel."

> The Common Gavel is an instrument used by operative Masons to break off the rough and superfluous parts of stones, the better to fit them for the builder's use. But we, as Free and Accepted Masons, are taught to make use of it for the more noble and glorious purpose of divesting our hearts and consciences of all the vices and superfluities of life; thereby fitting our minds, as living stones, for the spiritual building, that house not made with hands, eternal in the heavens.[48]

Biblical Response

Again, in response we must keep in mind that Freemasonry, as an institution, admits men of different faiths into its ranks. We have seen earlier in this chapter that men who deny the deity of Christ and His atonement on the cross may become Masons. From a biblical perspective these men are lost and in need of Christ if they are to have eternal life and enjoy everlasting rest in the presence of God. There is no other way for them to be saved. Without faith in Christ only eternal judgment and condemnation will be theirs (John 8:24; 14:6; Acts 4:12). Masons may call this "bigoted,"[49] but it is nevertheless the message of the New Testament.

The symbolism of the Common Gavel alludes to the "spiritual building" not made with human hands, eternal in the heavens. This reminds the Mason to live his life divesting his heart and conscience of all the vices and superfluities of life. The word "thereby" in the quotation above is fundamental to our interpretation that the Common Gavel is a symbol of works righteousness. "Thereby" is an adverb connecting the works (divesting) with the main point (fitting the mind for the spiritual building in heaven), which is the *outcome* of the works. The "thereby" functions grammatically to make the divesting essential for the fitting. Thus, preparation of the candidate's mind for heaven is accomplished by the divesting.

Once again, such teaching is contrary to Christian theology. Any divesting of the heart and conscience of the vices and superfluities of life is done by the Holy Spirit at the point of regeneration and throughout the Christian's life. That occurs only if a person acknowledges Jesus Christ as Lord and Savior.

In addition, the lecture pertaining to the Common Gavel involves a mixture of 1 Peter 2:5 and 2 Corinthians 5:1. The passage from 1 Peter says that *Christians* are like "living stones" who are "being built up as a spiritual house into a holy priesthood to offer up spiritual sacrifices acceptable to God *through Jesus Christ*" (v. 5). The passage from 2 Corinthians says that if *our* (Christians') "earthly tent" is destroyed, *we* have "a building of God, an house not made with hands, eternal in the heavens" (KJV).

The problem the Masonic Lodge faces with these two passages is that they are Christ-centered (thus my emphases above—*Christians, our, we*). Even a cursory reading of 1 Peter and 2 Corinthians 4 (as it leads into chap. 5) reveals this. Peter's first letter was written to Christians who were being persecuted "because[50] of the name of Christ" (4:14). Thus, Peter exhorts them with what strongly appears to be the main point of the letter: "Forasmuch ["Therefore"[51]] then as Christ hath suffered for us in the flesh, arm yourselves likewise with the same mind" (4:1, KJV). Believers are called to this purpose because *Christ* has suffered for them (2:21). Christians are the living stones, not any Mason who rejects Christ. Second Corinthians 5 begins by giving a reason[52] for hope to Christians who were being persecuted for Jesus' sake (4:11). That is, we should not despair, *because* we have a house in heaven to look forward to. The point is that the Lodge's symbolism of the Common Gavel is void of these considerations.[53] It is guilty of taking the Bible out of context by (1) missing the point of these two passages, and (2) applying them with a saving implication to Masons who reject Christ.

The Covering of a Lodge

In the *Colorado Craftsman,* a monitor for the Grand Lodge of Colorado, we read about the "covering" of a Masonic Lodge.

> Its [a Lodge's] covering is no less than the clouded canopy or starry decked heaven, where all good Masons hope at last to arrive, by the aid of that ladder which Jacob, in his vision, saw extending from earth to heaven, the three principle rounds of which are denominated Faith, Hope, and Charity; which admonish us to have faith in God, hope of immortality, and charity to all mankind. The greatest of these is Charity: for our faith may be lost in sight; Hope ends in fruition; but Charity extends beyond the grave, through the boundless realms of eternity.[54]

Incidentally, both Mackey and Coil mention the symbolism of the ladder, which represents moral and intellectual progress, found in the ancient Mystery Religions.[55]

Biblical Response

Candidates are taught that the "covering" of a Lodge symbolizes the "canopy" of heaven. Further, the quotation above states that "all good Masons" hope to arrive there "by the aid of the ladder." One rung of the ladder symbolizes "faith in God." But *which* God is alluded to? Although Freemasonry calls God T.G.A.O.T.U., a canopy designation that subsumes all of the various Masons' deities, I argue that Freemasonry actually does define who God is. If this is true, then the God of Freemasonry (as an institution, notwithstanding differences among individual Masons) is the God that Masons are "admonished" to put their faith in. And if this God is not the God of the Bible, then the Lodge promotes an unbiblical idea. According to the Bible, heaven is not promised to those who put their faith in other deities (Acts 4:12; 1 Cor. 8:5–6; Gal. 4:8).

The reader who disagrees with my observation concerning the canopy designation must still face the fact that Masonry as an institution leaves it up to the individual Mason to read his particular God into this ritual segment. Here I ask non-Christian Masons to consider why Christians would have problems with the Craft's teaching that "all good Masons" hope to arrive in heaven. There can be no promise of heaven for those who do not believe (place their trust) in Jesus Christ. For Masons who claim to follow Christ, and thus have the biblical conviction that Christ is the only way (John 14:6), the reality is that the Lodge teaches heresy on this point. All good Masons will not arrive in heaven with the help of "Jacob's ladder."

We now turn to the meaning of the Old Testament passage mentioning Jacob's ladder. The similarity to Abraham's vision (Gen. 15) is easily seen. Just as the Lord revealed Himself to Abraham in a vision and established a covenant of promise,[56] which included the gift of the land and the promise of prosperity and blessing to all nations, so Jacob's vision (Gen. 28) follows in the same way (28:13–15). Thus, the purpose of this passage "is to show that in all the events of the narratives [contained in Gen. 29–35] that follow we are to see a fulfillment of the promise here to Jacob."[57]

In the New Testament the apostle Paul relates this Old Testament passage to the salvation of all God's people. The phrase "Jacob I loved, but Esau I hated" (Rom. 9:13; cf. Mal. 1:2) shows the purpose of God's divine election of those whom He saves through faith in His Son Jesus Christ. This is to show that those who have faith in Christ, though they are not necessarily of the blood line of Abraham (Rom. 9:6–8) and Jacob, are the "seed" of Abraham (Gal. 3:7) and Jacob by God's grace. We see then the further fulfillment of God's promise to Jacob, communicated through the vision of the ladder in Genesis 28,[58] *when people believe in Christ as Lord and Savior* (Rom. 3:21–26; also chaps. 9–11). Applying these Old and New Testament passages to our situation today, this further fulfillment continues, but belief in Christ is absolutely necessary for its continuation.

The Lodge's interpretation of Jacob's ladder is faulty. There is no warrant for the ladder itself containing rungs that represent "Faith, Hope, and Charity." This phrase is found in 1 Corinthians 13:13 (KJV). Yet no mention of Jacob is made in 1 Corinthians 13 or in all of 1 or 2 Corinthians. Further, the *meaning* of the rungs of the ladder is nowhere mentioned in Genesis 28.[59] Here is an example of the Lodge's reading into the Bible a meaning it never intended to convey.

Summing up our observations, we see that the Lodge symbolizes one of the rungs of the ladder to mean "Faith in God," and yet either "God" is not defined by the Lodge, or it is the Masonic "God" (or designation) that the Mason is to place his faith in. Also, the meaning of Jacob's vision is not what the Masonic Lodge says it is; the Lodge uses this biblical passage out of its context.[60] The passage points in fulfillment to those whom God saves through faith in Christ, not to the attainment of heaven by "all good Masons" with the aid of Jacob's ladder. Finally, if the passage points to Christ as its ultimate basis of fulfillment, and Christ is the only way of salvation for all peoples, then the Masonic Lodge's application of it to men of faiths that reject Christ is opposed to the doctrine of salvation revealed in the Bible.

The Rough and Perfect Ashlars/Trestle-Board

A common type of symbolism in most, if not all, American and Canadian Lodges is that of the "Rough and Perfect Ashlars." As is usually the case, the lesson begins with the operative masonic significance and moves to the Speculative, or Freemasonic, significance.

> The Rough Ashlar is a stone as taken from the quarry in its rude and natural state. The Perfect Ashlar is a stone made ready by the hands of the workman, to be adjusted by the tools of the Fellow Craft. . . .
> The Rough Ashlar *reminds us* of our rude and imperfect state by nature; the Perfect Ashlar, of that state of perfection at which we hope to arrive by a virtuous education, our own endeavors and the blessing of God.[61]

Biblical Response

Just what is meant by "perfection" in the symbolic instruction of the Perfect Ashlar? How is one to "arrive" at this perfection? These two questions are most important to theological discussion and deserve answers based on (1) the logical relationships of the words to one another in the above quotation (the first question), and (2) the overall teachings of the Craft (the second question).

The key to answering the first question lies with the phrase "by nature." The Rough Ashlar reminds the Mason of his "rude and imperfect state *by nature*." If we take the two Ashlars to symbolize opposite states, we then can see the logical relationship (and thus the conclusion) emerging that the Perfect Ashlar reminds the Mason of "that state of perfection" *by nature*. Perhaps this led Henry Wilson Coil to suggest that the Rough Ashlar and the Perfect Ashlar represent, respectively, "material man and spiritual man."[62]

From a biblical perspective, perfection of our imperfect state (the flesh or fallen nature) can only come through Christ (Gal. 5:24; Rom. 8:9–17; 2 Cor. 5:17–19). With all that has been stated regarding the Lodge's view of God, the biblical view that the perfected state is reached *only* through Christ clashes with the Craft's symbolism of the Rough and Perfect Ashlars. It clashes because this symbolism can apply to the Muslim, the Hindu, the Unitarian, etc., all of whom deny the biblical Christ and His sacrifice on the cross for sin. The Mason who claims Christ as Savior and Lord must not sidestep the issue by appealing to *his* bringing of Christ into the lesson of the Rough and Perfect Ashlars. The issue is one of *allegiance* rather than individual interpretation. That is to say, the Masonic Lodge as an institution makes it possible for the person who denies Christ to apply the Ashlars' symbolism to his own life. The issue is whether this symbolic lesson is a *false* reminder (again, on the ontological level) to the Unitarian, Muslim, or Hindu. Should Christians who by definition hold to the exclusivity of Christ therefore be a part of the Lodge, which teaches something contrary to that exclusivity?

As to the question of *how* this perfection is arrived at, the ritual states that it is "by a virtuous education, our own endeavors and the blessing of God." The ritual does not define what a "virtuous education" is. It can perhaps be viewed as meaning education in the arts, trades, sciences, etc. "Endeavors" may simply mean working a job and thus earning a good reputation, or earning the respect of the community by being a model citizen.

Because principles of interpretation require us to examine a phrase in its immediate and overall contexts, we cannot really find the above interpretations of endeavors and virtuous education accurate. Considering the immediate context, the *Official Iowa Monitor* offers this interpretation of the Rough and Perfect Ashlars:

> . . . our own endeavors and the blessing of God; and by the Trestle-board we are reminded that as the operative workman erects his temporal building agreeably to the rules and designs laid down by the master on his trestle-board, so should we, as speculative Masons, endeavor to erect our spiritual building agreeably to the rules laid down by the Supreme Architect of the Universe in the Book of Life, which is our spiritual trestle-board.[63]

It is interesting to note the parallelism in the lessons of the Rough and Perfect Ashlars and the Trestle-Board (in operative masonry, that upon which building plans are laid). In various Masonic monitors they are taken as one lesson. One therefore may see "virtuous education" operatively as knowledge of the *trade* of masonry, paralleling speculative knowledge of Freemasonry and its teachings.[64] "Endeavors," understood *operatively,* may mean the endeavors of the trade, paralleling *speculatively* the "endeavor to erect our spiritual building" (note the repetition of "endeavor" in the above quotation). If this is the case—and a strong argument for it can be made by appealing to principles of interpretation—then works are an essential part of arriving at that perfection mentioned in the symbolism of the Perfect Ashlar. But we must ask what God is behind these works, for, in the Christian sense, works are the natural outgrowth of the salvation given to us by grace through faith in Christ (Eph. 2:8–10). Moreover, works testify to the fact that the process of being made perfect is continuing in a believer's life, making faith complete (James 2:14–26).

The use of the phrase "the blessing of God" prompts the question Which God? As has been stated before, Freemasonry either offers no definition of God, leaving it up to its initiates to fill in the blank (scenario number one), or does indeed find its Deity in the Great Architect of the Universe (scenario number two and my view). Further complicating things theologically is that the Mason is reminded of *that state of perfection at which he hopes to arrive* with "the blessing of God." Now, taking scenario one or two, and the biblical affirmation that people reach perfection only through Christ, the conclusion we reach is that Freemasonry teaches that perfection may be reached (or at the very least hoped for) outside of Christ.

Conclusion

In this first degree of Freemasonry, Christ may be both included and excluded. He can be included if the Mason receiving the degree claims to be a Christian, and this inclusion is not by any direct mention of Christ in the ritual, but by the candidate's *inserting Christ for himself* into the theological teachings of the Entered Apprentice degree.[65] We admit that in this sense it is technically incorrect to state that the Masonic Lodge excludes Christ. But He *can* be excluded in that no direct mention is made of Him in the ritual, and a man who believes in Krishna instead of Christ may see Krishna as his God and the giver of the saving benefits mentioned in the ritual.

But this is not the issue. Over and over again in this chapter the point has been made that it is possible for the person who rejects Christ to inculcate into his life the lessons of the Lambskin Apron, the Common Gavel, the

Rough and Perfect Ashlars, and the covering of a Lodge room. Although a man is perfectly free to do so, we must, as Christians, commit ourselves to what God has revealed to us in Christ. When we do this, we find that the Lodge, in its silence regarding the mention of Christ, and in its provision of this inculcation, comes into direct conflict with the exclusive claims of Christ Himself.

Notes

1. In response, Masons often quote biblical passages out of context in the effort to quell their Christian opponents' arguments. See the preface, and its n. 1 for an example. Yet another example occurs in the May 1993 issue of *Northern Light* magazine (the official publication of the Supreme Council, 33rd, Ancient Accepted Scottish Rite of Freemasonry, Northern Masonic Jurisdiction, USA). In his article "Freemasonry Can Take It on the Chin," Sovereign Grand Commander Francis G. Paul writes, "Let the record be clear. *Masonry stands in direct opposition to inquisition in any form.* We affirm the truth of the biblical words, 'Come, let us reason together,' as the true basis of peace and brotherhood, believing, as we do, that human beings are capable of reaching more noble heights." Notice that Paul leaves out *what* the "reasoning" pertains to in Isaiah 1:18. It is concerning *sin* and the forgiveness of it, which is based on repentance on the sinner's part (v. 19). The intent of Isaiah 1:18 is to convey that the Lord is willing to forgive sinners if they are willing to turn to Him. The intent of the text is *not* to convey "the basis of peace and brotherhood." This is shown by the overall theme of the book of Isaiah, which is to call an unrepentant and stubborn people (Israel) to repentance toward the Lord; and by 1:19–20, which connects with v. 18 in a "blessing/cursing" theme. It is necessary to read biblical passages in their proper contexts before quoting them to justify Freemasonry's position or stifle its opponents' arguments.
2. The Grand Orient in France does not require of its initiates a stated trusting belief in Deity. It is, of course, possible that there are other Lodges that do not require a profession of belief in a Supreme Being. I simply do not know about them.
3. It may be said that this is one of the "Landmarks" of Freemasonry. I do not use the term in this paragraph because Landmarks (stated beliefs, customs, laws, and fundamental principles of any particular Grand Lodge) differ from one Grand Lodge to the next. Some Grand Lodges do not appeal to any stated Landmarks. When one examines several of the rituals from various Grand Lodges worldwide, however, it is clear that trusting belief in Deity is expressed.
4. Henry Wilson Coil, *Coil's Masonic Encyclopedia* (New York: Macoy Publishing and Masonic Supply Co., 1961), 518.
5. Albert G. Mackey, *Mackey's Revised Encyclopedia of Freemasonry,* 3 vols. (Richmond, Va.: Macoy Publishing and Masonic Supply Co., 1946), 1:409.

Mackey's well-founded opinion concurs with this statement in the Blue Lodge ritual: "It [Masonry] demands of its initiates a trusting belief in God. . . . Around its altar, consecrated to T.G.A.O.T.U., men of all creeds may kneel in one common worship, each holding in his heart with all tenacity his own particular faith" (*The Scottish Workings of Craft Masonry* [London: Lewis Masonic, 1967], xviii).

6. Mackey, *Mackey's Revised Encyclopedia of Freemasonry*, 1:410.

7. *Blue Lodge Text-Book* (Grand Lodge of Mississippi, 1978), 7.

8. *The Standard Work and Lectures of Ancient Craft Masonry* (Grand Lodge of the State of New York, 1973), 30.

9. *Emulation Ritual* (London: Lewis Masonic, 1986), 67.

10. See John Robinson, *A Pilgrim's Path* (New York: M. Evans and Co., 1993), 35. Here Robinson takes issue with anti-Masonic writers who say that Freemasonry's name for God is "the Great Architect of the Universe." It is not a name, says Robinson, but a designation.

11. Rituals may vary as to the first initial. Some read *Supreme* instead of *Great.* There is also debate as to whether "G" stands for *Great* or *Grand.* In any event, the term came into use by at least 1730. See *Coil's Masonic Encyclopedia* (p. 517) for more on the subject.

12. The Unitarian, like the Muslim and the Hindu, denies the unique and eternal deity of Jesus Christ as the second person of the eternal triune God. As a result he denies the true nature of God and therefore does not worship the true and living God (see chap. 1, n. 10 for the exegetical reasons for this).

13. *Mackey's Revised Encyclopedia of Freemasonry,* 2:847.

14. *Coil's Masonic Encyclopedia,* 517.

15. Carl H. Claudy, *Introduction to Freemasonry,* 3 vols. (Washington, D.C.: The Temple Publishers, 1959), 1:37, emphasis added.

16. The *Masonic Square,* a Masonic magazine from England, mentions Robinson's joining of the Craft. He became a member of a Lodge in Cincinnati, Ohio, sometime after the publication of his book *Born in Blood.* In this magazine he is called "the anti-mason dragon-slayer," debating those who oppose the Craft "in head-to-head competition . . . and usually came off best." The article also mentions that to many American Masons, "Robinson was the champion of the Craft" (*Masonic Square* [Addlestone, Surrey: Lewis Masonic, June 1993], 108–9).

17. See chap. 1, n. 7.

18. Robinson, *A Pilgrim's Path,* 98.

19. Lest there be any confusion about what a Christian is, and lest any Mason who calls himself a Christian say that he does not have a problem with the following quotation by Roberts, let us define the term. The New Testament defines a Christian as a follower of Jesus Christ, having been born again through faith in Jesus Christ. If a person claims to follow Christ, it necessarily follows that he or she must believe in His claims about Himself and the Bible's claims about Him.

The nature of Christ's claims, and those of His apostles, prohibit anyone from rightly asserting that there are other ways for humanity to be saved. Consequently, there can be no truth to the claim that the other deities of humanity ontologically exist, for the Bible is clear that there is in reality only one true and living God (see Gal. 4:8), and that this God reveals Himself as Father, Son, and Holy Spirit. For this reason, and others not mentioned here, the person who calls himself a Christian must have no part in an eclectic atmosphere that fosters "acceptance" of other peoples' deities (i.e., "to accept as true"). Christians cannot biblically hold that other conceptions of deities are really the God of the Bible called by different names, especially if these other concepts of God exclude Jesus as God in human flesh, the second person of the Trinity. This may seem harsh to the person who desires to defend other Masons' personal beliefs concerning Deity. "They believe it is true," comes the reply. From the biblical perspective the oft-repeated statement "It is true for him" is not the issue. We must distinguish between "It is true *for him*" (the person *thinks* it is true) and "It is *true*" (it is ultimately or ontologically true) for him. The Bible concerns itself with the latter in this context. See the illustration given in the *Biblical Response* section under "Masonic Apron."

20. See n. 10. The very word that Robinson rejects ("name") is used here by Roberts, whom Robinson endorses as a universally recognized authority!

21. Allen E. Roberts, *The Craft and Its Symbols: Opening the Door to Masonic Symbolism* (Richmond: Macoy Publishing and Masonic Supply Co., 1974), 6.

22. Here we encounter two distinct issues that Masons often confuse. Though it is true that any single Mason may read his particular God into the prayers, lectures, and lessons of the ritual, we must also make the distinction that Freemasonry *as an institution* views all the different deities as being subsumed under the Great Architect of the Universe.

23. I assume here that since Freemasonry accepts the Bible as *a* valid sacred revelation, there is no need to argue about the authenticity of the claims of Christ and of the Bible's record of His statements.

24. The Greek *monogenēs*, in some translations reading "only begotten," implies uniqueness. There are both etymological reasons (see W. Bauer, W. F. Arndt, and F. W. Gingrich, *A Greek-English Lexicon of the New Testament and Other Early Christian Literature* [Chicago: University of Chicago Press, 1979], 527; Leon Morris, *The New International Commentary on the New Testament: The Gospel According to John* [Grand Rapids: Eerdmans, 1971], 105–6) and contextual reasons. John distinguishes between those who become children of God (v. 12), that is, those born of God (v. 13), and Jesus, who is God's unique Son (v. 14). For John to identify Christ with all others who become God's sons and daughters would contradict John's testimony that Christ is God, existing from all eternity with the Father (John 1:1). Humanity does not share this with Christ.

25. The biblical doctrine of the Trinity states essentially that there is one God who is Father, Son, and Holy Spirit.

26. I recognize that a pantheistic framework could allow a person to worship a tree as Brahman. Even this, however, must be defined cognitively, whether subjectively or objectively.

27. For an *implicit* statement to this effect, see Robert A. Gilbert, "Casting the First Stone," *The Northern Light* (Lexington, Mass.: Supreme Council, 33rd, Ancient Accepted Scottish Rite, Northern Jurisdiction, USA, August 1993): 11. Writing about intolerance, Gilbert states that religious fundamentalism and intolerance are not confined to Christians only, but "can also be observed among Muslims and Jews."

28. A contradiction is two or more concepts or statements that cannot be true at the same time and in the same relationship. For example, the statements "Jesus is the Son of God" and "Jesus is not the Son of God" cannot both be true. Either both statements are false or only one of them is true.

29. Most Masonic rituals and monitors in America state that the Bible is God's inestimable gift to man. In countries where the more accurate term "Volume of the Sacred Law" is used, my point is all the more valid, for any holy book binding on the candidate may be used in ritual. The *Emulation Ritual* of England, for example, states that "the Sacred Volume is derived from God to man in general," and that it has a "Divine Author" (pp. 245–46). Obviously this is worded for *any* candidate affirming belief in a Supreme Being.

30. For a discussion of the problem, see *Coil's Masonic Encyclopedia,* 518.

31. Some Grand Lodges add to this necessary qualification the belief in the immortality of the soul or a future existence.

32. These are various orders that have their origin in the Middle Ages and in ancient times. See Oliver Day Street, *Symbolism of the Three Degrees,* 3 vols. (Washington, D.C.: Masonic Service Association, 1924), 1:41.

33. *Florida Masonic Monitor* (Grand Lodge F. & A.M. of Florida, 1977), 27.

34. Ibid., 35–36. It is interesting to note that the *Florida Masonic Monitor* prefaces this statement with the following: "Without the explanation given in this section the mind of the Initiate would still be in darkness; all would be mysterious and incomprehensible" (p. 32).

35. Masons may at times attempt to confuse Christians by stating, "That's not what *my* ritual says!" In such cases Christians can stress similarity in content.

36. The mention of the Lamb, or Lambskin, does *not* carry a Christian meaning. The Lamb is viewed by Freemasonry as a symbol of purity for all cultures. Scholars of religion outside Masonry would agree. See S. Angus, *The Mystery Religions* (New York: Dover Publications, 1975), 83, for a brief mention of an inscription dated 91 B.C. which contains an explicit statement concerning a sacrifice of two lambs followed by a sacrifice of one hundred lambs. In a Kikuyu prayer (Kenya) another lamb is offered to a mountain god for rain; see Andrew Wilson, ed., *World Scripture: A Comparative Anthology of Sacred Texts* (New York: Paragon House, 1991), 612.

37. *The Oxford Ritual of Craft Freemasonry* (London: Lewis Masonic, 1988), 47.

38. By "church" I mean the body of Christ worldwide, which is made up of people believing in the essentials of the Christian faith, including the Trinity, the deity of Christ, the Virgin Birth, Christ's bodily resurrection, the deity and personality of the Holy Spirit, Christ's atonement on the cross, etc.

39. The Interfaith Witness Department of the Home Mission Board, Southern Baptist Convention, issued a 75-page study of Freemasonry in 1993. About the lesson of the Lambskin Apron they write, "Masons find puzzling the use of this quote to prove that Masons believe in a works salvation. They insist that neither this statement nor its context says anything about salvation; rather, it simply states that the Lambskin should *remind* the Mason that 'purity of life and conduct . . . is necessary to obtain admittance into the Celestial Lodge.' This statement does not say that wearing the lambskin or doing good works brings salvation. . . . Do all Masons believe all Masons will reside in the Celestial Lodge in the Sky for all eternity? Masons emphatically answer *no.*" (*A Study of Freemasonry* [Atlanta: Interfaith Witness Department, Home Mission Board, Southern Baptist Convention, 1993], 52).

   The IWD correctly points out the semantic difference between "reminder" and "assurance," but it misses the point in two instances. First, is it a *false* reminding? *Yes,* according to the Bible. And the ritual *does* state that "purity of life and conduct are *essentially* necessary to gaining admission into the Celestial Lodge Above." In the greater context of Masonry, this statement does not square with Christian theology. Second, the point is *not* whether "all Masons believe all Masons will reside in the Celestial Lodge." This is irrelevant, for we cannot base the truth or falsity of a phenomenon on whether or not all people believe it to be so. To reason like this is beyond the parameters of logic. The point is whether the *institution* of Freemasonry perpetuates this false reminder and false theology. Here we must answer *yes.* For these and other reasons I find the IWD's study and several of its conclusions to be weak and compromising.

40. "Mason" here meaning by title only. In this sense there are two types of Masons—those who are largely ignorant of the teachings of the Craft (Masons in name only) and those who are learned (Masons in the true sense of the word). The overwhelming majority fall within the first group. I believe that it is highly unlikely (if not impossible) that a man can be an *informed* Mason and a Christian at the same time.

41. *Official Cipher* (Boston: Grand Lodge of Masons in Massachusetts, 1978), 26, decoded. Other rituals, like that of the state of New York, do not contain this wording. No "darkness" is mentioned in this portion of the ceremony. It is, however, mentioned later in the Lecture Section, part 2 (*The Standard Work and Lectures of Ancient Craft Masonry,* 70).

42. Ibid., 28, decoded.

43. Ibid., 30, decoded.

44. Ibid.

45. See *Mackey's Revised Encyclopedia of Freemasonry*, 1:593–94: "Light is an important word in the Masonic System. It conveys a far more recondite meaning than it is believed to possess by the generality of readers. It is in fact the first of all symbols presented to the neophyte, and continues to be presented to him in various modifications throughout all his future progress in his Masonic career. It does not simply mean, as might be supposed, *truth* or *wisdom*, but it contains within itself a far more abstruse allusion to the very essence of Speculative Freemasonry, and embraces within its capacious signification all the other symbols of the order."

46. Henry Wilson Coil states, "Light is everywhere the symbol of intelligence, information, knowledge, and truth and is opposed to darkness which symbolizes ignorance and evil. So, in the ceremonies, the candidate is said to be brought from darkness to light" (*Coil's Masonic Encyclopedia*, 375).

47. "Speculative" means the symbolized intellectual deduction from operative masonry (actual stone masonry). *Mackey's Revised Encyclopedia of Freemasonry* states, "Speculative Masonry, which is but another name for Freemasonry in its modern acceptation, may be briefly defined as the scientific application and the religious consecration of the rules and principles, the language, the implements, and materials of Operative Masonry to the veneration of God, the purification of the heart, and the inculcation of the dogmas of a religious philosophy" (2:959).

48. *California Cipher* (Richmond: Allen Publishing Co., 1990), 29–30. European rituals may contain the following: "The Common Gavel represents the force of Conscience, which should keep down all vain and unbecoming thoughts which may obtrude during any of the before-mentioned periods, so that our words and actions may appear before the Throne of Grace pure and unpolluted" (*Ritus Oxoniensis* [London: Lewis Masonic, 1988], 52). In essence this is similar to the California Cipher.

49. "To say that one has the truth, all of the truth and the One Truth, and that those who differ are wrong is by definition bigotry" (John Canoose, "A Christian Mason Looks at Masonry and Religion," *The Scottish Rite Journal*, May 1993, 54–55). One has to wonder what Mr. Canoose would say to Christ, who proclaimed, "I am the way, the truth and the life; no one comes to the Father except through me" (John 14:6). Would he try to reinterpret the text? Masons must be made aware, first, that a bigot is a person who holds *blindly* to a particular creed or opinion; and second, that Christians do not hold to the exclusivity of Christ in a blind fashion, for if the Bible is the Word of God (and it can be shown to be just that in a rational way) and it testifies that Christ (who is God the Son, the second person of the Trinity) is the only way, then that is far from *blindly* holding to the position. Let critics either produce evidence against the trustworthiness of the Bible or offer other interpretations of passages such as John 14:6 and Acts 4:12, which teach of the exclusivity of Christ. The first may not be necessary, because (1) Freemasonry believes that the Bible is one of many VSLs, and (2) Mr. Canoose claims to be a Christian, as the title of the article suggests. But

he and others like him must offer another interpretation of John 14:6 and Acts 4:12 (using sound principles of interpretation) or be guilty of implying that Jesus Christ is a bigot.

50. The Greek preposition *en* is an instrumental of cause, meaning here "because of" the name of Christ.

51. The Greek preposition *oun* ("forasmuch," in the sense of "therefore") signals this.

52. Based on the subordinating conjunction *gar* ("because" or "for").

53. The Home Mission Board (HMB) of the Southern Baptist Convention, in its *Study of Freemasonry,* writes, "The ritual for the Fellow Craft degree in the *Murrow Masonic Monitor* used by Oklahoma Masons includes the 'Doxology,' with the phrase 'Praise Father, Son, and Holy Ghost.' Also found in the *Murrow Monitor,* from the ceremony for laying a cornerstone, is, 'According to the grace of God which is given unto me, as a wise master-builder, I have laid the foundation, and another buildeth thereon. But let every man take heed how he buildeth thereupon. For other foundation can no man lay, than that is laid, which is Jesus Christ'" (p. 47). As far as I can tell, these are the only quotations from the *Murrow Monitor* that the HMB cites in its study. The HMB study fails on several accounts. First, it fails to take the whole of Freemasonry into consideration, in that candidates for Masonry in Oklahoma must declare their belief in *a* Supreme Being, not necessarily the God of the Bible (see *Murrow Monitor,* "Fundamental Principles," 6). Second, it does not find it peculiar that Jesus should be mentioned in ritual. (Could this not be because Oklahoma is in the "Bible belt" and therefore all candidates have *some kind* of "profession" in Christ?). Third, it does not take into consideration the charge given to the Grand Chaplain at his installation: "We are sure that in ministering at the Masonic altar the services you may perform will lose nothing of their vital influence, because they are practiced in that spirit of universal tolerance which distinguishes our institution" (*Murrow Masonic Monitor* [Grand Lodge of A.F. and A.M. of the state of Oklahoma, 1988], 177–78). (In the context of Freemasonry and the *Murrow Monitor* itself, "tolerance" most likely means the adaptation of prayers and ritual to each candidate's belief system or God. Here the Grand Chaplain is asked to do nothing that the Craft has not already spelled out in ritual and in the fundamental principles of the Order. Though Christians should practice tolerance of other people's beliefs, for them tolerance is rather respect and recognition of another's right to hold and practice beliefs within the boundaries of the law of the land, even while the Christian opposes those beliefs by this same right and by the mandate of the Bible.) Fourth, what would the Lodge do if a Jew, a Muslim, a Hindu, etc., were to be initiated into the mysteries of Freemasonry in their jurisdiction, expunge these quotations from ritual if they were to offend these candidates? Finally, the HMB does not take into consideration the symbolism of the Entered Apprentice degree: "The Entered Apprentice candidate is typical of unregenerate man groping in moral and mental

darkness and seeking for the light which is to guide his steps, and point him to the path which leads to duty and to Him who gives its reward" (*Murrow Monitor,* 46).

By selectively citing from the *Murrow Monitor,* the HMB has not properly exegeted it. They fail to consider the overall worldview of Freemasonry (see chap. 1) and thus fail to see the above citations in their proper context. If they had, they would have found them either inconsistent with other parts of the *Monitor,* or inconsistent with the universal principles of Masonry and its worldview.

54. *The Colorado Craftsman: or Masonic Monitor,* rev. ed. (Colorado: Grand Lodge of Colorado, 1985), 24.

55. *Coil's Masonic Encyclopedia,* 330; *Mackey's Revised Encyclopedia of Freemasonry,* 1:498–99.

56. This and the following points are taken from John H. Sailhamer in *The Expositor's Bible Commentary,* 12 vols. (Grand Rapids: Zondervan, 1990), 2:196.

57. Ibid.

58. According to Keil and Delitzsch, the ladder symbolized the fellowship between God and His people (*Commentary on the Old Testament in Ten Volumes* [Grand Rapids, Mich.: Eerdmans, reprinted 1985], 1:281).

59. It is one thing to arrive at a *possible* meaning for the ladder based on word studies and cultural analysis, but quite another to read a meaning into the text without evidence, as the Lodge does.

60. *The Colorado Craftsman* continues its monitorial instruction by immediately following the above citing (from n. 54) with this: "The greatest of these is Charity [KJV; translated "love" in most modern translations]: for our Faith may be lost in sight; Hope ends in fruition; but Charity extends beyond the grave, through the boundless realms of eternity" (p. 24). The mention of "love" by Paul in 1 Corinthians 13, however, has its foundational and supreme example in Christ. Christ laid down His life as the Suffering Servant (Phil. 2:5–11), who died on the cross for our sins (Rom. 5:6–8; Eph. 5:1–2). This theme is reflected outside the Pauline Epistles as well (1 John 4:9–10). In this quote contained in *The Colorado Craftsman,* the "for" is used in an explanatory way. "Charity" being "Love" in modern translations (Roberts says, "Masonic charity is in reality love" [*The Craft and Its Symbols,* 29]), the explanation given by the Lodge as to *why* the greatest is Love is not biblical. It is the greatest not because "our Faith may be lost in sight," but because Christ died for our sins.

61. *Official Iowa Monitor* (Most Worshipful Grand Lodge of Iowa, 1991), 23–24.

62. *Coil's Masonic Encyclopedia,* 72.

63. *Official Iowa Monitor,* 24–25.

64. For the curious reader I note here Allen Roberts' initial words about the symbolisms of the Entered Apprentice degree: "You have entered into a new world. Symbolically and spiritually you have been reborn. This started the moment you were prepared to become a Freemason. As you progress in Masonic knowl-

edge your vision will broaden; you will become more vitally alive than ever before; you will become more aware of your fellow man, your family, your church and your country. Your whole philosophy of life will become richer. This will take place, but only if you become Masonically educated" (*The Craft and Its Symbols,* 3).

65. Despite the SBC, HMB's various citations of certain rituals mentioning Jehovah or Jesus Christ, the overall view of God for Freemasonry does not change, as can be seen in Lodge requirements in the same monitors the HMB cites. For example, in its section titled "God," the HMB mentions the Grand Lodge of Texas's consecrating their Lodge "to the honor and glory of Jehovah, the Grand Architect of the Universe" (*A Study of Freemasonry,* quoted from *Monitor of the Lodge* [Grand Lodge of Texas, 1982], 148). First, this quotation does not occur in the first three degrees of Blue Lodge ritual, and it is stated by the autonomous right of the Texas Grand Lodge without interfering with the *common* teachings in Blue Lodge ritual. Second, the HMB again fails to interpret this statement in light of the immediate context. The *Texas Monitor* states, in the "Preparation of the Candidate" section of the Entered Apprentice degree, "You have seriously declared, upon your honor, that you firmly believe in the existence of God" (p. 11). It does not state *which* God. It later states that "our ancient and honorable fraternity welcomes to its doors, and admits to its privileges, *worthy men of all faiths and creeds* who possess the indispensable qualifications . . . [one of Freemasonry's grand purposes is] to inculcate a wider knowledge concerning the existence of the Grand Architect of the Universe" (p. 12, emphasis added). One can only (1) be puzzled therefore at the mentioning of "Jehovah" in this monitor, (2) conclude that the Grand Lodge of Texas would expunge "Jehovah" from this ceremony if a Muslim or a Hindu Lodge were being consecrated, or (3) be both puzzled *and* conclude number two, as I have.

CHAPTER 3

THE FELLOW CRAFT AND MASTER MASON DEGREES

"Every candidate for the Mysteries of Masonry, at the proper time and in an appropriate manner, should be taught the truth that the rite of Initiation means much more than a formal ceremonial progress through the Degrees." —Grand Lodge of Texas, Monitor of the Lodge

In this chapter I shall examine a small portion of the second degree (Fellow Craft). The majority of the chapter is devoted to the third degree, that of Master Mason. In it we find the foundation for all Masonic philosophy and theology. Because of the teachings of the third degree millions of Masons find hope and peace in life, and millions of pages have been written concerning these teachings.

The Fellow Craft

The second degree in Blue or Symbolic Lodge Masonry is called "Fellow Craft." We continue with our critique of some of the symbolic teachings of the Craft.

The Letter "G"

It is in this degree that we learn the meaning of the popular symbol that characterizes Freemasonry in the United States and Canada. The Square interwoven with the Compass and with the letter "G" placed in the middle garnishes license plates, belt buckles, the lapels of sport coats, and various other items. This symbol also crowns many Masonic Lodges. In ritual one is told that the "G" represents the science of Geometry.

> By Geometry we may curiously trace Nature through her various windings to her most concealed recesses. By it we discover the power, wisdom and goodness of the Grand Artificer of the Universe, and view with delight the proportions of this vast machine. By it we discover how the planets move in their respective orbits, and demonstrate their various revolutions. By it we account for the return of seasons, and the variety of scenes which each season displays to the discerning eye. Numberless worlds are around us, all framed by the same Divine Artist, which roll through the vast expanse, and are all conducted by the same unerring law of Nature.[1]

The Worshipful Master continues, however,

> But, my Brother [or Brethren], the letter G has a still further and most solemn allusion. It alludes to the sacred name of God, to whom should we all, from the youthful Entered Apprentice who stands in the north-east corner of the Lodge to the Worshipful Master who presides in the East, most humbly and reverently bow.[2]

Biblical Response

Three questions need to be raised here. First, does the ritual imply that *Freemasonry* does have a "sacred name" for God? Second, if so, what is this sacred name? And third, does ritual allow *each individual Mason* to read his particular Deity into the symbolic lecture?

That Freemasonry has a sacred name for God is obvious. One would have to totally ignore the above lecture in ritual to believe otherwise. And as we have seen from quotations from rituals and Masonic scholars in chapter 2, Freemasonry has its designation, or special name, for the Deity: T.G.A.O.T.U. (the Great Architect of the Universe). In answer to our third question, again from chapter 2, each Freemason may read his God into T.G.A.O.T.U.[3]

Although each Mason is free to find his God within the Great Architect of the Universe, in ironic fashion he relinquishes his claim that his God is the *only* true and living God! Masons who claim to be Christians are no exception here. But how is this? The answer is that during ritual, *prayers are offered, addressing T.G.A.O.T.U., and the person praying uses the pronouns "we" and/or "our," meaning that T.G.A.O.T.U. is addressed by someone praying in behalf of all Masons assembled.* In other words (just as Allen Roberts observes; see n. 3), one Deity is petitioned on behalf of all the Masons assembled. And since it is possible, or even likely, that many differing deities are represented in any given group of Masons, it strengthens my observation that T.G.A.O.T.U. is a canopy designation for the Masonic God.

In the following prayers from Masonic ritual, we see exactly that:

Most holy and glorious Lord God, the Great Architect of the Universe, the giver of all good gifts and graces, in Thy name *we* have assembled and in Thy name *we* desire to proceed in all *our* doings.[4]

Supreme Architect of the Universe, as *we* are about to separate, accept *our* humble praises and the gratitude of *our* hearts for the many mercies and blessings Thy bountiful goodness has conferred upon *us.* . . . May *we* practice Thy precepts, that *we* may obtain the fulfillment of Thy promises, and gain an entrance through the gates into the Temple and City of *our* God. Amen.[5]

The lesson of "brotherly love" adds weight to the evidence that Freemasonry does have a sacred name for God, and buttresses my thesis of a Masonic canopy designation. In the ritual of the Entered Apprentice degree candidates are told,

By the exercise of brotherly love we are taught to regard the whole human species as one family; the high and the low, the rich and the poor; who, as created by one Almighty Parent and inhabitants of the same planet, are to aid, support and protect each other. On this principle, Masonry unites men of every country, sect and opinion, and conciliates true friendship among those who might otherwise have remained at a perpetual distance.[6]

Who is this "one Almighty Parent"? If Masonic ritual proclaims T.G.A.O.T.U. and contains prayers addressed to T.G.A.O.T.U., we have no reason to doubt that from a Masonic perspective this Almighty Parent *is* the Great Architect. Additionally, though it is true that by *creation* we are one family,[7] and that we are all created by one Almighty Parent, the Bible identifies this Parent as God—Father, Son, and Holy Spirit. The biblical God is not referred to in Blue Lodge ritual as being this "one Almighty Parent." Rather—and this on the basis of an interpretive principle, that is, taking *the whole* of Blue Lodge ritual into consideration—we find T.G.A.O.T.U. referred to in the prayers and lessons of the first three degrees. And, as we have seen, T.G.A.O.T.U. represents *all* the different deities of Masons. Thus, it is the Great Architect that ritual calls this "one Almighty Parent."

In our last quotation we read that "Masonry unites men of every country, sect and opinion." Notice that men of every *sect* are united. Freemasonry unites men of differing religions[8] (and thus men with different gods) by employing the designation T.G.A.O.T.U in prayers, lessons, and lectures. This is far more than a simple fraternal organizational uniting. It is a spiritual uniting, and one that Christians are warned against being a part of (2 Cor. 6: 14–18).

The Master Mason

The third degree of Blue Lodge Masonry, that of Master Mason, is considered the pinnacle of Freemasonry.[9] Though there are higher numbered degrees in, for example, the York Rite and the Scottish Rite (see Introduction),[10] from a strictly Blue Lodge perspective these are best seen as concentric circles extending outward from the pinnacle. In all probability this third degree was not added to Masonry until six to fifteen years after the Grand Lodge in England was formed in 1717.[11]

One reason why this degree is called the pinnacle of the Craft is that the three degrees of Blue Lodge Freemasonry represent man in his various stages of life. The Entered Apprentice degree represents youth in time of learning; the Fellow Craft, manhood in time of work; and the Master Mason, old age in wisdom and the culmination of life leading to death. The third degree thus represents the time when death calls and the wearied workman is summoned by the Great Architect of the Universe to heavenly refreshment.[12] Perhaps that is why England's *Emulation Ritual* states that "the working tools of a Master Mason teach us to bear in mind, and act according to, the laws of our Divine Creator, that, when we shall be summoned from this sublunary abode, we may ascend to the Grand Lodge above, where the world's Great Architect lives and reigns forever."[13]

The Three Steps

"The Three Steps" are found within a series of "emblems" (certain items emblematic of something) in the third section of the Master Mason degree. Keeping with the theme of youth, manhood, and old age, we learn,

> The Three Steps usually delineated upon the Master's carpet,[14] are emblematical of the three principal stages of human life: *Youth, Manhood,* and *Age.* In *Youth,* as Entered Apprentices, we ought industriously to occupy our minds in the attainments of useful knowledge; in *Manhood,* as Fellow Crafts, we should apply our knowledge to the discharge of our respective duties to God, our neighbor, and ourselves; that so, in age, as Master Masons, we may enjoy the happy reflection consequent on a well-spent life, and die in the hope of a glorious immortality.[15]

Various forms of Masonic art portraying three steps leading up to radiant beams of light in the heavens most likely are inspired by the Three Steps.

Biblical Response

In the beginning of the previous chapter I dealt with the crux of the matter in detail. Briefly, however, a basic requirement for all candidates for the mysteries of Freemasonry is that they believe in *a* Supreme Being. Thus the Unitarian, Muslim, Hindu, Christian, etc., may all be Masons. So it is possible to be a Mason and at the same time reject who Christ claimed to be.

My critique of the lesson of the Three Steps focuses on its last statement. We will concern ourselves not with the individual Mason who reads his particular God or hope into the lesson, but rather with the *institution* of Freemasonry. If the Mason is a Muslim, what is the ritual communicating to him? That the Muslim will die "in the hope of a glorious immortality." Based on the revelation of God in Jesus Christ, who claimed that no one comes to the Father except through Him (John 14:6), this is a false hope.

The Pot of Incense

In the *Missouri Cipher* (a Blue Lodge ritual book) we read that "the Pot of Incense is an emblem of a pure heart, which is always an acceptable sacrifice to the Deity; and as this glows with fervent heat, so should our hearts continually glow with gratitude to the Great Beneficent Author of Our Existence for the manifold blessings and comforts we enjoy."[16]

Let us see what the Bible says about pure hearts.

Biblical Response

The psalmist states in Psalm 24, "Who shall ascend into the hill of the LORD? or who shall stand in his holy place? He that hath clean hands, and a pure heart; who hath not lifted up his soul unto vanity, nor sworn deceitfully. He shall receive the blessing from the LORD, and righteousness from the God of his salvation" (vv. 3–5, KJV). For our purpose, the important question is Who and what makes a pure heart?

The setting of the psalm makes it unjustifiable to claim that the phrase "he will receive . . . vindication from the God of his salvation" (Ps. 24:5) refers to *any* individual's particular God. Rather, it refers to Yahweh, who has acted to bless His people.[17] As for a pure heart, no one can boast, "I have kept my heart pure; I am clean, without my sin" (Prov. 20:9). This cleansing comes only by God's grace. Not just any god can accomplish this; only the God of the Bible can give us clean hearts (Ps. 51:10) and declare our hands clean[18] (see Deut. 30:6).[19]

It is by grace through faith in Christ that one's heart is made pure. Once again Freemasonry implicitly refers to a biblical and theological concept that may seem innocent but is not. Given the selective universalism of Masonry,[20] which portrays in rituals saving hope for its variously religious candidates, teachings such as that symbolized by the Pot of Incense threaten the very exclusiveness of the God of the Bible, who gives a pure heart to whom *He* wills. Allah cannot do this; Brahman cannot do this; Krishna cannot do this; no "god" can do this except the triune God of the Bible.

Masons who claim to be Christians are hard-pressed to deny this. Thus they are faced with the fact that they belong to an institution that espouses unbiblical lessons like the Pot of Incense. Masonic scholars or apologists who disagree must either disprove my interpretation of ritual or offer an alternative interpretation of the Bible regarding the exclusiveness of Christ's claims.

Other Emblems from the Third Degree

The following key components form the basis of my critique of the emblems: (1) the exclusivity of Christ and His claims, (2) the God of the Bible's being the only true and living God, and (3) how Freemasonry admits men of differing creeds and sets forth in symbolic lectures the hope of a glorious immortality. Therefore, I will not give a biblical response to the following selection of emblems. The reader is asked, however, to answer this question: From a biblical perspective, can the lessons of these emblems apply to those outside the Christian faith?

The All-Seeing Eye, "whom the Sun, Moon, and Stars obey, and under whose watchful care even Comets perform their stupendous revolutions, pervades the inmost recesses of the human Heart, and will reward us according to our merits."[21] The Anchor and Ark are "emblems of a well-grounded hope and a well-spent life. They are emblematical of that divine ark which safely wafts us over this tempestuous sea of troubles, and that anchor which shall safely moor us in a peaceful harbor, where the wicked cease from troubling, and the weary shall find rest."[22] The Scythe is

an emblem of time, which cuts the brittle thread of life, and launches us into eternity. Behold what havoc the scythe of time makes among the human race! If by chance we should escape the numerous ills incident to childhood and youth, and with health and vigor attain the years of manhood; yet, withal, we must soon be cut down by the all-devouring scythe of time, and be gathered into the land where our fathers have gone before us.[23]

The Legend of Hiram Abif

The greatest distinguishing mark of the Master Mason degree, and its central focal point, is the legend of Hiram Abif. Many Freemasons claim, though there is no supporting evidence, that Freemasonry can be traced back to ancient times and the building of King Solomon's Temple. The Old Testament mentions that Hiram of Tyre, a skilled bronze worker, helped build the house of the Lord (1 Kings 7:13–45). Hiram[24] is also mentioned in 2 Chronicles 2:13–14 (also 4:16).

At this point Freemasonry departs from the biblical account of Hiram and enters into the realm of speculation in its dramatic presentation of the death of the "Grand Master Hiram Abif." Hiram is the central figure in the second section of the Master Mason degree.[25]

One early source for the legend of Hiram Abif is Dr. James Anderson. In his *Constitutions* of 1723, Anderson states that *King* Hiram of Tyre (not Hiram Abif) "sent his Masons and Carpenters to Jerusalem. But above all, he sent his namesake Hiram, or Huram, the most accomplished Mason upon Earth."[26] Later, in his 1738 edition, Anderson embellished his previous statement, saying that after the completion of the Temple, "their joy was soon interrupted by the sudden death of their dear Master, Hiram Abif, whom they decently interred in the Lodge near the Temple, according to ancient Usage."[27] The Bible nowhere mentions the death of Hiram.

In ritual the candidate plays the legendary hero Hiram Abif in a dramatic reenactment. He is confronted by three "ruffians" who ask that they each be given the secrets of a Master Mason. Each time the candidate (or his conductor) answers "I will not" (thus remaining true to the obligation of a Master Mason).[28] The third ruffian counters, "Then die!" and slays the candidate (though all three admit to the conspiracy). The candidate is instructed to lie motionless on the floor of the Lodge room. Seeing that they have slain their Grand Master Hiram Abif, the three then conspire to "bury the body in the rubbish of the Temple (of Solomon) until low twelve [midnight]," when they plan to return to give the body proper burial. They then take the body on a westerly course from the Temple to a hill west of Mount Moriah, where they bury it in a grave dug due east and west, placing on top of the grave a "Sprig of Acacia." The three ruffians plan to escape, but their plan is foiled when a search party of Fellow Craft Masons sees the Sprig of Acacia in the ground. One of them pulls it up easily, signaling something strange. The ruffians are captured, are taken before King Solomon (played by the Worshipful Master of the Lodge), confess to their vile crime, and are executed. The search party then returns to the site of the Sprig and digs up the dirt over the putrid remains of Hiram Abif.

Attempts to raise the body of Grand Master Hiram now commence, first by the "grip of an Entered Apprentice," which is accomplished by gripping the candidate's right hand with the right hand and placing the thumb on the knuckle of the candidate's forefinger. This is not successful, as "the skin slips from the flesh"[29] because the body has been dead for such a lengthy time. Another attempt is made, this time with the "grip of a Fellow Craft," which is made in the same manner as above, though this time by placing the thumb on the second knuckle. Again the attempt fails because "the flesh cleaves from the bone."[30]

A question is now put forth: "What shall we do?" The answer comes, "Pray."[31]

Thou, O God, knowest our down-sitting and our up-rising, and understandest our thoughts afar off. Shield and defend us from the evil intentions of our enemies, and support us under the trials and afflictions we are destined to endure while traveling through this vale of tears. Man that is born of woman is of few days, and full of trouble. He cometh forth as a flower, and is cut down; he fleeth also as a shadow, and continueth not. Seeing his days are determined, the number of his months is with Thee; Thou hast appointed his bounds that he cannot pass; turn from him that he may rest till he shall accomplish his day. For there is hope of a tree if it be cut down, that it will sprout again, and that the tender branch thereof will not cease. But man dieth and wasteth away; yea, man giveth up the ghost and where is he? As the waters fail from the sea, and the flood decayeth and drieth up, so man lieth down, and riseth not up till the heavens shall be no more. Yet, O LORD! have compassion on the children of Thy creation; administer them comfort in time of trouble, and save them with an everlasting salvation. Amen.[32]

After this prayer King Solomon (the Worshipful Master) states that he will endeavor to raise the body "by the strong grip of a Master Mason, or the Lion's Paw of the Tribe of Judah."[33] Some Lodge rituals omit the phrase "of the Tribe of Judah,"[34] while still others from Europe state, "taking a more firm hold of the sinews of the hand,"[35] not even mentioning the strong grip or the Lion's Paw. Hiram (the candidate) is then raised to "the five points of fellowship," which are foot to foot, knee to knee, breast to breast, hand to back, and cheek to cheek (or mouth to ear). Legend then states that Hiram was afterward given a proper burial near the Temple of Solomon.

To recap and conclude the legend, the body of Grand Master Hiram was first buried in the rubbish of the Temple, then in the ground on a hill west of Mount Moriah, "and thirdly, near the Sanctum Sanctorum or Holy of Holies of King Solomon's temple and Masonic tradition informs us that there was erected to his memory a Masonic monument."[36]

Interpretations of the Hiramic Legend

What are we to make of all this? A charge commonly made by Christian critics of Freemasonry is that the Master Mason degree assures the candidate of a future resurrection[37] and/or salvation. Masonic apologist John Robinson denies the charge pertaining to resurrection.[38]

The act referred to in the allegation of resurrection is easily identified. In the initiation drama of the third degree, the master builder of Solomon's temple is murdered by three assassins, who hide the body in an obscure grave in the wilderness. By the time the grave is discovered, the body is decomposing. It is dug up and brought back to Jerusalem for a proper burial. Taking a body from one grave to put it in another is called "re-interment," or reburial. It meets no one's definition of *resurrection*.[39]

Robinson has his facts straight. That is exactly the story line of the drama of the Master Mason degree. It does seem puzzling that critics would make these allegations. Henry W. Coil writes, "Who ever heard of reinterring a resurrected person? What would be the sense of resurrection, if it were to be followed by reinterment?"[40] So, why do some say that the drama of the third degree does teach what critics allege?[41]

For example, on page 87 of his book *The Craft and Its Symbols,* Allen Roberts states, "Freemasonry teaches the immortality of Man; *the resurrection of the body* and eternal life" (emphasis added). This statement was made in the section titled "Freemasonry's Great Legend," referring no doubt to the Legend of Hiram Abif.

The eminent Masonic scholar Albert Mackey saw the following symbolism in the dramatic legend of the third degree:

Here, then, in Masonry, is what was called the *aphanism*[42] in the ancient Mysteries. The bitter but necessary lesson of death has been imparted. The living soul, with the lifeless body which encased it, has disappeared, and *can nowhere be found.* All is darkness—confusion—despair. Divine truth—the Word—for a time is lost, and the Master Mason may now say, in the language of Hutchinson, "I prepare my sepulchre. I make my grave in the pollution of the earth. I am under the shadow of death." But if the mythic symbolism ended here, with this lesson of death, then were the lesson incomplete. That teaching would be vain and idle—nay, more, it would be corrupt and pernicious—which should stop short of the conscious and innate instinct for another existence. And hence the succeeding portions of the legend are intended to convey the sublime symbolism of a resurrection from the grave and a new birth into a future life. The discovery of the body, which, in the initiations of the ancient Mysteries, was called *euresis,*[43] and its removal, from the polluted grave into which it had been cast, to an honored and sacred place within the precincts of the temple, are all profoundly and beautifully symbolic of that great truth, the discovery of which was the object of all the ancient initiations, as it is almost the whole design of Freemasonry, namely, that when man shall have passed the gates of life and have yielded to the inexorable fiat of death, he shall then (not in the pictured ritual of an earthly lodge, but in the realities of that eternal one, of which the former is but an antitype) be raised, at the omnific word[44] of the Grand Master of the Universe, time to eternity; from the tomb of corruption to the chambers of hope; from the darkness of death to the celestial beams of light; and that his disembodied spirit shall be conveyed as near to the holy of holies of the divine presence as humanity can ever approach to Deity. Such I conceive to be the true interpretation of the symbolism of the legend of the Third Degree.[45]

Mackey *could* be interpreted as relating a doctrine of resurrection (note Mackey's use of "resurrection" and "raised"), though it is improbable, considering his mention of the "disembodied spirit" coming near to Deity.

Mackey is joined by Masonic scholar Carl Claudy, who writes that "the Entered Apprentice passes through the period of early Masonic youth. The Fellowcraft is emblematic of manhood; while the Master Mason learns that true Freemasonry gives to a man a well-spent life, and assurance of a glorious immortality."[46] Claudy also states, "The whole drama of the Master Mason Degree is of immortality."[47] Though the teaching of the immortality of the soul is not the same as the teaching of resurrection or salvation, the overall teachings of Blue Lodge Masonry strongly portray the hope of being in the presence of T.G.A.O.T.U., as we saw in the symbolism of the Lambskin Apron. Thus, the Masonic doctrine[48] of the immortality of the soul, if we take the whole of Masonic Blue Lodge ritual into consideration, necessarily carries with it an allusion to salvation.

Finally, one other respected Masonic scholar, Joseph Fort Newton, recalls in a footnote of his famous work *The Builders,*

> How many Masons fail to grasp the master truth of the Master Degree! And yet the candidate is not altogether to blame since the historical lecture does not even mention it, much less expound it. That lecture only reminds the candidate that Masonry cherishes the hope of a glorious immortality—that is all. Whereas in the Degree itself immortality is not a vague hope to be cherished here and realized hereafter. It is a present reality into which the candidate is symbolically initiated; a fact to be realized here and now. If our ritual does not convey this truth, it behooves us to see that it does, first by laying hold of the truth ourselves, and second by so shaping our ceremony, or at least by so explaining it, as to make the truth unmistakable. Manifestly, if we are immortal at all, we are immortal now, and to know that fact is the one great human experience.[49]

Let us also review the teachings of various Grand Lodges. In their respective rituals (monitors) they express their views on the meaning of the legend. The *North Dakota Monitor* and monitors from other states, such as Louisiana, New Mexico, and Florida, state,

Then let us imitate the good man [Hiram] in his virtuous and amiable conduct; in his unfeigned piety to God; in his inflexible fidelity to his trust; that we may welcome the grim tyrant Death, and receive him as a kind messenger sent from our Supreme Grand Master, to translate us from this imperfect to that all-perfect, glorious and celestial Lodge above, where the Supreme Architect of the Universe presides. . . . By its legend and all its ritual, it is implied that we have been redeemed from the death of sin and the sepulchre of pollution. "The ceremonies and the lecture," as a distinguished writer has observed, "beautifully illustrate this all-engrossing subject, and the conclusion we arrive at is, that youth, properly directed, leads us to the honorable and virtuous maturity, and that the life of man, regulated by morality, faith and justice, will be rewarded at its closing hour by the prospect of eternal bliss."[50]

The *Murrow Masonic Monitor* sees in the legend the teaching of resurrection.

Remember, then, that as the body of G. M. H. A. [Grand Master Hiram Abif] was buried in the rubbish of the Temple, so must yours be buried in earth's friendly bosom; as he was raised, so likewise must you be raised—not, indeed, by the brotherly grip of an earthly master, but at the awful command of Him who rules the heaven and the earth, and in answer to whose summons and word graves will be opened, seas give up their dead, and all stand before His judgment seat to render unto Him their dread account. . . . Let the Temple, which you have this evening partly raised, be so beautiful, so adorned with Charity's choicest jewels, and so acceptable to the All-Seeing Eye, that when, at the close of a virtuous life, you are summoned hence by the Omnific Word, you may be admitted to that glorious and celestial Temple, "that house not made with hands, eternal in the heavens."[51]

Other Grand Lodges opt for immortality of the soul. The monitor of the Grand Lodge of Texas states that the legend of Hiram Abif "embodies the symbolic lesson of life, death and immortality."[52] The *Washington Monitor and Freemason's Guide* explains that the Hiramic legend "symbolizes our faith in the immortality of the soul";[53] the *Louisiana Masonic Monitor,* that "it is intended to impress upon our minds—the immortality of the soul";[54] and Alberta, Canada's *Lodge Plan for Masonic Education,* that "it is a drama

of the immortality of the soul."[55] Lastly, the Grand Lodge of New York interprets the legend as portraying "the solemn and sublime doctrine it is intended
to impress on our minds—the fidelity of true manhood and the immortality of
the soul."[56]

Based on the testimony of Masonic apologists and monitors, we may
safely say that the Legend of Hiram Abif teaches either the future resurrection of the body (the minority view) or the immortality of the soul (the majority view). The Sprig of Acacia plays a major part in interpreting the legend in
these ways. Observe three separate Blue Lodge rituals regarding the Sprig of
Acacia or Evergreen.

> The good Freemason is revived by the ever green and ever living
> Sprig of Faith, which blooms at the head of the grave. It reminds him
> that there is an immortal spark in man, bearing a close affinity to the
> Supreme Intelligence of the Universe, which shall survive the grave
> and never, never die. This strengthens him to look forward with con-
> fidence and composure to a blessed immortality, and he doubts not
> that in the glorious morn of the resurrection his body will rise and
> become as incorruptible as his soul.[57]

> . . . but, when we look forward to the acacia, which budded and
> bloomed at the head of the grave, we are reminded of the immortal
> part, the spirit or soul of man, which will live when time shall be no
> more. It [the soul or spirit] is the inspiration of that great Divinity
> whom we adore, and bears the nearest resemblance or affinity to that
> Supreme Intelligence which pervades all nature, and which shall nev-
> er, never die.[58]

> . . . but when we reflect on the Sprig of Acacia found blooming at the
> head of the grave, we are reminded that we have an immortal part
> within us which shall survive the grave, and which will never, never,
> never die.[59]

So far we have established what the legend is, what it inculcates, and
what some Masonic writers and Grand Lodges have said about it. It remains
for us to form our own interpretation of the legend.

Our Interpretation of the Legend

To interpret any body of literature, one must understand the context. For example, we know that the phrase "a trunk full of bugles," if the context sur-

rounding it is a traveling marching band, means a car trunk full of musical instruments called "bugles." To interpret that phrase as meaning an elephant trunk full of munchy snack food would be to interpret it outside its context, thereby misinterpreting the phrase. So it is with the Masonic legend of Hiram Abif contained in the second section of the Master Mason degree. We must interpret the legend in light of what surrounds it—the first and third sections of the degree; and we must examine what may be included as an interlude (a hymn) within the second section itself.

Masons generally agree that the Hiramic legend symbolizes the immortality of the soul. What is hotly debated is whether or not *salvation* is included in this symbolism. I believe it is.

First, as stated above, we must assume that the three sections of the Master Mason degree are connected in some logical way with some kind of agenda. Confusion and lack of direction would result if the sections and their particular ingredients were simply thrown together haphazardly. Second, what is the point of a teaching concerning the immortality of the soul without a view on *where* the soul goes after death? The two go hand in hand. That is the case in Freemasonry, as we will see.

Heading our list of surrounding phenomena that allude to eternal life in God's presence is a portion from the first section of the third degree. Here Ecclesiastes 12:1–7 is recited, the end of which reads, "Then shall the dust return to the earth as it was: and the spirit shall return unto God who gave it."[60] Here "dust" represents the body, and "spirit" represents that immortal part of human beings that survives the grave and shall never, never die.[61]

Second is the funeral dirge sung during the second section of the degree. This is known also as *Pleyel's Hymn.* It is sung before the attempts to raise Hiram's body. Part of the last verse reads, "Lord of all! below, above, fill our hearts with truth and love; When dissolves our earthly tie, take us to Thy Lodge on high."[62] Again, the implication is that there is a hope that accompanies the doctrine of the immortality of the soul, and this hope is a future life in God's "Lodge on high."

Third is the prayer (already cited) before the raising of the candidate. The end of the prayer reads, ". . . save them with an everlasting salvation." In European rituals one is likely to find a prayer in the beginning of the working of the degree that states, "Endue him [the candidate] with such fortitude that in the hour of trial[63] he fail not; but that passing safely under Thy protection, through the valley of the Shadow of Death, he may finally arise from the tomb of transgression,[64] to shine as the stars for evermore."[65] Here again something more than mere belief in the immortality of the soul is set forth.

Last on our list of salvific phenomena surrounding the legend of Grand Master Hiram are the several emblems or symbols contained in the third section of the degree. These have already been mentioned earlier in the chapter. The reader is asked to review the symbolism of the Three Steps, the All-Seeing Eye, the Anchor and the Ark, and the Scythe. Respectively, these refer to a glorious immortality, a reward according to one's merits, rest for the weary in a peaceful harbor, and a gathering into the land (see n. 23) where our fathers have gone before us.

It would seem strange if the second section (the Hiramic legend) were not connected in any way to the first and third sections. And, as we have seen, these latter two do contain elements of a salvific nature. Thus we can only conclude that the legend of the Master Mason degree must have something to do with the gist of the first and third sections.

We have to agree with various Grand Lodges that say, in essence, the following: The Hiramic Legend symbolizes man in his later years. Struggling through the toils of life, he finally meets the last and terrible grim messenger of death. Though death may seem to end existence as we know it, there remains the hope that all Master Masons have. This hope arises from faith in the immortality of the soul and is symbolized by the Evergreen or Sprig of Acacia. Through the lesson of the great drama of the Grand Master Hiram Abif, we learn that, though death overtakes us, our souls may bloom in eternal spring.

This we take to be the teaching of the third degree of Blue Lodge Freemasonry. It teaches the doctrine of the immortality of the soul, and with it the degree as a whole is flooded with the teaching of a glorious afterlife. We come to this conclusion because the principles of sound interpretation lead us to it.[66]

The Lion of the Tribe of Judah

The raising of the candidate with the Lion's Paw might cause some Masons to state that the whole meaning of the degree is Christ-centered. Christ, in Revelation 5:5, is called "the lion of the tribe of Judah." Here are some observations concerning this. First, not all rituals contain the phrase. They either omit the portion "of the tribe of Judah" or omit the whole phrase and use another phrase, as documented above.

Second, the story of the death, burial, and raising of Hiram Abif bears astonishing similarities to the legend of the Egyptian god Osiris. The legend of the death, burial, and resurrection of Osiris tells of a plot by Typhon to slay Osiris. Typhon induces Osiris to lie down in a chest. Thereafter Typhon and his fellow conspirators shut the chest tight and bring it to the mouth of the Nile River. Isis, Osiris's wife, sets out to find her husband's body and eventually hears that the chest was found among the branches of a tamarisk tree and enclosed within the tree's trunk. Isis eventually recovers the chest and her husband's body, but Typhon finds this out, tears the body into fourteen pieces, and scatters the pieces throughout the land. Isis, hearing the news, sets out once again, and collects the pieces of her beloved's body, building a tomb at each site were she finds a piece.[67] Osiris is eventually resurrected[68] and becomes king of the underworld. In ancient funeral inscriptions from pyramid texts, and inscribed upon simple coffins during the ancient Roman dynastic period, the dead are identified with the god Osiris. If Osiris lives forever, the deceased shall live forever.[69] Moreover, for numerous centuries drama plays depicting the sufferings, death, and resurrection of Osiris were performed.[70] Before Masons jump too quickly toward a Christian allusion from the passion play of Hiram Abif, they should consider this legend of Osiris, to which some Masonic scholars point as very much resembling the Hiramic legend.[71]

Third, it is alleged that the collection of Montfaucon, at the Austin-Friars of La Place des Victoires, contains a painting representing the death and resurrection of Osiris.[72] The picture, in Egyptian hieroglyphic style, portrays the body of Osiris atop a figure of a lion transformed into a couch. Here the body is raised by the strength of the lion's paw and figuratively represents the ascent of the soul of Osiris or his resurrection.[73] Though a scant possibility, it is nonetheless *a* possibility that this could be the source for the Lion's Paw in Masonic ritual, with "of the Tribe of Judah" later added to allude to Solomon, since he was from the tribe of Judah. The word "lion" would refer to Solomon since in ancient Mesopotamia the lion was used figuratively to refer to kings or rulers. Also, there appears a reproduced hieroglyphic picture in Albert Pike's *Morals and Dogma*.[74] Copied from an ancient Egyptian monument, a lion stands over a corpse grasping the left arm of the body with its left paw and holding up high in its paw the Ankh, the Egyptian symbol for life. This, if authentic, provides a powerful historical background source for interpreting the phrase in Masonic rituals.

Fourth, in light of Freemasonry's eclectic environment, it seems rather odd to claim that the Lion of the Tribe of Judah refers to Christ. Still, the phrase is found in some Grand Lodge rituals. What would a Lodge do if, for example, a Muslim were to be initiated into the third degree? If indeed it refers to Christ, would they expunge it from the ritual to accommodate the candidate? That is a good question for the Christian Mason to ask the Worshipful Master or his Grand Lodge. The monitor of the Grand Lodge of Texas offers an opinion true to the spirit of Freemasonry, stating, "LION OF THE TRIBE OF JUDAH—Refers in its original interpretation to Christ; Him who 'brought life and immortality to light'; also describes the Messiah of the Jewish Mason, or the mediator of some of the ancient religions of the East; also one of the titles of King Solomon."[75]

Fifth, building on our third observation (from Pike's *Morals and Dogma*), I believe that this is the most plausible explanation of the phrase: The lion is a symbol of strength and power. In the ancient Near East the lion was a symbol for rulers or kings.[76] Solomon was king over Israel and was of the tribe of Judah. Solomon is also the person who, in the Legend of Hiram Abif, raises the body of Hiram. Recall that the raising of Hiram's body by the Lion's Paw is synonymous with "the strong grip of a Master Mason." Thus the phrase "Lion's Paw of the Tribe of Judah" refers to king Solomon's method of raising up the corpse of Hiram and "Lion of the Tribe of Judah" refers to Solomon.[77]

Given the above observations, it is far-fetched to read into the legend of Hiram Abif an allusion to Jesus Christ.

The Ancient Mysteries and Freemasonry

Many Masonic scholars and critics of Freemasonry find parallels in content with the ancient mysteries of Greece, Rome, Egypt, etc.[78] According to one scholar,

> The mysteries (mostly in the plural, *mustēria* [the Greek here and following is transliterated]) were societies with secret rites and doctrines, admission to which was through instruction, discipline, and initiation (*teletē*, literally "a making perfect"), the celebrant being called a hierophant (one who discloses the holy), and the one initiated or being initiated a mystic (*mustēs*).[79]

Another scholar writes, "Mysteries were initiation rituals of a voluntary, personal, and secret character that aimed at a change of mind through experience of the sacred," later adding that they are "a form of personal religion, depending on a private decision and aiming at some form of salvation through closeness to the divine."[80]

Their secrecy contributes to the scholar's dilemma of not knowing *exactly* what went on in these cults that existed from the sixth century B.C. to the fifth century A.D.[81] We can nevertheless gather data from ancient writers who told of the ideas of certain of the mysteries into which they were initiated without disclosing the secret rites of their specific cults.[82] Still, Angus notes,

> We have extant but a few literary works dealing with the Mysteries, many scattered references, verses of poetry, fragments of hymns and prayers, mutilated inscriptions, damaged papyri, cult emblems, bas-reliefs, frescoes, painted vases, ruined chapels and temples. These are the varied and imperfect material out of which we have to attempt reconstruction.[83]

Some of the scattered references that Angus mentions come from Plato (late fifth century B.C.), who said,

> The founders of the mysteries would appear to have had a real meaning, and were not talking nonsense when they intimated in a figure long ago that he who passes unsanctified and uninitiated into the world will lie in a slough, but that he who arrives there after initiation and purification will dwell with the gods.[84]

This, among other references that will follow, is what causes modern researchers to believe that the mysteries carried with them the teaching of some kind of blessed afterlife, provided that one was properly initiated into the society, having gained adequate *gnosis* (knowledge) of divine secrets. As Plato explains, "The latter sort they call mysteries, and they redeem us from the pains of hell, but if we neglect them no one knows what awaits us."[85]

From Plutarch (first–second century A.D.) comes another allusion to the mysteries' promise of a blessed afterlife: "[They] think that some sort of initiations and purifications will help: once purified, they believe, they will go on playing and dancing in Hades in places full of brightness, pure air and light."[86] Speaking of the mysteries at Eleusis (Eleusinian mysteries), Cicero (first century B.C.) writes that they show "how to live in joy, and how to die with better hopes."[87] Though evidence about the ancient Mystery Religions remains sparse, we can nonetheless state that in all probability they concerned themselves (though not exclusively) with the promise of a blessed afterlife.[88] Consider the following from Plutarch in his *Letter of Consolation to His Wife:*

> You are hearing from some people, who persuade many to believe them, that the dead have no feeling or consciousness at all. But I

know you are kept from believing that by your father's teaching and by the mysteries of Dionysus, into which we have both been initiated. Remember that the soul, which is immortal . . .[89]

Characteristics of Mystery Religions

Samuel Angus, in his book *The Mystery-Religions,* lists multiple characteristics that these ancient cults shared.[90] While many of these characteristics are similar, in essence, to those of Christianity, there are several marks that distinguish the mysteries from Christianity. Freemasonry shares these distinguishing marks.[91] The following is Angus's list of characteristics:

1. *The ancient mysteries were religions "of symbolism, which, through myth and allegory, iconic representations, blazing lights and dense darkness, liturgies and sacramental acts, and suggestion quickened the intuitions of the heart, and provoked in the initiate a mystical experience conducing to palingenesia (regeneration), the object of every initiation."*[92]

In the religion of Freemasonry we have, as Masons state, "a system of morality, veiled in allegory and illustrated by symbols." The ritualistic acts of Freemasonry make use of light and darkness (literally and figuratively), while the enacted drama play of the Master Mason degree is designed to bring the initiate to realize the immortality of the soul and, when the third degree is considered, a blessed afterlife. Angus even observed that "in the enacted passion-drama of the resurrection of Osiris [an Egyptian deity played by the initiate in the mysteries of Osiris] the initiate read the promise of his own triumph over death: 'as truly as Osiris lives shall he live; as truly as Osiris is not dead shall he not die.'"[93] In many of the Masonic rituals previously cited, we have the assurance of triumph over the grave.

2. *"A Mystery-Religion was a religion of Redemption which professed to remove estrangement between man and God, to procure forgiveness of sins, to furnish mediation."*[94]

All the evidence from the various Masonic rituals and monitors points to Freemasonry's concern for the removal of estrangement between God and man. The whole ritualistic practice of prayer offered to T.G.A.O.T.U., the symbolism of darkness characterized by the Hoodwink, the coming of the candidate to light as symbolized by the Volume of the Sacred Law, and the doctrine of the immortality of the soul (in some Grand Lodges the doctrine of a resurrection to a future life) have the sole purpose of removing the estrangement between God and man. In this sense the Masonic Lodge mediates between its candidates and God. Forgiveness of sins is strongly implied in Blue Lodge rituals and in the burial services (see chap. 4) of certain Masonic Grand

Lodges. The symbolism of the Lambskin Apron, the Common Gavel, the Covering of a Lodge, and the Three Steps allude to a glorious afterlife in the presence of God, implying that one's sins have been forgiven; it is not uncommon to find Masonic magazines stating that brother so-and-so has entered the "Celestial or Grand Lodge Above."[95] Masonic scholar Carl Claudy once stated that "true Freemasonry gives to a man a well-spent life, and assurance of a glorious immortality."[96] In Freemasonry, as in the ancient mysteries, the initiate dies with hope. In the death and resurrection of the cult Deity, whether Osiris or Attis,[97] or in the rites of Dionysus or Eleusis, the enacted death and resurrection drama plays of the ancient Mystery Religions formed the basis of their initiates' hope of life beyond the grave.[98] Freemasonry offers the same hope.

3. *"The Mystery-Religions were systems of* Gnosis. . . . *There was something, whether doctrine, symbol, or divine drama, which could not be imparted except by initiation to those duly qualified to receive, a supernatural revelation which gave the recipient a new outlook upon life, the world, and the deity, and a security denied to the uninitiated. The 'mystery' consisted in an objective presentation of the history of the cult-deity in his or her struggles, sorrows, and triumphs."*[99]

In the system of Blue Lodge Freemasonry, "knowledge" (Greek, *gnosis*) of the teachings of the Craft is a must. As the candidate proceeds in his initiation into "the mysteries of Freemasonry"[100] he must learn of the great symbols of the Craft and inculcate them into his life. He gains this knowledge as he progresses up the Three Steps, or grades of initiation, of the three degrees of Freemasonry. With the first degree comes "light," with the next two degrees comes "further light." With knowledge of the symbols of the Craft comes a lifestyle worthy of the institution. Also, a man must *qualify* to partake of the mysteries of Freemasonry, declaring his belief in a Supreme Being and being himself moral and upright in character. The mysteries of Freemasonry are intended only for those worthy of receiving them; they are not for the profane. As I have heard numerous times, "Masonry makes a good man better."

Through the dramatic presentation of the Legend of Hiram Abif, where the struggles, sorrows, and triumphs of Hiram are acted out, the candidate learns that his own life will be filled with such struggles, but that he will ultimately triumph. This is symbolized by the doctrine set forth in the Legend of Hiram Abif, namely, the immortality of the soul. Through the valleys of life the candidate is to draw on the legend for strength until that day he is summoned to that Great Abode where the Great Architect of the Universe dwells.

4. *"A Mystery-Religion was a Sacramental Drama which appealed pri-marily to the emotions and aimed at producing psychic and mystic effects by which the neophyte might experience the exaltation of a new life. . . . A Mys-tery-Religion was thus a divine drama which portrayed before the wondering eyes of the privileged observers the story of the struggles, sufferings,[101] and victory of a patron deity, the travail of nature in which life ultimately tri-umphs over death, and joy is born of pain. This was impressed on the behold-er by a solemn mimic representation."[102]*

A great design of the ancient mysteries was to change the initiate's view of the world, his life, and his purpose in life. Masonic scholar Allen Roberts makes the same claim for Masons:

> As you progress in Masonic knowledge your vision will broaden; you will become more vitally alive than ever before; you will be-come more aware of your fellow man, your family, your church and your country. Your whole philosophy of life will become rich-er. This will take place, but only if you become Masonically edu-cated.[103]

The passion plays of the mysteries of Attis, the finding of the body of the Egyptian god Osiris, and the legend of Dionysus[104] were all concerned with dying to the old life and coming into the new life. So it is with Freema-sonry. Albert Mackey writes, "Thus in the Egyptian Mysteries we find a representation of the death and subsequent resurrection of Osiris; in the Phoenician, of Adonis; in the Syrian, of Dionysus; in all of which the scenic apparatus of initiation was intended to indoctrinate the candidate into the dogma of a future life."[105] Mackey concludes, "The idea, therefore, proposed to be communicated in the myth of the ancient Mysteries was the same as that which is now conveyed in the masonic legend of the Third Degree."[106]

5. *"The Mysteries were eschatological religions having to do with the interests and issues of life and death."[107]*

The word *eschatology* means the study of last things or end times. The doctrine of the immortality of the soul was of chief concern to the ancient mysteries. This was the object of the passion plays. The struggles, sufferings, death, and consequent afterlife of the patron deity were enacted with the hope that initiates would one day enjoy the benefits of a blessed hereafter conse-quent on a well-spent life. Masonry is, as we have seen, no stranger to this kind of passion play, featuring Hiram Abif. The candidate for the degree of Master Mason not only plays the part of Hiram, but he learns some important lessons from Grand Master Hiram's struggles, sufferings and death. He learns that there is an immortal spark in man that survives the grave and never, never dies.[108]

6. *"A Mystery-Religion was a personal religion to which membership was open not by the accident of birth but by a religious rebirth."*[109]

Sometimes reacting to the state religions of Greece and Rome, where one was of a particular religion due to birth, the ancient mysteries made membership in their cults a matter of religious rebirth. In this way the ancient mysteries provided the initiate with a new way of life, a new way to view and relate to the world, and the hope or promise of salvation regarding the age to come. Allen Roberts, obviously no stranger to the study of the ancient Mystery Religions, writes, "You have entered a new world. Symbolically and spiritually you have been reborn. This started the moment you were prepared to become a Freemason."[110]

When a man becomes a Freemason, the claim is that his whole philosophy of life becomes richer. He now has a new way to relate to the world. Indeed, he has become part of a worldwide brotherhood under the Fatherhood of God. The principles of Freemasonry serve to mold his mind into a living stone for that spiritual building not made with hands, eternal in the heavens. The working tools of the Craft provide him with the knowledge to build his spiritual temple, so that finally, when his labors on earth are finished, being level, square, and plumb, he will meet the approval of the Great Architect of the Universe.

A Common Element

According to Angus, an interesting phenomenon accompanies the above six points.

> In these personal cults the worshippers were united by the ties of fellowship with the deity of their choice, by the obligation of common vows. . . . The Mysteries made terms with polytheism and pantheism by making their respective deities all-comprehensive, and with monotheism by equating the gods of competing religions with their cult-deity.[111]

No doubt the reader sees similarities between Freemasonry's concept of an all-comprehensive Deity (T.G.A.O.T.U) and the ancient mysteries' all-comprehensive deities that subsumed polytheistic, pantheistic, and monotheistic deities.[112]

Conclusion

In the legend of the third degree one can see the promise of a resurrection—a glorious bodily immortality. Or one may see in it the doctrine of the immortality of the soul. Freemasonry teaches through the legend of Hiram Abif the immortality of the soul. The ritual of the third degree thunders with the hope of a blessed afterlife, perhaps bodily, perhaps not. The questions Christians need to ask are: Does the Masonic Lodge set forth this teaching to those who reject Christ as God and Savior? Does the Lodge avail the great lesson of the Master Mason degree to those who reject Christ's atonement on the cross and believe in some other way of salvation? Remember that the issue for the Mason who claims to be a Christian is not what *he* reads into the degree, but rather what Blue Lodge Freemasonry *as an institution* provides for every Mason, which is the *framework* to embrace a doctrine of the immortality of the soul and a blessed afterlife. Yet many Masons reject the deity of Christ and His saving work on the cross. This should concern the Christian because, in light of the teachings of the New Testament, Christ is the only way of salvation, rendering false the hope that the Lodge gives to Unitarians, Muslims, Jews, Hindus, etc.

It has been necessary to study briefly the ancient mysteries, to see that the subject of the immortality of the soul concerned them, and to observe the similarity of content between them and Blue Lodge Freemasonry. Scholars of Freemasonry have noted the evidence pointing to Freemasonry's similarities to the ancient Mystery Religions. What has not been answered is *Why* the similarity? Here we can only speculate.[113] We don't really know why. We do, however, know *that* there is great similarity between the two. Of all the similarities between the two, no other ingredient of Freemasonry so strongly attests to its being a successor of the ancient mysteries than the legend of Hiram Abif.

Though there is no definite historical tie linking Freemasonry with the ancient mystery cults, there are striking similarities. Freemasonry shares with the ancient mysteries the teaching of the immortality of the soul, the reenactment of the passion play or simulated murder,[114] the enabling of the initiate to die with the hope of a blessed afterlife, the exclusion of women from its ranks,[115] secret recognition signs,[116] a sacred plant (the Sprig of Acacia or Evergreen),[117] knowledge gained by secret initiatory rituals,[118] access to *gnosis* for the chosen few, the acquisition of *gnosis* in initiatory steps, belief in an all-encompassing Deity,[119] and oaths of secrecy sworn by the initiate—he must never divulge the secrets of the cult.[120] Freemasonry is indeed a modern Mystery Religion.

Notes

1. *Maine Masonic Text Book* (Maine Printing Exchange, 1992), 49–50.
2. *Official Cipher* of the Grand Lodge of Masons in Massachusetts, 104, decoded.
3. Allen Roberts, in his book *The Craft and Its Symbols,* agrees: "You have learned that Freemasonry calls God 'The Great Architect of the Universe.' This is the Freemason's special name for God, because He is universal. He belongs to all men regardless of their religious persuasion. All wise men acknowledge His authority. In his private devotions a Mason will pray to Jehovah, Mohammed, Allah, Jesus, or the Deity of his choice. In a Masonic Lodge, however, the Mason will find the name of his Deity within the Great Architect of the Universe" (p. 6).
4. *Masonic Manual of the Grand Lodge of Georgia* (1983), 7, emphasis added.
5. *Washington Monitor and Freemason's Guide* (Grand Lodge of Washington, 1976), 10–11, emphasis added.
6. *Masonic Manual of the Grand Lodge of Georgia* (1983), 27.
7. This does not imply that all are God's children pertaining to salvation. The New Testament teaches that we are saved by *adoption*. Being saved is becoming a child of God in a *salvific way* through faith in Jesus Christ (Gal. 4:5; Eph. 1:5; Rom. 8:15). Only these have eternal life (1 John 5: 13).
8. There is a striking similarity between the "Brotherly Love" lesson and Anderson's First Charge in *Anderson's Constitutions* of 1723. The First Charge, "Concerning God and Religion," reads in part, "But though in ancient Times Masons were charged in every Country to be of the Religion of that Country or Nation, whatever it was, yet 'tis now thought more expedient only to oblige them to that Religion in which all Men agree, leaving their particular Opinions to themselves; that is, to be good Men and true, or men of Honour and Honesty, by whatever Denominations or Persuasions they may be distinguished; whereby Masonry becomes the Center of Union, and the Means of conciliating true Friendship among Persons that must have remained at a perpetual Distance" (*Little Masonic Library,* 5 vols. [Richmond: Macoy Publishing and Masonic Supply Co., 1977], 1:233).
9. Roberts, *The Craft and Its Symbols,* 61.
10. *Coil's Masonic Encyclopedia* (New York: Macoy Publishing and Masonic Supply Co., 1961), 165–82, contains a list of approximately 1,100 names of various degrees.
11. Ibid., 189–90. For a discussion of the Master Mason degree, see *Mackey's Revised Encyclopedia of Freemasonry,* 2:651–54.
12. This theme is seen in various burial services of Masonry. It is also interesting that in most American Lodges no Mason can be buried with a Masonic ceremony unless he has received the degree of Master Mason. As we study the degree, the reasons for this will become obvious.
13. *Emulation Ritual* (London: Lewis Masonic, 1986), 199.

14. In earlier times Lodge meetings were held in homes or taverns. As a result "carpets" were drawn on the floor with chalk. Contained in the drawing were "The Three Steps." After the meeting the "carpet" was erased. Later, cloths or carpets were specially decorated with the Three Steps and placed on the floor when the ritual was performed. Today one may find them, as carpets or charts, hanging or suspended in the lodge room.

15. *California Cipher* (Richmond: Allen Publishing Co., 1990), 173–74. This cipher (coded ritual) is also used by Lodges in Hawaii.

16. *Missouri Cipher* (Grand Lodge, A.F. & A.M. of Missouri, 1991), 111.

17. For example, see 1 Chron. 11: 4–5, where David captures the fortress of Zion; and 1 Chron. 14: 8–17, where David attacks the Philistines and is victorious. In both instances it was the Lord who defeated David's enemies by David's hand (see 1 Chron. 11:9; 14:10). In the setting for our psalm, David and his people are ascending the hill of Zion to the city of Jerusalem, praising the Lord and Him alone.

18. The Hebrew for "clean," *nqi*, communicates a *declaration* of innocence. See R. Laird Harris, Gleason Archer, and Bruce Waltke, eds. *Theological Wordbook of the Old Testament,* 2 vols. (Chicago: Moody Press, 1980), 2:598.

19. Other references that allude to a command to circumcise our heart (Deut. 10:16), or to "love from a pure heart" (1 Tim. 1:5), must be understood in the overall message of the Bible, which concerns God's initial work of grace in one's heart to produce a pure heart. Matt. 5:8 ("Blessed are the pure in heart, for they shall see God") has as its backdrop Ps. 24, which teaches that it is the God of the Bible (v. 6) who gives to whom He wills a pure heart. Thus, universalistic reading into Matt. 5:8 is exegetically unsound.

20. Blue Lodge ritual does not speak of salvation or the hope of salvation for those outside the Craft. It does, however, for those who are Masons, making it selective. This, coupled with Blue Lodge Freemasonry's provision of a ritualistic framework for Masons of various faiths (including those who view Freemasonry as their only religion) to have a hope of salvation (in the burial services this hope is turned into a positive affirmation that the deceased is in the presence of the Great Architect), gives rise to the phrase "selective universalism."

21. *New Mexico Monitor and Ceremonies* (The Grand Lodge of A.F. & A.M. of New Mexico, 1992), 57.

22. *Cipher of the Grand Lodge of Minnesota,* 127, decoded.

23. *The Standard Work and Lectures of Ancient Craft Masonry* (Grand Lodge of Free and Accepted Masons of the State of New York, 1973), 239–40. There is the possibility that "land" may refer in a general way to the land where graves are located.

24. In 2 Chron. 2:13 the Hebrew transliterated is *churam abi* (in 4:16, it is *churam abiv*). This is translated as "Hiram [Huram] my father's" (KJV), though *abi* may mean "master," and thus "master Huram." The "f" in the Masonic "Hiram Abif"

may come from the transliteration of the Hebrew of 2 Chron. 4:16, the *waw* (*abiv*) being transliterated as "f."

25. See *Coil's Masonic Encyclopedia,* 306.

26. Anderson's *Constitutions,* 193–94.

27. Taken from *Coil's Masonic Encyclopedia,* 309. See this source for an in-depth discussion of the history of source materials contributing to the "Legend of Hiram Abif" (pp. 306–9).

28. In his obligation the candidate swears never to reveal the secrets of a Master Mason.

29. *Official Cipher,* Grand Lodge of Massachusetts, 162, decoded.

30. *Official Cipher,* Grand Lodge of Minnesota, 106, decoded.

31. Ibid., 107, decoded.

32. *Manual of the Miami Valley Lodge,* no. 660 (Dayton: Free and Accepted Masons of Dayton, Ohio, 1920), 50–51. This prayer is essentially the same in all rituals.

33. *Official Cipher,* Grand Lodge of Massachusetts, 164.

34. See, for example, the *Official Cipher,* Grand Lodge of New Hampshire (reprinted 1975), 101.

35. *Emulation Ritual* of London, England, 181; *Sussex Ritual of Craft Freemasonry,* 134.

36. *The Ceremonies of Craft Masonry,* Grand Lodge of New Brunswick, 103, decoded.

37. See Steven Tsoukalas, *Freemasonry: Is It a Cult? Should a Christian Belong to a Masonic Lodge?* (Exeter, N.H.: Sound Doctrine Ministries, 1989), and Jack Harris, *Freemasonry: The Invisible Cult in Our Midst* (Orlando: Daniels Publishing Co., 1983), 71–75, if by "resurrection" Harris means resurrection of the body.

38. When I began writing this book, Robinson was still alive. He died of cancer in 1993 (see "John J. Robinson Enters Celestial Lodge Above," *The Scottish Rite Journal* [November 1993], 34).

39. Robinson, *A Pilgrim's Path,* 36.

40. *Coil's Masonic Encyclopedia,* 309.

41. See *Coil's Masonic Encyclopedia,* 309, for a list of 19 theories as to what the degree teaches. See options 9 and 18. Also, some argue for a resurrection teaching on the basis that when the candidate (Hiram) is raised to the five points of fellowship, he speaks, and *dead men do not speak.* I have not found in any official ritual any evidence of the candidate speaking after he is slain. He does speak in *Duncan's Ritual* (Chicago: Charles T. Powner Co., 1974), but this is not published under the authority of any Grand Lodge. It may be that official ritual workings make room for the candidate to speak, though the speech is not specifically worded in the ritual. If this is the case, the resurrection argument is strengthened, but one must still account for the fact that Hiram's body is finally buried near the Holy of Holies near King Solomon's Temple (see the *Official*

Cipher of the Massachusetts Grand Lodge, 166). Conversely, resurrected men do not get reburied!

42. Meaning an occurrence of death with a resulting concealing of the remains.
43. Meaning a finding or a discovery.
44. At the raising of the candidate to "the five points of fellowship," the word *Mah-Hah-Bone* is whispered in the candidate's ear. This is the secret word of the legend; no one is really sure of its meaning. I think the phrase could be a corruption of a Hebrew phrase *mah* (interrogative "who?" or "how?"), *ha* (definite article "the"), and *boneh* (masculine singular participle, which, when used with the definite article, translates as "the one building" or "the one who builds"). Thus the translation "How is the builder?" or "What! is this the builder?" The possible connection with the biblical Hebrew should not be surprising, since we are dealing with an Old Testament character in the person of Hiram Abif, and it is King Solomon (in the person of the Worshipful Master) who whispers the phrase. The phrase may come from the Hebrew. Hiram was a builder of King Solomon's Temple!

   For further discussion on this phrase, consult Albert Pike, *The Book of the Words* (Kila, Mont.: Kessinger Publishing Co., n.d.), 88–92. Here Pike wrestles with Albert Mackey's theory (which is much like mine) that the phrase means "What! is this the Builder?" Pike does display some knowledge of Hebrew, though he is deficient in the finer points, not showing a "feel" for the language. In *The Magnum Opus* (Kila, Mont.: Kessinger Publishing Co., 1992), xiv...16, the revised ritual of the Scottish Rite, Pike states that the translation of the phrase is what Mackey says it is, with no discussion, probably because it is in the ritual, thereby rendering discussion out of place.

   We shall see in later chapters, by our examination of some of the degrees of the Scottish Rite, that *Mah-Hah-Bone* is but a pithy substitute for the Lost Word, or Sacred Name of Deity, the search for which (and continued loss of which) occupies much of the time of the Scottish Rite ritualistic system.

45. Albert G. Mackey, *The Symbolism of Freemasonry* (Chicago: The Charles T. Powner Co., 1975), 233–34.
46. Carl H. Claudy, *Foreign Countries* (Richmond: Macoy Publishing and Masonic Supply Co., 1971), 11.
47. Ibid., 136. Claudy mentions the possibility of a resurrection interpretation by Christians, but that "modern students, however, are reasonably well agreed that the Hiramic legend is a retelling of the immortality of the soul" (pp. 98–99).
48. The *Louisiana Masonic Monitor,* 134, uses this word to describe the teaching of the immortality of the soul.
49. Joseph Fort Newton, *The Builders* (Lexington, Mass.: The Supreme Council, 33rd Degree, A.A.S.R., Northern Masonic Jurisdiction, United States of America, 1973), 262–63.
50. *North Dakota Monitor* (Grand Lodge, A.F. & A.M. of North Dakota, 1965), 144–47. I am aware of a preceding section in this monitor mentioning "faith in

the merits of the Lion of the Tribe of Judah." I shall address this later in this chapter.

51. *Murrow Masonic Monitor* (Grand Lodge of A.F. & A.M. of Oklahoma, 1988), 94.

52. *Monitor of the Lodge* (Grand Lodge of Texas, A.F. & A.M., reprinted 1992), 78.

53. P. 67.

54. P. 134.

55. *Lodge Plan for Masonic Education: Mentor's Guide* (Alberta: The Grand Lodge of Alberta, A.F. & A.M., 1993), 66.

56. *The Standard Work and Lectures of Ancient Craft Freemasonry,* 222, decoded.

57. *Missouri Cipher,* 114.

58. *California Cipher,* 178; first sentence decoded.

59. *The Standard Work and Lectures of Ancient Craft Masonry* (Grand Lodge of New York), 223, decoded.

60. Taken from the *Colorado Craftsman* (Monitor of the Grand Lodge of Colorado), 57. Though not a part of various ritual workings in Europe, this is contained in the overwhelming majority of rituals in the United States and in rituals for other Grand Lodges throughout the world that use the "Webb" form (from Thomas S. Webb's *Masonic Monitor*).

61. Informed Masons should be well acquainted with this phraseology, which the "Sprig of Acacia" or "Evergreen" symbolizes. Remember that it was the Sprig of Acacia that signaled to the searching Fellow Crafts the whereabouts of Hiram's corpse.

62. *Maine Masonic Text Book,* 56. Again, this is found in the majority of rituals in the United States. According to *The Colorado Craftsman,* the dirge was written by David Vinton, a Masonic lecturer during the early part of the nineteenth century (p. 60).

63. "Trial" most likely refers to the testing of Hiram Abif.

64. Here alluding figuratively to Hiram's tomb or burial place.

65. *The Scottish Workings of Craft Masonry,* 100–101.

66. See Art deHoyos and S. Brent Morris, *Is It True What They Say About Freemasonry?* (Silver Spring, Md.: Masonic Service Association, 1994), 49–52. Here deHoyos and Morris take issue with the stretched conclusions that the legend of Hiram teaches the resurrection of the body or reincarnation. I am arguing that the legend teaches the glorious (i.e., salvific) immortality of the soul (however, in my earlier work, *Freemasonry: Is It a Cult?,* the conclusion that the Legend teaches resurrection is reached). In their criticism, however, they mention only anti-Masons, stating (regarding the legend), "There is no resurrection nor doctrine of reincarnation" (p. 52). Here I ask that deHoyos and Morris address not only anti-Masonic writers, but Mackey (perhaps) and the Grand Lodges of Oklahoma and Missouri, for example, who see in the legend the doctrine of resurrection (see quotations from the sources listed in nn. 45, 51, and 57.

67. The legend of Osiris can be found in Wallis Budge's *The Book of the Dead* (Secaucus, N.J.: University Books, 1960), 52–58.
68. Ibid., 178.
69. Ibid., 56.
70. Ibid., 202.
71. See, for example, *Mackey's Revised Encyclopedia of Freemasonry,* 1:318.
72. See R. Swinburne Clymer, *The Mysteries of Osiris or Ancient Egyptian Initiation* (Quakertown, Pa.: The Philosophical Publishing Co., 1951), 49–51, and Edmond Ronayne, *Ronayne's Hand-Book of Freemasonry* (Chicago: Ezra A. Cook Publications, 1985), 375–79.
73. I was unable to find any mention of the Lion's Paw in the resurrection of Osiris in the more recognized and scholarly sources on Egyptian religion. I therefore advise caution.
74. Albert Pike, *Morals and Dogma of the Ancient and Accepted Scottish Rite of Freemasonry* (Washington, D.C.: The Supreme Council of the Ancient and Accepted Scottish Rite, 1906), 80.
75. *Monitor of the Lodge,* 252.
76. See G. Johannes Botterweck and Helmer Ringgren, eds., *Theological Dictionary of the Old Testament,* currently 7 vols. (Grand Rapids: Eerdmans, 1974), 1:378, 380.
77. Pike states that Solomon is "the Lion of the Tribe of Judah" (*Morals and Dogma,* 210).
78. See, for example, the *Monitor of the Lodge,* Grand Lodge of Texas, which states, "The presence in the modern Masonic system, of many of the emblems, symbols and allegories of the ancient Temples of Initiation, as well as certain rites performed therein, has persuaded the most learned among Masonic scholars to conclude that *Masonry* is of very ancient origin, and is, in some aspects, the modern successor of, and heir to, the sublime Mysteries of the Temple of Solomon, and of the Temples of India, Chaldea, Egypt, Greece, and Rome, as well as the basic doctrine of the Essenes, Gnostics and other mystic Orders" (p. xiv).
79. Jack Finegan, *Myth and Mystery: An Introduction to the Pagan Religions of the Biblical World* (Grand Rapids: Baker, 1989), 172.
80. Walter Burkert, *Ancient Mystery Cults* (Cambridge, Mass.: Harvard University Press, 1987), 11–12.
81. Samuel Angus, *The Mystery-Religions* (New York: Dover Publications, 1975), 41, and Burkert, *Ancient Mystery Cults,* 2.
82. Angus, *The Mystery-Religions,* 39–40. Angus goes on to state that "we are in a worse position with regard to these ancient cults than a present-day historian would be in regard to Freemasonry. A mason may not disclose the secrets, while an outsider could record only such elements of Freemasonry as are obvious to all or such features as are openly spoken of by the brotherhood" (p. 40). The fact is, however, that secret rituals *do* get into the hands of the uninitiated,

as this book displays. Yet some Grand Lodges, such as many European Lodges, have no problem with rituals getting into the hands of the public, as, so they claim, no uninitiated person could make sense of them if they did. Walter Burkert, in his book *Ancient Mystery Cults,* mentions this very same phenomenon with regard to the ancient mysteries: "A mystery must not be betrayed, but it cannot really be betrayed because told in public it would appear insignificant; thus violations of the secrecy that did occur did no harm to the institutions" (p. 9).

83. Ibid., 40–41.
84. B. Jowett, trans., *The Dialogues of Plato,* 2 vols. (New York: Random House, 1937), 1:452–53, *Phaedo.*
85. Ibid., 627–28, *Republic II.*
86. Quoted in Burkert, *Ancient Mystery Cults,* 23.
87. Ibid., 21.
88. See Robin Lane Fox, *Pagans and Christians* (San Francisco: Harper and Row, 1986), 96–97.
89. Taken from *Plutarch: Selected Lives and Essays,* trans. Louise Ropes Loomis (Roslyn, N.Y.: Walter J. Black, published for the Classics Club, 1951), 326.
90. See pp. 45–75.
91. For the Mason to make the former an issue, however, begs the question: Is Freemasonry a religion? And if so, are its teachings opposed to the central teachings of Christianity?
92. Angus, *The Mystery-Religions,* 45.
93. Ibid., 45–46.
94. Ibid., 50.
95. See n. 38.
96. Claudy, *Foreign Countries,* 11.
97. Walter Burkert states that "there is no evidence for a resurrection of Attis; even Osiris remains with the dead" (*Ancient Mystery Cults,* 75). Burkert, however, is not necessarily admitting that Osiris was not resurrected, only that he remains with the dead. Wallis Budge, in his *Egyptian Religion* (Secaucus, N.J.: Citadel Press, 1987), states that "he [Osiris] rose again and became king of the underworld." (p. 61; cf. p. 121). This is, most likely, what Burkert is alluding to.
98. Of course, Hiram Abif is not a Masonic Deity in the same sense as Osiris and Attis were (some, including critics, may say that it is implied). Nonetheless Mackey and others make a solid case for the similarities of these legends to that of Hiram.
99. Angus, *The Mystery-Religions,* 52–53.
100. This is a common phrase used in the preparation room for the Entered Apprentice degree. There the candidate is asked a series of questions, one of which is whether he offers himself "as a candidate for the mysteries of Freemasonry" (*Masonic Manual of the Grand Lodge of Georgia* [1983], 12). This question is found in many other monitors of Grand Lodges, such as those of Louisiana,

Washington, Texas, North Dakota, Oklahoma, Iowa, Colorado, New Mexico, Maine, Massachusetts, North Carolina, and Florida.

101. Clement of Alexandria (second–third century A.D.) makes mention of the mysteries, writing, "Demeter and Proserpine have become the heroines of a mystic drama; and their wanderings, and seizure, and grief, Eleusis celebrates by torchlight processions" (Alexander Roberts and James Donaldson, eds., *The Ante-Nicene Fathers*, 9 vols. [Grand Rapids: Eerdmans, 1977], 2:175); quoted in Clement's *Exhortation to the Heathen*, chap. 2.

102. Angus, *The Mystery-Religions*, 58, 59–60.

103. Roberts, *The Craft and Its Symbols*, 3.

104. See Clement's *Exhortation to the Heathen*, chap. 2, in *The Ante-Nicene Fathers*, 2:176. Here the dismembered and cooked body of Dionysus is recovered by the god Zeus and properly interred. Other accounts of slaying of bodies, finding these bodies, and burying them in sacred places are recounted by Clement in this work.

105. Mackey, *The Symbolism of Freemasonry*, 231.

106. Ibid.

107. Angus, *The Mystery-Religions*, 63.

108. See the body of the text from n. 61.

109. Angus, *The Mystery-Religions*, 65.

110. Roberts, *The Craft and Its Symbols*, 3.

111. Angus, *The Mystery-Religions*, 66, 71. See also Burkert, *Ancient Mystery Cults*, 49–50, where it is stated, "Isis would claim that she has 'infinitely many names' around the world."

112. The *Liturgy of the Ancient and Accepted Scottish Rite* (The Supreme Council, Mother Council of the World, of the Inspectors General Knights Commanders of the House of the Temple of Solomon of the Thirty-third Degree of the Ancient and Accepted Scottish Rite of Freemasonry of the Southern Jurisdiction of the United States of America 1962) states, "There was peace between us, and we made a league together, notwithstanding that my Gods were not thine; because we were brethren in the Sacred Mysteries" (p. 45).

113. See W. L. Wilmshurst, *The Meaning of Masonry* (New York: Bell Publishing, 1980), 170–216, especially 172. Wilmshurst makes a gallant effort to trace the relation between Freemasonry and the ancient mysteries, but stretches his thesis, given the lack of historical ancestral evidence that plagues all researchers. Also, Wilmshurst's personal Gnostic–New Age theology is read into Masonic ritual, which in turn becomes strange to many Masons who may hold differing personal beliefs.

114. See Franz Cumont, *The Mysteries of Mithra* (New York: Dover Publications, 1956), 161. Quite interesting is a remark by Clement of Alexandria in the context of his naming two mystery cults' death and burial scenes, "These mysteries are, in short, murders and funerals" (*Exhortation to the Heathen*, chap. 2; quoted in *The Ante-Nicene Fathers*, 2:176).

115. Cumont mentions that "since men only were permitted to take part in the secret ceremonies of the Persian liturgy, other Mysteries to which women were admitted must have formed some species of alliance with the former, to make them complete" (*The Mysteries of Mithra,* 179). This is similar to the Masonic Lodge and one of its allied organizations—the Order of the Eastern Star for women. See also Burkert, *Ancient Mystery Cults,* 42–43.

116. See Kurt Rudolph, *Gnosis: The Nature and History of Gnosticism* (San Francisco: Harper & Row, 1987), where, speaking of the Gnostic cults, Rudolph states, "As in the mystery religions the gnostic communities were also acquainted with their own secret distinguishing signs . . . according to Epiphanius the (Barbeliote) gnostics, by way of greeting, made a tickling stroke on the palm of the hand" (p. 214). Masons distinguish themselves from others by a series of hand grips. These are described earlier in this chapter in connection with the attempts to raise the body of Hiram Abif, first with the Entered Apprentice grip, then with the grip of a Fellow Craft, then, successfully, with the grip of a Master Mason. When these grips are given by someone to a Mason, that Mason immediately returns the grips in recognition. See also Burkert, *Ancient Mystery Cults,* 45.

117. See Mackey, *The Symbolism of Freemasonry,* 247–62.

118. Burkert mentions "initiations performed by secret clubs. The best parallel, which is often invoked, may be the Masons" (*Ancient Mystery Cults,* 41–42).

119. See the quotations from the sources in nn. 111, 112, and Cumont, *The Mysteries of Mithra,* 187.

120. See Burkert, *Ancient Mystery Cults,* 45–46.

CHAPTER 4

THE MASONIC BURIAL SERVICE

"Freemasonry has a religious service to commit the body of a deceased brother to the dust whence it came and to speed the liberated spirit back to the Great Source of Light. Many Freemasons make this flight with no other guarantee of a safe landing than their belief in the religion of Freemasonry. If that is a false hope, the Fraternity should abandon funeral services and devote its attention to activities where it is sure of its ground and its authority."—Henry Wilson Coil, Coil's Masonic Encyclopedia

In the United States, Masonic Lodges perform funeral or burial services for their deceased brethren. The particular Lodge to which the deceased belonged may come to the funeral home and perform a service during the wake, or perform a burial service at the grave site. For the vast majority of non-Masons, these services provide the only public exposure to Freemasonry they will ever have. And the many Grand Lodges throughout the United Sates know this. All too often I have read articles in Masonic publications that exhort members to faithfully participate in the funeral services of deceased brethren, stating that the glamor and solemnity of the service should make an everlasting impression upon the public. Observed with the Christian theological eye, these services *do indeed* make an everlasting impression, an impression that Freemasonry is not simply a fraternal organization.

As the reader works through the following eight ceremonies, common elements will arise. The *Ahiman Rezon* or *Book of Constitutions of the Grand Lodge of Ancient Free Masons of South Carolina*[1] mentions five "essentials" in a Masonic funeral:

> (1) that the services shall be conducted by a Lodge that has been duly congregated and opened; (2) that a lambskin apron shall be deposited with the body; (3) that a sprig of evergreen shall be deposited with the body; (4) that the Public Grand Honors be given;[2] (5) that the Lodge which takes charge of the body shall consign it to its last resting place, without intermingling its services with any others.[3]

We may add other common elements, if not essentials, to this list: (6) that prayers be offered to the Grand Architect of the Universe; (7) that passages from the Volume of the Sacred Law be read throughout the ceremony; (8) that the Masonic dogma of the immortality of the soul be set forth; (9) that a hope or reminder of a glorious immortality be conveyed; (10) that the hope of one day being reunited with the deceased be stated or prayed for; (11) that a firm faith (trust) in God should characterize the service; (12) that faith in the immortality of the soul, symbolized by the Evergreen, be clearly set forth; (13) that the teachings of the first three degrees play a part in the makeup of the service; and (14) that the root of all the preceding is the first three degrees.

Some of the Grand Lodges in the United States observe the following rule for burial or funeral services:

> No Freemason can be buried with the formalities of the Fraternity, unless it be at his own request, or that of his next of kin, communicated to the Worshipful Master of the Lodge of which he died a member, foreigners or sojourners excepted; nor unless he be a Master Mason in good standing. There can be no exception to this restriction.[4]

There are some Grand Lodges, given their autonomy, that do not make this rule mandatory. For example, the Grand Lodges of New Mexico[5] and Washington[6] provide Masonic services for any Mason in good standing, whether Entered Apprentice, Fellow Craft, or Master Mason. When a Grand Lodge restricts services to Master Masons only, Entered Apprentices and Fellow Crafts typically may not even take part in the service.[7]

Among the various Grand Lodge Masonic monitors of the United States the funeral services are essentially the same in content, though the wording, prayers, and format of the services may vary.[8] Masonic funeral clothing is usually dark, with white gloves, plain white Masonic Lambskin Aprons, and the Sprig of Acacia (Evergreen) on the lapel.[9] The plain white Lambskin Apron is to be placed on the remains of the deceased brother[10] or upon the casket. In the case of cremation the Apron may be placed upon the urn at the appropriate time.

Following are excerpts from the funeral services, memorial services, and Lodges of Sorrow[11] of eight randomly chosen United States Grand Lodges. This will enable the reader to get a feel for the general content of Masonic funeral services and to recognize the ingredients common to all eight Grand Lodge services. An asterisk (*) indicates where a biblical text has been misquoted, taken out of context, or only partially quoted, and is followed by discussion in the notes. Unless otherwise noted, all Lodge monitor funeral services quoted here use the King James Version of the Bible. I shall also use the KJV.

Florida (Funeral at the Grave)

WORSHIPFUL MASTER:
We have assembled here today as Freemasons to pay our respects to the memory of a deceased Brother whose remains lie before us and to inter them with Masonic Rites. Brother Chaplain, lead us in prayer.

CHAPLAIN:
Almighty and most merciful Father, we adore Thee as God of time and eternity. As it hath pleased Thee to take from the light of our abode, one dear to our hearts, we beseech Thee to bless and sanctify unto us this dispensation of Thy providence. . . . And when our toils on earth shall have ended, may we be raised to the enjoyment of fadeless light and immortal life in that kingdom where faith and hope shall end, and love and joy prevail through eternal ages. And Thine, O Righteous Father, shall be the glory forever. Amen!

BRETHREN:
So mote it be!

WORSHIPFUL MASTER:
The solemn notes that betoken the dissolution of this earthly tabernacle have again alarmed our outer door, and another spirit has

been summoned to the land where our fathers have gone before us . . . stones and lettered monuments symbolize the affection of surviving friends, yet no sound proceeds from them, save that silent but thrilling admonition, "Seek ye the narrow path and the strait gate that lead unto eternal life."*[12] . . . May our Faith be evinced in a correct moral walk and deportment; may our Hope be bright as the glorious mysteries that will be revealed hereafter; and our Charity boundless as the wants of our fellow creatures. And, having faithfully discharged the great duties which we owe to God, to our neighbor, and ourselves, when at last it shall please the Grand Master of the Universe to summon us into His eternal presence, may the Trestle-board of our whole lives pass such inspection that it may be given unto each of us to "eat of the hidden manna," and to receive the "white stone with a new name"*[13] that will insure perpetual and unspeakable happiness at his right hand.

(The Master, displaying the apron, continues:)

The Lambskin, or white leather Apron, is an emblem of innocence and the badge of a Mason. . . . This emblem I now place on the coffin of our deceased Brother. . . .

(The Master deposits it upon the coffin.)

(The Master, holding a sprig of evergreen, continues:)

The evergreen, which once marked the temporary resting place of the illustrious dead,[14] is an emblem of our faith in the immortality of the soul. By it we are reminded that we have an immortal part within us, that shall survive the grave, and which shall never, never, never die. By it we are admonished that, though like our Brother whose remains lie before us, we too shall soon be clothed in the habiliments of death and deposited in the silent tomb, yet through our belief in the mercy of God, we may confidently hope that our souls will bloom in eternal spring. This, too, I deposit in the grave *with the exclamation,* "Alas, my Brother!"

WORSHIPFUL MASTER:

. . . *(Gives the Public Grand Honors.*[15]*)*

(The third time—with arms crossed over the breast.)

We cherish his memory here.

(Bring the palms together above the head, looking upward.)

We commend his spirit to God who gave it.

(Bring the hands quickly to the thighs with the head bowed.)

And consign his body to the earth.

... There to remain until the trump shall sound on the resurrection morn. We can confidently leave him in the hands of a Being who doeth all things well; who is glorious in holiness, fearful in praise, doing wonders.

. . . Then let us improve this solemn warning, so that when the sheeted dead are stirring, when the great white throne is set, we shall receive from the Omniscient Judge the thrilling invitation, "Come, ye blessed, inherit the kingdom prepared for you from the foundation of the world."*[16]

WORSHIPFUL MASTER:
Brother Chaplain, lead us in prayer.

CHAPLAIN:
Most glorious God, Author of all good and Giver of all mercy, pour down Thy blessings upon us, and strengthen our solemn engagements with the ties of sincere affection . . . and that after our departure hence in peace and Thy favor, we may be received into Thine everlasting kingdom, and there join in union with our friend, and enjoy that uninterrupted and unceasing felicity which is allotted to the souls of just men made perfect. Amen!

BRETHREN:
So mote it be!

WORSHIPFUL MASTER:
The will of God is accomplished.

BRETHREN:
So mote it be! . . . May we all be recompensed at the resurrection of the just. Amen![17]

Maine (Funeral Service)

CHAPLAIN: [Reads Ps. 121 in its entirety.]

MASTER: Death and the dead are with us again, my brethren, teaching us the brevity and uncertainty of human life. . . . The body of our late brother lies before us, overtaken by the relentless fate which is sooner or later to overtake us all. . . . But this body is not our brother, but that which was his material part until God laid his finger on him and he slept. He was mortal but now has put on immortality.

CHAPLAIN: Let us pray.

Almighty and Most Holy God, in whom we live and move and have our being, we bow in thy presence with a profound sense of dependence in thee. . . . In thy keeping we leave our brother, assured that in the larger life of the spirit upon which he has entered thou wilt do for him more abundantly than we can ask or think. Remember in thy great mercy his sorrowing relatives and friends. Give to them thy peace which passeth all understanding*[18] that they may be comforted. May they not sorrow as those who have no hope, but with Spiritual vision see beyond the grave the glories of the eternal life to which thou hast called their loved one. Teach us anew the brevity of this earthly life, even at its longest. Help us to live as becometh immortals, giving ourselves in goodly and loving service to thee and to humanity, that when this earthly house of our tabernacle is destroyed we may have an abundant entrance into that house not made with hands, eternal in the heavens, where parting will be no more. Amen.

ALL: [The Lord's Prayer is recited.] . . . (The Master now takes the Apron and deposits it on the casket . . . [or] in the grave . . . and continues as follows):

MASTER: The Lamb-Skin Apron is an emblem of innocence and the badge of a Mason. Here we have no permanent lodge or place of abode, but we look for one to come. Not trusting in ourselves, but in God, who preserveth the living and enliveneth the dead, we hope to pass an everlasting day of blissful brotherhood in a lodge in that house not made with hands, eternal in the heavens.

This Evergreen is an emblem of our faith in the immortality of the soul. By it we are reminded there dwells within our tabernacle of clay an imperishable, immortal spirit over which the grave has no dominion and death no power.

(The Master then brings his right hand to his left breast; then extends it, palm downward, over the grave [or casket if at the house], depositing the Evergreen, then carries it above his head, pointing to heaven, and then drops it to his side.)

Master continues: . . . Friend and brother, farewell. Thou art at rest from thy labor. Raised by the Supreme Grand Master's word[19] may you hereafter share the honors of perfection, the joys of bliss immortal.

CHAPLAIN: Let us pray.

Our gracious Father, with a glorious faith in the resurrection we consign the body of our brother to its grave. Help us, we beseech thee, so to fulfill the remaining duties of life that our entrance into the Eternal Life of the Beyond may bring us into the joy of our Lord and the reward of a well-spent life.[20] Assist us in all our laudable undertakings; comfort us in our afflictions; forgive us all that thou seeth amiss; bring us finally to the Celestial Lodge above to be with thee forevermore. Amen.

RESPONSE: So mote it be.

CHAPLAIN: [Gives benedictions from Num. 6:24–26 and I Tim. 1:17.][21]

Washington (Service at the Grave or Crematory)

MASTER: From time immemorial it has been a custom of the Society of Free and Accepted Masons, on proper request, to accompany the remains of a brother to their final resting place. . . .

CHAPLAIN: Almighty and Eternal God—in Whom we live and move and have our being, we beseech Thee to be present with us in this hour and during all the days of our earthly life. . . . Pour out Thy continual blessing upon the relatives and friends of our departed brother. Lead them to know that he is waiting to greet them in a world where light and bliss are eternal. Grant us Thy divine assurance, oh! most merciful God, to redeem our mis-spent time, and, in the important duties which Thou hast assigned us in the erection of our spiritual temple, give us *wisdom* to direct us, *strength* to support us and the *beauty* of holiness to adorn our labors and render them acceptable in Thy sight, so that, when our labors here on earth are ended, we may be with Thee amidst the radiant splendor of eternal truth. Amen!

RESPONSE: So mote it be.

MASTER: We commit the body of our brother to the kindly embrace of mother earth . . . but his spirit has winged its flight to that blissful Lodge which will remain open during the endless ages of eternity. . . .

MASTER (*holding up apron, unfolded*): The Lambskin, or white leather apron, is an emblem of innocence, and the badge of a Mason. Its pure and spotless surface is an ever-present reminder of that purity of life so essentially necessary to gaining admission into the Celestial Lodge above. . . .

SCROLL[22]

MASTER: This scroll, on which is inscribed the name of our departed Brother, I now deposit with his remains (*drops it in the grave*). He has passed away, never more to return. His name is inscribed in the Book of Life.

THE SPRIG OF ACACIA

MASTER: The Evergreen, which once marked the temporary resting-place of one illustrious in Masonic legend,[23] is an emblem of our faith in the immortality of the soul. By it we are reminded that we have an imperishable, immortal spirit, which survives this death, and which will never, never, *never* die. By it we are admonished that we, too, like our brother, whose remains now lie before us, shall soon be clothed in the habiliments of death; yet, through the loving-kindness of the Supreme Grand Master, we may confidently hope that our souls will hereafter flourish in eternal spring.

FUNERAL HYMN [Pleyel's hymn, third verse]: Lord of all! below,—above,—Fill our hearts with Truth and Love: As dissolves our Earthly Tie, Take us to Thy Lodge on High! . . .

MASTER: Reverently we commit the body of our brother to the grave (flames). . . . Though our brother has passed beyond our mortal view, yet we can trustingly leave him in the hands of a beneficent Being, who doeth all things well; who is glorious in His holiness, wondrous in His power, and boundless in His goodness and love.

. . . With firm faith and reliance in the Supreme Grand Master of the Universe, we know that we shall meet once more in realms beyond the skies. Until then, dear friend and brother, until then, farewell!

CHAPLAIN: [Gives benediction from Num. 6:24–26.]

RESPONSE: So mote it be.[24]

New Mexico (Memorial Service at a Lodge, Church, Chapel, Cemetery, or Crematory)

Let us resolve to seek the favor of the eternal God, so that when the moment of passing comes, even as it has to our Brother, we may be enabled to prosecute our journey without dread or apprehension, to that far-distant land from whose bourn no traveler returns.

To the relatives and friends of our Brother, we have but little of this world's consolation to offer; we can only sincerely, deeply, and most affectionately sympathize with them, and assure them that He, who looks with infinite compassion upon the afflicted, will fold the arms of His love and protection around those who put their trust in Him.

The Lambskin, or White Leathern Apron, is an emblem of innocence and the badge of a Mason. It reminds us of that purity of life and conduct so essentially necessary to gaining admission into the Celestial Lodge above, where the Supreme Architect of the Universe presides.

(The Master deposits apron on the coffin and, displaying an evergreen sprig, continues.)

The evergreen is an emblem of our faith in the immortality of the soul. By this we are reminded that we have an immortal spark within, which shall survive, and springing into newness of life in realms beyond the skies, shall never, never die.

(The Master drops the evergreen on the coffin.) . . .

MASTER OR CHAPLAIN: Almighty and most merciful Father, we adore Thee as God of time and of eternity. . . . May we realize Thine All-Seeing Eye is upon us, and be influenced by the spirit of truth and love to faithfully perform the duties assigned to us here, so that we may ever enjoy Thy divine approbation. And when our work on earth shall cease, and we are called to depart this life, may we be cheered by the enjoyment of Thy presence and the assurance of immortal life in that world where faith and hope shall end, and love and joy prevail through eternal ages.

CHAPLAIN: Amen.

BRETHREN: So mote it be. . . .

MASTER OR CHAPLAIN: [Gives benediction from Num. 6:24–26.]

BRETHREN: So mote it be.[25]

Mississippi (Ritual for a Lodge of Sorrow[26])

MASTER: We dwell in houses of clay, whose foundation is in the dust, which are crushed before the moth. Our days upon earth are a shadow. Soon we go whence we shall not return, to the land of darkness and the shadow of death. . . .

CHAPLAIN: Just and true are Thy ways, thou King of Saints. Righteousness and judgment are the habitation of thy seat. Shall we receive good at the hands of God, and shall we not receive evil? It is the Lord; let Him do what seemeth to Him good. We know that if our earthly house of this tabernacle were dissolved, we have a building from God, an house not made with hands, eternal in the heavens. . . .

Let us pray. . . . Inspire our hearts with wisdom from on high that the days of our pilgrimage here below may not be unprofitable to us and to our fellow-men, so that when, in Thy good time, we have run our race and reached the end of life's journey, we may go down into the grave having the testimony of a good conscience, in the confidence of a certain faith, in the comfort of a reasonable, religious, and only hope, in favor with Thee, our God, and in perfect charity with the world. Console his relatives in their affliction and sustain them in all the adversities and trials which they may have to encounter in this world; and may they and we, loving and serving Thee, and trusting in Thy infinite beneficence, be, in Thy good time, gathered in peace unto our fathers, and again meet our friend and brother at Thy Throne of Glory. *Amen.*

Response by the brethren. *So mote it be. . . .*

MASTER: . . . Brother Chaplain, we will attend to the reading of a lesson from the Holy Scriptures.

The Chaplain will then read the following:

[Chaplain reads 1 Cor. 15:35–57.]

[v. 35] "But some man will say, How are the dead raised up? ... [vv. 56–57] The sting of death is sin; and the strength of sin is the law. But thanks be to God which giveth us the victory." (I Cor. 15:35–57.)*27

[The Junior Warden sprinkles wine on the coffin and the Senior Warden sprinkles oil on it.]

Calling up the brethren, who form around the coffin, the Master holding in his hand a lamb skin apron, or the apron usually worn by the deceased, says:

This apron, an emblem of innocence and the badge of a Mason, free from spot or blemish, denotes the hope we cherish that the soul of our departed brother, released from its earthly encumbrance and purified from all its imperfections, has met a welcome reception in the Supreme Grand Lodge above. . . .

The Master, holding a sprig of Evergreen, says:

This sprig of evergreen is an emblem of Masonic Faith in the immortality of the soul, of that ever-living principle in man which survives the grave, and blooms in perpetual verdure through an endless eternity. Though the body of our brother is clothed in the habiliments of the dead, and is consigned to the silent tomb, this living sprig denotes our trust that his immortal spirit has passed the portals of that celestial temple not made with hands, eternal in the heavens, and accepted through the mercy of our Supreme Grand Master, will enjoy His presence through an eternity of glory, and in a happiness as endless as it is perfect.

The sprig of evergreen is then laid upon the coffin.

The Master, still standing beside the coffin, calls up the brethren, and all say together:

Farewell, brother! Our faith, our hope, our assurance is that we shall meet again around that celestial altar, where with songs of praise we unite to hail the Supreme Grand Master. Until then, farewell, farewell.28

Massachusetts (Funeral Service)

MASTER: My Brethren the roll of the workmen has been called and one Master Mason has not answered to his name. He has laid down the working tools of the Craft and with them he has left that mortal part for which he no longer has use. His labors here below have taught him to divest his heart and conscience of the vices and superfluities of life, thereby fitting his mind as a living stone for that spiritual building—that house not made with hands, eternal in the heavens.[29] Strengthened in his labors here by faith in God and confident expectation of immortality, he has sought admission to the celestial lodge above.

Here the Master reads the Sacred Roll.[30] . . .

CHAPLAIN: Almighty Father! Into thy hands we commend the soul of our departed Brother. . . .

[CHAPLAIN]: [Reads 1 Cor. 15:35–58]*[31]. Let us pray.

O God, most mighty and most merciful, we thank thee that amidst all the labor and the turmoil, the perplexity and the apparent confusion of life thou hast not left us to wander unguided and alone. Thou hast set up the Ancient Landmarks[32] to guide our course. Thou hast displayed the Great Lights[33] to disclose our path. . . . We thank thee for the revelations of the deeper meanings of life which show us its oneness and continuity so that we know that here and now we are immortal, that life on earth is but a phase of that abounding and eternal life which we share with thee. . . . My [*sic*] we go from this place with deeper sympathy, warmer love, stronger faith, more earnest purpose, so that we may govern our thoughts, words, and deeds in such wise that when we are summoned hence we may hear the words, "Well done, good and faithful servant; thou hast been faithful over a few things: I make thee ruler over many things: enter thou into the joy of thy Lord."*[34]

[All the brethren recite the Lord's Prayer.] . . .

MASTER: . . . Our paths lead not *to* the grave but *through it*. Immortal we are and ever shall be. We look not to another life, but to the perfecting of this one. In God's good time we shall be raised by His right hand[35] to that higher, fairer phase of life for which this is only the preparation. . . .

At the close of his address, or after the music following it, the Master will deposit the lambskin in the casket, or upon it if it is closed . . . saying as he does so:

This lambskin, or white leather apron, is an emblem of innocence and the badge of a Mason. It reminds us of that purity of life and conduct so essentially necessary to gaining admission into the Celestial Lodge above, where the Supreme Architect of the Universe presides. . . .

The Master then deposits the evergreen in the casket . . . saying as he does so:

This evergreen is an emblem of our faith in the immortality of the soul. By this we are reminded that we have an immortal part within us which shall survive the chilling blast of death and springing into newness of life in realms beyond the grave shall never, never die.

CHAPLAIN: O God, our heavenly Father, grant that we sorrow not as those who know not the promises contained in thy Holy Word; but may we look forward to the great gathering of thy faithful servants and children into their everlasting home. O thou in whom we trust, keep us by thy grace that we may live as the heirs of this blessed and glorious hope which thou hast so graciously set before us. [Chaplain then gives the benediction from Num. 6:24–26.] . . .

. . .Unto the Grand Architect of the Universe, we commit our departed Brother; earth to earth, ashes to ashes, dust to dust (optional); and we commit his soul to him who gave it; cheerfully leaving him in the hands of a being who doeth all things well. *Amen.* So mote it be.[36]

Michigan (Lodge Service)

The Master, taking the roll[37] in his hand, says:
May we die the death of the righteous, and may our last end be like his.

The Brethren answer:
God is our God forever and ever: He will be our guide even unto death.

The Master reads the roll, and says:
Almighty Father! Into Thy hands we commend the soul of our departed Brother.

The Brethren answer three times, giving the Grand Honors each time:
The will of God is accomplished. So mote it be. . . .

Prayer by the Chaplain:
Most glorious God, Author of all good and giver of all mercy, pour down Thy blessing upon us and strengthen our solemn engagements with the ties of sincere affection . . . and after our departure hence in peace and in Thy favor, may we be received into Thine everlasting kingdom, and there enjoy, in union with the souls of our departed friends, the just rewards of a pious and virtuous life. Amen.

Response: So mote it be.

The Brethren proceed . . . to the house of the deceased. (House or Church Service) . . .

W.M.: Death and the dead are with us again, my brethren, teaching us the brevity and uncertainty of human life and the instability of human fortune, and demanding of us the last sad offices of charity and brotherhood. The body of our beloved Brother _____ lies before us. . . . But this body over which we now mourn is not our brother, but only that which was his human and material part until God laid His finger upon him and he slept. He was mortal but now has put on immortality. He sleeps, but he shall wake again.

S.W. [Senior Warden]: I know that my Redeemer liveth, and that He shall stand at the latter day upon the earth. And though, after my skin, worms destroy this body, yet in my flesh I shall see God; whom I shall see for myself, and mine eyes shall behold, and not another.

J.W. [Junior Warden]: I am the resurrection and the life, saith the Lord; he that believeth in Me, though he were dead, yet shall he live; and whosoever liveth and believeth in Me shall never die.*[38]
. . .

Chaplain or Master: Let us pray.
Most glorious and merciful Lord God, author of all good and giver of every perfect gift, pour down, we beseech Thee, Thy blessing upon us and under the deep solemnities of this occasion, bind us yet closer together in the ties of brotherly love and affection . . .

and may we be enabled to work an entrance into the Celestial Lodge above, and in the Glorious Presence, amidst its ineffable mysteries, enjoy a union with the souls of our departed friends, perfect as is the happiness of heaven, and durable as is the eternity of God. Amen!

BROS.: So mote it be.

The procession is then formed. . . . On arriving at the grave. . . . The Worshipful Master then says:
Brethren, the solemn notes that betoken the dissolution of this earthly tabernacle have again alarmed our outer door, and another spirit has been removed to the land where our fathers have gone before us. . . . Stones and lettered monuments symbolize the affection of surviving friends, yet no sound proceeds from them, save that silent but thrilling admonition: "Seek ye the narrow path and the strait gate that leadeth to eternal life."*[39] . . .

The coffin is then lowered into the grave, the apron having been previously taken from the coffin and handed to the Master, who raises it in his hand and then says:
The lambskin or white leathern apron is an emblem of innocence and the badge of a Mason. . . . This emblem I now deposit in the grave of our deceased brother (deposits it). By it we are reminded of that purity of life and conduct so essentially necessary to our gaining ready admission into the Celestial Lodge above, where the Supreme Architect of the Universe presides. . . .

W.M.: (Taking off his white glove and holding it up.) This glove is a symbol of fidelity, and is emblematic of that Masonic friendship which bound us to him whose tenement of clay now lies before us. It reminds us that while these mortal eyes shall see him not again, yet, by the practice of the tenets of our noble order and a firm faith and steadfast trust in the Supreme Architect, we hope to clasp once more his vanished hand in friendship and in love.

W.M.: (Holding up sprig of evergreen.) This evergreen, which once marked the temporary resting place of the illustrious dead,[40] is an emblem of our faith in the immortality of the soul. By it we are reminded that we have an immortal part within us which survives the grave and which shall never, never, no, never die. This, too, I deposit in the grave. Alas, my brother.

The Master brings his right hand holding the evergreen to his left breast; then extends it downward over the grave, palm down; drops the evergreen into the grave at its head; then quickly points upward over his head with his hand closed, except the index finger; then drops the open hand down by his side. All then move around the grave as before, singing the following stanza:

Lord of all below, above; Fill our hearts with truth and love; When dissolves our earthly tie; Take us to Thy Lodge on high.

As each member passes the head of the grave he drops his evergreen in the same manner as did the Master. . . .

[W.M.]: We deposit the body of our deceased brother in the grave: We treasure his memory in our hearts; We commend his spirit to God, who gave it. [When the first phrase is uttered, all the brethren raise their hands up in front of their own bodies, level with the elbow and palms down; the second phrase—they cross hands over their breasts; the third phrase—they raise their hands above their heads, lowering them as the third phrase ends.]

W.M.: . . . Then, my brethren, let us so live that when our dissolution draws nigh, the entrance to the dark valley and shadow of death may be illuminated by the consciousness of a well-spent life and the hope of a glorious immortality. . . .

CHAPLAIN: May the blessing of Heaven rest upon us and all regular Masons. May brotherly love prevail and every moral and social virtue cement us. Amen.

RESPONSE: So mote it be.[41]

Oklahoma (Lodge of Sorrow[42])

WORSHIPFUL MASTER:
Brother Senior Warden, for what purpose are we assembled?

SENIOR WARDEN:
To honor the memory of those brethren whom death hath taken from us; to contemplate our own approaching dissolution, and, by the remembrance of immortality to raise our souls above the consideration of this transitory existence.

WORSHIPFUL MASTER:
Brother Junior Warden, what sentiments should inspire the souls of Masons on occasions like the present?

JUNIOR WARDEN:
Calm sorrow for the absence of our brethren who have gone before us, earnest solicitude for our own eternal welfare, and a firm faith and reliance upon the wisdom and goodness of the great Architect of the Universe.

WORSHIPFUL MASTER:
Brethren, . . . I declare this Lodge of Sorrow opened.

[CHAPLAIN PRAYS]:
Grand Architect of the Universe, in whose holy sight centuries are but days, to whose omniscience past and future are but as one eternal present. . . . Look down, we beseech Thee, from Thy glorious and eternal day into the dark night of our error and presumption and suffer a ray of Thy divine light to penetrate into our hearts, that in them may awaken and bloom the uncertainty of life, reliance upon Thy promises, and assurance of a place at Thy right hand.[43] Amen.

RESPONSE:
So mote it be. . . .

WORSHIPFUL MASTER (rising and taking up skull):
. . . Behold this emblem of mortality, once the abode of a spirit like our own; beneath this smouldering canopy once shone the bright and busy eye; within this hollow cavern once played the ready, swift and tuneful tongue; and now sightless and mute, it is eloquent only in the solemn lesson it teaches us. . . . Think how soon death, for you, will be a reality. . . . The cradle speaks to us of remembrance, the coffin of hope, of a blessed trust in a glorious immortality, and a never ending existence beyond the gloomy portals of the tomb! . . . [Ps. 90:1–12 and Job 14:1–12 are recited.]

An interval of profound silence follows, all the lights in the hall are put out, save the three small burning tapers in the East, West and South stations . . . after another period of silence, Low Twelve[44] will be sounded on the gong, very slowly.

WORSHIPFUL MASTER:
Brother Senior Warden, in this hour of gloom and darkness, when

death stares us in the face, when the skin slips from the fingers and the flesh cleaves from the bones,[45] what shall we do?

SENIOR WARDEN:
Worshipful Sir, the light of nature and of reason fails us here. The feeble rays penetrate not the darkness of the tomb! Let us look above to him whose omniscience rules both death and the grave.

WORSHIPFUL MASTER: (calling up the Lodge):
Brother Chaplain, lead us in addressing our earnest petitions to that Almighty Father, who ever lends a listening ear to His suffering children.

CHAPLAIN:
Our Father who Art in heaven, it hath pleased Thee to take from among us those who were our brethren. . . . When it comes to us also to die, may a firm and abiding trust in Thy mercy dispel the gloom and dread of dissolution. Be with us now, that we may serve Thee in spirit and understanding. And to Thy name shall be ascribed the praise forever. Amen.

RESPONSE:
So mote it be.

WORSHIPFUL MASTER:
. . . Brothers Senior and Junior Warden, join me around these solemn emblems of mortality, and assist me in paying the last Masonic honors to our departed brethren. . . .

JUNIOR WARDEN:
In memory of our departed brethren, I deposit these white flowers, emblematical of that pure life to which they have been called, and reminding us that as these children of an hour will droop and fade away, so, too, we shall soon follow those who have gone before us, and inciting us to fill the brief span of our existence that we may leave to our survivors a sweet savor of remembrance. . . .

SENIOR WARDEN:
. . . Let these flowers be to us a symbol of remembrance of all the virtues of our brethren who have preceded us to the silent land, and a token of that fraternal alliance which binds us while on earth and which we hope will finally unite us in Heaven. . . .

WORSHIPFUL MASTER:

It is appointed unto men once to die, and after death cometh the resurrection.*[46] . . . While, therefore, nature will have its way, and our tears will fall upon the graves of our brethren, let us be reminded by the evergreen, symbol of our faith in immortal life, that the dead are but sleeping, and be comforted by the reflection that their memories will not be forgotten . . . let us prepare to meet them where there is no parting, and where with them we shall enjoy eternal rest. . . .

[1 Cor. 15:35–55 is read in responsive style.]

As the concluding words are pronounced, "O grave where is thy victory?" the light in the hall will be raised to great brilliancy . . . while a strain of triumphant music will be played. . . .[47]

Biblical Response

Masonic scholar Henry Wilson Coil cites the Masonic burial service as evidence that Freemasonry is a religion.[48] After surveying many Masonic burial and memorial services, I cannot help but agree with Coil. Freemasonry is a religion, and the theological teachings of the Craft's burial and memorial services certainly have all the necessary ingredients to provide an unchurched Mason with all the religion he may need.

Once again the "sole dogma of Freemasonry"—belief in *a* Supreme Being—plays a major role in our critique. The Lodge does not require the candidate to specifically name his Deity, but as we have seen, it subsumes all the different ideas of deity that individual Masons may have under the canopy designation T.G.A.O.T.U. (see chaps. 1 and 2).

This is a theological problem for the Christian. For example, the Lambskin Apron, which is placed on the deceased, on his coffin, or atop his ashes, teaches an ultimately false hope for those outside the Christian faith. John 14:6 states, "I [Jesus] am the way, the truth, and the life: no man cometh unto the Father, but by me" (KJV). Additionally, when the Lodge states (or implies) that a deceased Mason is "reminded of that purity of life and conduct so essentially necessary to his gaining admission into the Celestial Lodge above," it conflicts with the teachings of Christ and the New Testament. Though it is true *for him,* it is not *true.* Ultimately, ontologically, it is a false reminder.

The same criticism holds for the Evergreen, or ever-living Sprig of Acacia. In a few instances we saw that the Evergreen symbolizes the immortality of the soul, which is an immortal part within, which never dies but will spring to newness of life in realms beyond the grave (or which will bloom in eternal spring). The Mason may say, however, that in his ritual there is no mention of the soul blooming in eternal spring. What is symbolized is simply "the immortality of the soul." The overall context of the funeral service, however, explicitly teaches, through prayers, lessons, and symbols, that the deceased brother is in the Celestial Lodge. Therefore the symbolism of the Evergreen goes beyond simply teaching that the soul is immortal.

Faith plays an important part in Masonic funeral services. Faith is also a vital ingredient in religion. Though faith is not restricted to religion (one can have faith [trust] that his car will start in the morning), faith, in religion in general, is directed toward a supernatural Being or beings, and toward supernatural doctrine. Through prayer and lecture the Masonic funeral service is laden with the doctrine of faith, specifically faith in God (T.G.A.O.T.U.) and in the immortality of the soul.

Though Christians should be tolerant of other people's beliefs—in the sense of acknowledging people's right to their own beliefs—they should not hesitate to challenge other people's beliefs when they run contrary to biblical teachings. Thus, when a Masonic funeral service teaches faith in God or in the blooming of our souls in eternal spring, Christians need to ask (1) *Which* God is this faith being directed toward? and (2) *Why* and *how* are souls going to bloom in eternal spring? The answer to the first question is Jesus Christ (Acts 16:30–31[49]; cf. John 14:6; Acts 4:12); the answer to the second is that because of the Father's love and by grace through faith in Christ (John 3:16; Eph. 2:8–9) we may dwell in His presence forever (Rev. 21:3).

These assorted Masonic services clearly evidence the expunging of Christ from the biblical text and the wrenching of biblical texts from their proper contexts. By opting for nonsectarianism, Freemasonry is quite anxious to use the Bible but not as anxious to echo the Bible's exclusive claims. That unbiblical approach runs the Lodge into a theological dead end. In their services regarding the afterlife, Masons state with dogmatic certainty that brother so-and-so has entered into the Celestial Lodge above. Yet, according to the Bible a person is in heaven *only* if he has believed in the Jesus of the Bible.

If the Masonic Lodge in the United States does not wish to be called a religion or to be seen as opposing the teachings of Christianity, then one step it must take (though certainly not the only one) is to eliminate from its list of activities all funeral, burial, and memorial services.

Notes

1. Originally edited by Albert G. Mackey. Revised by Charles Inglesby, Grand Secretary, and assisted by Walter M. Whitehead, Deputy Grand Master. Seventeenth edition revised and augmented by O. Frank Hart, Grand Secretary (Columbia, S.C.: The R.L. Bryan Co., 1947). Compiled and arranged by the authority of the Grand Lodge, and published under its sanction.

2. Public Grand Honors are performed by the Masons assembled at the funeral service. They are performed by crossing the arms at the breasts, raising the hands above the head, and dropping them quickly to the sides of the thighs. See n. 15 for more detail. Though not mentioned every time in this work, the Public Grand Honors were contained in all of the ceremonies documented.

3. *Ahiman Rezon,* 274. The *Ahiman Rezon* took these five essentials from *Claudy's Digest* (n.p., n.d.).

4. *Florida Masonic Monitor* (Grand Lodge of Florida, 1992), 170.

5. *New Mexico Monitor and Ceremonies* (Grand Lodge of New Mexico, 1992), 197–201.

6. *Washington Monitor and Freemason's Guide* (Grand Lodge of Washington, 1983), 133.

7. See the *Florida Masonic Monitor,* 170.

8. The *Monitor of the Lodge* (Grand Lodge of Texas, A.F. & A.M., 1992) states, "They [Masonic funeral services] are uniform throughout the Masonic world in some general and essential matter, though they often differ in detail" (p. 205).

9. *Kentucky Monitor: Complete Monitorial Ceremonies of the Blue Lodge,* 13th ed. (Louisville, Ky.: The Standard Printing Co., 1946), 160.

10. *Louisiana Masonic Monitor* (Walker, La.: Lavergne's River Parish Press, 1988), 154.

11. The *Blue Lodge Text-Book: Official Publication of the Grand Lodge of Mississippi, F. & A.M.* (Grand Lodge of Mississippi, 1978), 63, states, "A Lodge of Sorrow should be held within a reasonable time after the decease of a brother, but only where it may be impracticable to perform the usual funeral ceremonies at the time of interment." Excerpts from a Lodge of Sorrow can be found in this chapter under the headings *Mississippi* and *Oklahoma.*

12. Matt. 7:14 reads, "Because strait *is* the gate, and narrow *is* the way, which leadeth unto life, and few there be that find it." This is sandwiched between vv. 13 and 15, which warn of the broad way leading to destruction and false prophets.

13. Rev. 2:17 reads, "To him that overcometh will I give to eat of the hidden manna, and will give him a white stone, and in the stone a new name written, which no man knoweth saving he that receiveth *it.*" The phrase "to him that overcometh" has been omitted in the service. In the book of Revelation this phrase occurs eight times, and, given the overall scheme of the New Testament, which teaches that obedience comes from faith (Rom. 1:5; here the Greek *pisteōs* is

taken to be a subjective genitive; faith produces obedience) and that believers in Jesus Christ *will* persevere until the end (Matt. 10:22), the phrase "to the one that overcomes" should be taken to mean the believer in Christ who, as a natural outgrowth of his or her faith, perseveres to the end. This one will receive, by the grace of God, the eternal reward of faith (Rev. 3:21; 21:7), and this faith is the gift of God to the Christian (Eph. 2:8–9).

14. This is most likely a reference to Hiram Abif. When the band that was looking for Hiram saw the Sprig of Acacia, it signaled the grave of Hiram. They took his body and later buried it near the Temple.

15. The *Florida Masonic Monitor* states that the Public Grand Honors are performed in the following manner: "Both arms are crossed on the breast, with the left over the right and the open palms of the hands striking the shoulders; they are then raised above the head, the palms striking each other, and then made to fall sharply on the thighs, with head bowed. This is given three times" (p. 201).

16. Taken from Matt. 25:34, which reads, "Then shall the King say unto them on his right hand, Come, ye blessed of my Father, inherit the kingdom prepared for you from the foundation of the world." Notice that "of my Father" has been deleted by the Lodge. Also, the "King" in this verse is the "Son of man" (Matt. 25:31), which is Jesus Christ. Thus, by removing "of my Father" from the text, the Lodge removes mention of Jesus Christ from the biblical text and from their funeral service. The Grand Lodge of Florida also misquotes Heb. 9:27, which says, "And it is appointed unto men once to die, but after this the judgment." The *Florida Masonic Monitor* states, "It is appointed unto all men once to die, and after death cometh the resurrection" (p. 273).

17. *Florida Masonic Monitor,* 195–206.

18. Phil. 4:7 reads, "And the peace of God, which passeth all understanding, shall keep your hearts and minds through Christ Jesus."

19. This may allude to the second section of the ritual of the Master Mason degree, where the Master's word "Mah-Hah-Bone" (see chap. 3, n. 44) is given.

20. This is an allusion to the symbolism of the Three Steps (see chap. 3).

21. *Maine Masonic Text Book* (Maine Printing Exchange, 1992), 98–102.

22. The Scroll (or Roll) contains the name of the deceased, his date of birth, the dates on which he received the first three degrees, the date of his death, the name of his Lodge, and the name of the state in which he was a member.

23. See n. 14.

24. *Washington Monitor and Freemason's Guide,* 142–46.

25. *New Mexico Monitor and Ceremonies,* 205–8.

26. See n. 11. Also, some Lodges, such as those of Florida (see *Florida Masonic Monitor,* 264) and Oklahoma (see this chapter under the heading *Oklahoma*), make use of a skull during the ritual for a Lodge of Sorrow.

27. The Grand Lodge of Mississippi includes this reference to 1 Cor. 15:35–57 at the end of the quotation. Notice that 1 Cor. 15:57 was cut short. The whole

verse reads, "But thanks be to God, which giveth us the victory through our Lord Jesus Christ."

28. *Blue Lodge Text-Book* (Grand Lodge of Mississippi), 63–74.

29. This is an allusion to the symbolism of the Common Gavel in the Entered Apprentice degree. See chap. 2.

30. See n. 22.

31. Omitting vv. 43a, 45, 47, 51–52, 55–57. After quoting v. 54, the monitor moves on to v. 58, with no ellipsis points in the text to indicate the omission of vv. 55–57.

32. Landmarks are the particular principles of each Grand Lodge. For example, the Grand Lodge of Massachusetts lists seven Landmarks: (1) monotheism, the sole dogma of Freemasonry; (2) belief in immortality, the ultimate lesson of Masonic philosophy; (3) the Volume of the Sacred Law, an indispensable part of the furniture of a Lodge; (4) the legend of the Third Degree; (5) secrecy; (6) the symbolism of the operative art (operative masonry); and (7) that a Mason must be a freeborn male adult. These are listed in Silas H. Shepherd's "The Landmarks of Freemasonry," in *Little Masonic Library,* 5 vols. (Richmond: Macoy Publishing and Masonic Supply Co., 1977), 1:77.

33. The Volume of the Sacred Law, the Square, and the Compass are the Three Great Lights in Masonry. See chaps. 1 and 2.

34. Taken from Matt. 25:23. Here the word "lord" appears in lowercase, though the Lodge writes "Lord" in its funeral service, making it allude to God. In exegeting the parable, we should see in "lord" the *immediate* allusion to the traveling man who is master of his servants (v. 14), though Jesus' *ultimate* point is that He is the one portrayed as this master, in an "end of the ages" judgment motif (see vv. 32–46). Thus, in v. 23, "lord" is figurative of the Son of man (v. 31), Jesus Christ. To enter into the joy of thy lord (v. 23) is to come into the eternal joy of fellowship with Jesus Christ. The Lodge misses this.

35. Perhaps alluding to "The Strong Grip of a Master Mason, or the Lion's Paw of the Tribe of Judah." See the discussion of the Lion's Paw in chap. 3.

36. *A Masonic Trestle-Board for the Use of Lodges Under the Jurisdiction of the Grand Lodge of Massachusetts, A.F. & A.M.* (Grand Lodge of Massachusetts, 1979), 108–28.

37. See n. 22.

38. Taken from John 11:25–26, which reads, "Jesus said unto her, I am the resurrection, and the life: he that believeth in me, though he were dead, yet shall he live: And whosoever liveth and believeth in me shall never die. Believest thou this?" V. 27 continues, "She [Martha, whose brother, Lazarus, Jesus raised from the dead in this same chapter] saith unto him, Yea, Lord: I believe that thou art the Christ, the Son of God, which should come into the world."

39. See n. 12.

40. See n. 14.

41. *Michigan Masonic Ceremonies: Adopted by the Grand Lodge, Free and Accepted Masons of Michigan* (Grand Lodge of Michigan, 1911), 4–17, bold added to assist the reader.

42. See n. 11. Bold print has been added to assist the reader. In addition, the *Murrow Masonic Monitor* (Grand Lodge of Ancient, Free and Accepted Masons of the State of Oklahoma, 1988) states, "There is no necessity for any attempt at secrecy in the ceremonies of Sorrow Lodges. They may be held in churches or public halls, or in the presence of friends at the Lodge room with benefit to all concerned" (p. 145).

43. For the Christian, this prayer is blasphemous. Christ alone, as the resurrected King and Messiah, is now seated at the right hand of God the Father (Rom. 8:34; Eph. 1:20; Col. 3:1; Heb. 1:3; 8:1; 10:12; 12:2; 1 Peter 3:22). The place at God's right hand symbolizes Christ's royal exaltation (Acts 2:33). In Mark 10:40 Jesus says that the Father will grant to those whom He wills a place at *Christ's* right and left, but this is not to be confused with the symbolic phrase "the right hand of God [the Father]," which alone is fulfilled by the Messiah and signifies Christ's divine authority and unique high priesthood.

44. Referring to midnight, when the murderers of Hiram Abif would return to move his remains from the rubbish of the Temple to a hill near Mount Moriah. See *The Legend of Hiram Abif* in chap. 3.

45. Again an allusion to the Great Drama of the third degree, this time to the attempts to raise Hiram from the grave.

46. Heb. 9:27 reads, "And as it is appointed unto men once to die, but after this the judgment" (Cf. v. 28.). See also the relevant comment in n. 16.

47. *Murrow Masonic Monitor,* 147–64.

48. *Coil's Masonic Encyclopedia* (New York: Macoy Publishing and Masonic Supply Co., 1961), 512.

49. In Acts 16:31, the Greek *pisteuson* ("believe"; here in the aorist imperative), coming from the noun *pistis* ("faith"), means "to place trust in." To believe is not merely to affirm existence.

PART TWO

THE SCOTTISH RITE

CHAPTER 5

AN INTRODUCTION TO THE SCOTTISH RITE

"We have heard, even to nausea, the assertion a thousand times repeated, that the Degrees of the Ancient and Accepted Scottish Rite are no higher than the Blue Degrees, and that they are no part of genuine Masonry. They are higher, nevertheless, because they are not conferred indiscriminately on all, nor intended to be popular; and because they illustrate and explain the Symbols of the Blue Lodge. And they are Masonic, if by Masonry we mean initiation into the mysteries. If we do not mean that, all Masonry is contained in the Apprentice's Degree."
—Legenda of the Lodge of Perfection

Visiting the Scottish Rite Temple (House of the Temple) in Washington, D.C., was an experience I will never forget. Architecturally, it fits in with the other stately buildings on the Mall. But atop the wide steps, to the left and right of the entrance, stand Isis and Nephthys, two Egyptian goddesses, as if guarding the entrance to the Temple. On the main floor is a bust of the great Scottish Rite past Sovereign Grand Commander Albert Pike. Various gods and goddesses line the stairs that lead up to the Temple room. In front of the Temple entrance is an inscription that reads, "Know Thyself."[1] In the center of the enormous Temple room is the altar. When Session meets once a year, holy books from many religions are placed side by side on the altar.

About the Rite

The Rite contains four "bodies" (sections). Degrees 4–14 make up the Lodge of Perfection; 15–18, the Chapter of Rose Croix; 19–30, the Council of Kadosh; and 31–32, the Consistory. These bodies of the Southern Jurisdiction will be treated in chapters 6–9.

Who Qualifies?

A man may seek membership in the Scottish Rite after completing the three degrees of Blue Lodge Freemasonry.[2] This Rite has a thirty-two–degree system, with an honorary thirty-third degree for those who have performed exceptionally as Masons. The Scottish Rite has nothing to do with Scotland—it is actually French in origin.[3] In the United States there are two Jurisdictions, Northern and Southern. In the United States alone, nearly one million men are Scottish Rite Masons. And numbers may rise quickly, since special "one day classes" have been adopted: in one day Blue Lodge Masons can become thirty-second–degree Masons!

When Is a Mason Not a Mason?

The ancient mysteries taught that the majority of initiates were not *really* initiates; only a chosen few were able to comprehend the "true" meaning of the mysteries of the cult. "In the Mysteries, those who misunderstood the Symbols and allegories were left to remain in the complacency of their ignorance."[4] The monitor of the Grand Lodge of Texas shares this belief.

> Every candidate for the Mysteries of Masonry, at the proper time and in an appropriate manner, should be taught the truth that the *rite of initiation* means much more than a formal ceremonial progress through the Degrees. In fact one may receive the entire work, conferred under the most favorable circumstances, and by competent officers, and yet not perceive the true Masonic *light,* which the symbols and allegories are designed to conceal, as well as to reveal. *Initiation* is to be attained only after real labor, deep study, profound meditation, extensive research and a constant practice of those vir-

tues which will open a true path to moral, intellectual, and spiritual illumination.[5]

The average Mason is not aware of the spiritual import of the Craft degrees. He may not even be aware of the above opinion, for many Masons do not read through their monitors, if they read them at all.[6]

The Scottish Rite thinks that the Blue Lodge is not enough, as is evidenced in the opening quotation. The ritualistic system of the Scottish Rite is therefore set up to unfold more fully the mysteries of the Blue Lodge.

> Masonry claims to be an advance toward the Light. That Light is Truth. How far does Symbolic or Blue Masonry advance toward it? . . . Blue Masonry utters a few of the commonest dicta of moral Truth, known and familiar to all men in all ages. It does no more. It limits itself to so much as is useful to bind together in a kind of Brotherhood the mass of a numerous order. In the lesser mysteries[7] no more was ever required. . . . The Masonry of the Higher Degrees teaches the great truths of Intellectual Science; but as to all these, even as to the rudiments and first principles, Blue Masonry is absolutely dumb. Its drama *seems* intended to teach the resurrection of the body; but it teaches nothing more. . . . Every man of high intelligence, Initiate of the Lesser Mysteries, but ignorant of the Greater, would still have known that the former were but preparatory, and that there must be some place in which their symbols were explained and their real purposes made known. . . . We do not demand your assent to these conclusions. We state them here, to lead you to reflect and study, that you may decide for yourself. All that we positively assert is, that so far from containing in themselves all Freemasonry, the Blue Degrees, especially in England and the United States, only conceal the Light from the Initiates, were at the beginning only a means of organization, and are now only preliminary and rudimental. The Degree of Perfection[8] is so called because it *completes* and *perfects* the Third Degree.[9]

Sources for Our Study

The ritualistic system of the Scottish Rite is highly esoteric. Meaning is hidden, and only the chosen few are capable of truly understanding its import. Compounding the phenomenon is a general ignorance of spiritual matters and of religion. This is one primary reason why the spiritual and religious aspects of Freemasonry, blatant as they are, escape the average Mason.[10] The average Mason comes from the general populace. So, although Masonic scholar Henry Coil clearly states that "the rituals [of the Scottish Rite] constitute something of a study in comparative religion, colored by Kabbalism,[11] Hermeticism,[12] Rosicrucianism,[13] and other mystical philosophies,"[14] most Masons either do not know what he means (if they read Coil) or are not alert enough to perceive it in ritual.[15] The *Legenda of the Lodge of Perfection* states,

> Masonry also has its ancient Symbols, inherited from the Mysteries and the Kabalah, and intended to veil and conceal the truth from all except the Adepts. Like the religions, also, Masonry gives false interpretations of its Symbols, to mislead those who would not value the highest philosophical truth, and the Profane to whom these interpretations may be divulged.[16]

Pike also says that "it is in its *antique* Symbols and their occult[17] meaning that the true secrets of Freemasonry consist."[18] Today, the Scottish Rite uses the *Legenda* to supplement teaching on its degrees.

For the teachings of the Scottish Rite, the most important source will be Albert Pike's *Liturgy of the Ancient and Accepted Scottish Rite.*[19] This is the monitor of the Ancient and Accepted Scottish Rite today. Next to the ritual, this is the most authoritative source one can possess.

Albert Pike was and is a Masonic giant.[20] His remains are contained in a vault at the Scottish Rite's Temple in Washington, D.C., reflecting the fact that he is held in the highest regard. In 1859 he was appointed Sovereign Grand Commander (chief officer; the head) of the Scottish Rite, not long after he had begun revising the rituals for the Rite. The finished product was called *The Magnum Opus.*[21] Today the Scottish Rite has revised this ritual by Pike, though it remains essentially the same. I will therefore cite from this work. Pike's monumental work, *Morals and Dogma,*[22] is his most popular, though most Masons do not understand it. It is highly esoteric and is written in a lofty and verbose style. *Morals and Dogma* is a voluminous work and contains lectures on the thirty-two degrees of the Scottish Rite.[23] The Scottish Rite still uses it to elaborate on its rituals[24]; much of the lecture portion of the ritual is taken from this work.[25] Sovereign Grand Commander C. Fred Kleinknecht says that, along with the rituals of the Rite, *Morals and Dogma* is "the apex of our teachings."[26] The last source from Pike that we will draw from here is *The Book of the Words.*[27] This work focuses on analyzing significant words in ritual (passwords, etc.).

Rex Hutchens's *A Bridge to Light*[28] is another source. This book explains the degrees of the Rite and significant portions of *Morals and Dogma,* and it is "unanimously approved" by the "Committee on Rituals and Ceremonial Forms."[29] Sovereign Grand Commander C. Fred Kleinknecht states that a lack of education in classical mythology and Greek and Latin has made it difficult to understand Pike's book. As a result, *"A Bridge to Light* seeks to overcome this difficulty by presenting passages from *Morals and Dogma* that best reinforce the teachings of the rituals of the degrees."[30] This book is given to all Scottish Rite candidates.

Methodology

A note on my methodology in chapters 6–9: For the most part I will endeavor to start with the most authoritative of the above sources, the *Liturgy of the Ancient and Accepted Scottish Rite.* The *Legenda, The Magnum Opus,*[31] *Morals and Dogma,* and *A Bridge to Light* follow in order of importance, and will be used to elaborate upon the *Liturgy* where needed. I have chosen to deal only with the Scottish Rite, Southern Jurisdiction.

With the *Liturgy* we have no real problems regarding the teachings of the Rite; it contains portions of the rituals themselves. The minute problem regarding *The Magnum Opus* is discussed briefly in note 31. A Mason could argue that the *Legenda, Morals and Dogma,* and *A Bridge to Light* are only the opinions of Pike and Hutchens. That is true, but what kind of opinions are they? Clearly, these sources hold *some* authoritative weight. The fact that the Rite uses the *Legenda* and *Morals and Dogma* to instruct its neophytes, and that *A Bridge to Light* is endorsed by the Committee on Rituals and Ceremonial Forms, must be reckoned with by the Mason.

The problem is that most Masons do not take the time to seriously reckon with the less authoritative sources. When they read, for example, quotations from Pike's *Morals and Dogma* in anti-Masonic books, they dismiss them as Pike's "opinions." I challenge these Masons to (1) consider how well schooled *they* are in the study of religion; (2) find out why Pike, Hutchens, Kleinknecht, and others are endorsed; (3) understand why Pike, Hutchens, Kleinknecht, and others hold their opinions; and (4) give adequate reasons for their disagreement, using their knowledge of comparative religion and the *Liturgy* or ritual to do so.

The chapters that follow will include "Biblical Response" sections. I will occasionally, however, include shorter biblical responses in the midst of the treatment of certain degrees.

Summary

In this chapter I have identified the various bodies of the Scottish Rite, documented its claim of the necessity of the Rite as regards its shedding of light on the Blue Lodge degrees, and identified the major sources for our study. We now move to the Lodge of Perfection, where the Legend of Hiram continues.

Notes

1. Plutarch, in his essay *Peace of Mind*, writes, "All things, therefore, are not in everyone's power, and we should heed the maxim inscribed in Apollo's temple, 'Know thyself'" (*Plutarch: Selected Lives and Essays,* trans. Louise Ropes Loomis [Roslyn, N.Y.: Walter J. Black, 1951], 348).

2. The Scottish Rite may confer its own Blue Lodge degrees, but most Masons attain the Blue degrees through their particular state's Grand Lodge, and then earn degrees 4–32 (and the honorary 33rd) in either the Northern or the Southern Jurisdiction of the Scottish Rite.

3. Kent Henderson, *Masonic World Guide* (London: Lewis Masonic, 1984), 36.

4. *Legenda of the Lodge of Perfection,* degrees 4–14 (Southern Jurisdiction, USA, 1956), 41. This is all the bibliographical information given.

5. *Monitor of the Lodge* (Grand Lodge of Texas, A.F. & A.M., 1992), xvi.

6. This apathy or disinterest reinforces for Masonic scholars the conviction that it takes hard work to be a true initiate. Alphonse Cerza, in his *Masonic Reader's Guide* ([Missouri Lodge of Research, 1980], ix), states, "Receiving the degrees in the Craft makes one a member, but he does not become a Mason until he has learned the meaning of the degrees, the moral lessons taught in the degrees, and how to make them a part of his life." It is for this reason, and for reasons given in the body of this work, that Carl Claudy, in *Foreign Countries* (Richmond: Macoy Publishing and Masonic Supply Co., 1971), wrote, "*True* Freemasonry gives to a man a well-spent life, and assurance of a glorious immortality" (p. 11, emphasis added).

7. There are lesser mysteries and greater mysteries, the former introducing the latter, which are superior in disclosing and unfolding spiritual content.

8. In the Scottish Rite, degrees 4–14 constitute the Lodge of Perfection.

9. *Legenda of the Lodge of Perfection,* degrees 4–14, pp. 37–43.

10. See, for example, the quote in the *Legenda* contained in chap. 6, n. 45.

11. From the Hebrew verb *qbl* ("to receive," thus dealing with oral tradition). Definitions of Qabbalah (also spelled Kabalah or Kabbalah) vary. Rabbi Simeon ben Yohai (second century A.D.) is said to have written a "spiritual" commentary on the Torah (the first five books of the Bible) of Moses, called *The Zohar.* Others (rightly so) attribute the work to Moses de Leon, a thirteenth-century esoterist. *The Zohar* supposedly reveals the inner and concealed truths of the Torah. Qabbalah focuses on the Sacred Tree made up of ten Sephiroth. Sephi-

roth (from the Hebrew word meaning "numbers") are the "branches" of the Tree bringing the light of God (*En Sof,* the Limitless and Unknowable One), through emanations of its attributes, to humanity. Here the creation is believed to have come into being through emanations of the *En Sof.* It is Jewish occultism, bringing true light to those desiring to "receive" it, and thus, in my opinion, *re*uniting the soul of a person (which is no different in essence from the *En Sof*) with the *En Sof.*

12. From Hermes Trismegistus (the thrice greatest Hermes). Hermes is the Greek name given to the Egyptian god Thoth. According to one occult source, he coined the teaching "as above, so below" (E. E. Rehmus, *The Magician's Dictionary* [Los Angeles: Feral House, 1990], 107). From this source we learn that "Hermetic science is based on universal symbols present within the collective unconscience and therefore available to inner revelation, rather than to objective experience."

13. A mystical brotherhood dating back to the early seventeenth century. Esoteric wisdom is gained through grades or degrees of initiation, thereby enabling one to achieve oneness with the divine.

14. Henry W. Coil, *Conversations on Freemasonry* (Richmond: Macoy Publishing and Masonic Supply Co., 1976), 137.

15. According to Coil, about half, sometimes less, of the Scottish Rite degrees are "conferred" (in scenic drama plays performed before large classes). The other half are simply "communicated," i.e., briefly described and explained (see Coil, *Conversations,* 137, 140).

16. *Legenda of the Lodge of Perfection,* degrees 4–14, p. 6.

17. Here the word *occult* means "secret" or "hidden."

18. *Legenda of the Lodge of Perfection,* degrees 4–14, p. 25.

19. By The Supreme Council (Mother Council of the World) of the Inspectors General Knights Commanders of the House of the Temple of Solomon of the Thirty-third Degree of the Ancient and Accepted Scottish Rite of Freemasonry of the Southern Jurisdiction of the United States of America. Part II, 4th–14th degrees, copyright 1962; Part III, 15th–18th degrees, copyright 1936, revised 1982; Part IV, 19th–30th degrees, copyright 1944.

20. For an extended historical account of Pike, refer to any standard Masonic encyclopedia.

21. Kila, Mont.: Kessinger Publishing Co., 1992.

22. Washington, D.C.: The Supreme Council of the Thirty-third Degree, Southern Jurisdiction, A.M. 5680 (1920). The charge has been made that Pike "lifted from the work of others," especially the great occultist Eliphas Levi and his work *Philosophia Occulta* (A. E. Waite, *A New Encyclopedia of Freemasonry* [New York: Weathervane Books, 1970], part 2, p. 278).

23. The Scottish Rite also confers Blue Lodge degrees. A Mason may receive the first three degrees from this Rite, though the majority receive them from local Lodges governed by the State Grand Lodge. From there they join the Scottish

Rite, beginning with the fourth degree. For this reason we have chosen not to treat the first three degrees of the Scottish Rite.

24. *Liturgy,* the monitor of the Scottish Rite degrees, includes sections from Pike's *Morals and Dogma* in the lecture portions of the degrees.

25. I, along with other Christian authors who have critiqued Freemasonry, continually hear and read the Masonic defense that *Morals and Dogma* represents Pike's opinions. My question is, why, then, are portions of it placed in the ritual, the authoritative source for the Scottish Rite? And how does the Rite's committee on ritual decide what is to be placed in the ritual from *Morals and Dogma?* Is all of *Morals and Dogma* authoritative, or are only certain portions of it?

26. Rex R. Hutchens, *A Bridge to Light* (Washington, D.C.: The Supreme Council, 33rd, Ancient and Accepted Scottish Rite of Freemasonry, Southern Jurisdiction, United States of America, 1988), vii.

27. Kila, Mont.: Kessinger Publishing Co., reprint, n.d.

28. See n. 26.

29. This book is personally signed by the eight-member committee: Jess W. Gern, Chairman; David O. Johnson; James R. Rogers; Paul T. Million, Jr.; Francis W. Douglas; David Kruger; Harry S. Barrows; and Thomas S. Perry.

30. Hutchens, *A Bridge to Light,* vii.

31. As stated before, *The Magnum Opus* is essentially the same ritual as is used by the Scottish Rite today, though it has been revised. Because of this revision we hesitate to place it first on our list.

CHAPTER 6

THE LODGE OF PERFECTION: THE CONTINUING LEGEND OF HIRAM AND THE INEFFABLE NAME OF DEITY

"You are in the path that leads up the slope of the mountain of Truth."
—*Albert Pike,* Morals and Dogma

Degrees 4–14 begin a portion of the Scottish Rite ritual system known as the Lodge of Perfection. The Lodge of Perfection elaborates the third degree's legend of Hiram Abif. Thus one will find additions to the already fictional accounts of Hiram.[1]

Historical Background

Rex Hutchens calls degrees 4–14 "the Ineffable Degrees because their principal purpose is the investigation of the ineffable name of Deity."[2] From here the Lodge of Perfection enters into legend. As Hutchens writes, "The threads of the legend dealing with Solomon and the Temple are then merged with an even older legend dealing with Enoch, one of the earliest of the Hebrew Patriarchs."³ According to this legend, Enoch had long ago built a Temple (later, according to this legend, King Solomon built his Temple near the ruins of Enoch's Temple). In Enoch's Temple were several vaults containing various kinds of esoteric information.⁴ One piece of information was the true pronunciation of the sacred name of Deity—the Hebrew consonants *YHVH*.⁵

*The Zohar,*⁶ a chief textbook of the Qabbalah (a Gnostic and occultic philosophical system), says of whoever understands the sacred name, "Happy is his portion in this world and in the world to come."⁷ As we shall see, Scottish Rite Freemasonry concerns itself with the ineffable name of Deity.

According to Masonic tradition, the vault containing the sacred name was discovered when Solomon's workmen, supervised by the Master Builder Hiram, were clearing the site to erect the Temple. The sacred name was lost, however, when Hiram was slain by the three ruffians (see chap. 3). Thus the Grand Omnific Word of the Master Mason degree, *Mah-Hah-Bone,* was only a substitute for the true pronunciation.⁸ Hutchens goes on to state that "the religious lessons of the Ineffable Degrees culminate in the realization of the ineffable name of Deity as a symbol of the ineffable, or indescribable, nature of God."⁹

What follow are prominent aspects of the Lodge of Perfection.

The Fourth Degree: Secret Master

In the fourth degree the Lodge represents the "Kadosh-Kadoshim" (the Most Holy Place).¹⁰ The ritual explains what this means.

> The East of this Lodge represents The Holy of Holies of the First Temple at Jerusalem, and the most Secret Mysteries of Masonry, from which you are now separated by a barrier at present impassable. But you bear the key; and some day it will be permitted you to unlock the gate, and pass the barrier.¹¹

The Apron

The Apron of the Secret Master is white and edged with black, signifying the grief of Masons who hear of Hiram's death and the loss of the Sacred Word.¹² Hutchens states that these colors "are illustrative of the dualist nature of the universe, containing light and darkness, good and evil, truth and error."¹³ The letter "Z" embroidered on the Apron "is esoteric and thus not proper to be discussed here [in Hutchens's book]."¹⁴ It is the password of the degree, most likely standing for "Ziza" or "Zizon."[15] Pike states that *"Ziz,* means 'Abundance, Riches, Strength, Power;' and . . . *on,* added, gives the meaning of *'great* abundance.' Also, 'what moves, movable.'"[16] The All-Seeing Eye on the blue flap of the Apron

> is a symbol of the Sun in the sky, Eye of the universe, and to the ancients an emblem and image of the Deity, the Great Archetype of Light. *"Light and darkness,"* said Zarathustra, *"are the world's eternal ways."* An eye was the Egyptian hieroglyphic for the word IRI [to perform religious ceremonies],[17] and the second syllable of the name of Osiris [OSH-IRI], the sun deified, personification of the Principle of Good.[18]

The Five-Pointed Star

The degree also features the emblem of the five-pointed star, with the Hebrew consonant *yodh* (or *yod* or *yud*), the first consonant of the Hebrew for *Yahweh* (LORD). The *Liturgy* explains its significance: "The blazing five-pointed star represents the Great Central Light, which so many nations have worshiped in the Sun, its representative; and the LETTER,[19] surrounded by its splendours, is the Hebrew Initial of the Name of the Great Source of Light, the True God, whom all Masons revere."[20]

The Ritual

During ritual the candidate has a cord placed around his neck, a bandage over his eyes, and a light in his left hand.[21] What is being sought is "Truth, and the Lost Word."[22] Eventually these three things are taken from the candidate and the Thrice Puissant[23] says, "My Brother, late in darkness, I restore you to Light, and set your feet in the path of Duty, which leads to that True Light of which this is but an emblem."[24] The Thrice Puissant then charges the candidate, "Begin now to rise above the earth, and climb the skies of spiritual knowledge, for there, and not upon the earth, are Truth and the Lost Word to be found."[25] The word "Begin" is essential, for later the *Liturgy* states, "You have yet many steps to ascend before you can reach the heights on which Truth sits enthroned, and discover the Lost Word, known to the ancient partriarchs [*sic*]."[26]

Later the candidate is crowned.

> I crown you with this garland of laurel and olive or laurel, emblem of victory and triumph, and sacred to Apollo, God of Light. Those

who went to consult the Delphic oracle wore garlands of it, as did the Roman Priests on festivals. You march toward an oracle greater than that at Delphi—that of Masonic Truth. . . . You now commence the upward course that is to fit you to be Truth's Minister and Priest.[27]

Thus when Hutchens states that the duties of a Scottish Rite Mason "form the path which leads to the object of the Masonic quest, the True Word," and, "The wreaths of laurel and olive symbolize the hopeful expectation of success in that search,"[28] he is alluding to those who consulted the oracles at Delphi to obtain a word of revelation from Apollo. One of the questions put to Apollo was "Who is God?" Many followers of Apollo believed that he was the Supreme God. Apollo's advice to a human being was to "know thyself."[29] The inscription "Know Thyself" is found in the Scottish Rite Temple *and* at a temple of Apollo (see chap. 5, n. 1). Just as these ancients relentlessly pursued divine wisdom, so should the Mason.

The allusions to religions other than Christianity continue in this fourth degree. The sign of the degree is formed by placing the two forefingers of the right hand on the lips.[30] This "is a symbol of silence or secrecy" and "is derived from statues of the Greek child-deity Harpocrates, who was adopted from the Egyptian deity Horus."[31]

The Sixth Degree: Intimate Secretary

The Apron of this degree is white lambskin, with crimson lining. Two Phoenician letters represent "the mysterious name of the Deity."[32] They correspond to the Hebrew *yodh* and *hey*, the first two consonants of the tetragrammaton.[33] Three other Phoenician letters, corresponding to the Hebrew *bet, nun,* and *shin,* are found in the upper right and left, and bottom center of the Apron.[34] Of these three letters the ritual states,

> The three other letters upon it are the initials of words that mean a *Covenant, Alliance; Agreement* or *Divine Law;* and *Completion, Salvation;* . . . the new alliance between the two kings, the promise made by Solomon to Khirum,[35] which the latter imagined had been broken; and its perfect and complete performance, in the spirit as well as in the letter. They also have a profounder meaning to us as Masons; the *Covenant* made by God with man, by the Creator with his erring creatures; his *Promise* of mercy and for-

giveness; and that *Salvation* and state of *Perfection* which await those who emulate the virtues and follow the example of the Master Khirum. When you wear the apron, remember the covenants you have made at the altars of Masonry, with God and your Brethren; your vows in the degrees of this Rite especially; and that perfection which a Mason must ever aim at, though he can never reach it here below.[36]

The Sacred Word of the degree is *Yeva*[37] (or *Jova* or *Ivah*).[38] In the Qabbalah these consonants are "the representative signs of male and female, of the generative and productive energies of Deity."[39] One of the passwords of the degree is "Joabert." Pike explains that this is a compound of the Hebrew for *Yah* ("the Deity of the Hebrews") and *Aber*[40] (meaning "to rise up"). Pike then notes that "Yu-Aber means the Energy or Uprising of Deity, and has a phallic signification, meaning the *'generative* Energy.'"[41]

The Eighth Degree: Intendant of the Building[42]

The eighth degree provides a "history"[43] of the events following the death of the Grand Master Hiram Abif. Here the candidate represents one of the five builders appointed by King Solomon to erect the Temple.[44]

The degree also contains an admonition to candidates that is found in many Masonic books in various ways. Keeping in step with the true milieu of Freemasonry, those Masons who are content with simply receiving their degrees and not investing in deep study and reflection are warned,

> You have been taught the important lesson, that none are entitled to advance in the Ancient and Accepted Scottish Rite who have not by study and application made themselves familiar with Masonic learning and jurisprudence. The degrees of this Rite are not for those who are content with the mere work and ceremonies, and do not care to explore the mines of wisdom that lie buried beneath the surface.[45]

The Nine-Pointed Star

Some of the symbols and their meanings are heavily Qabbalistic. One of the Lodge decorations for this degree is a nine-pointed star with a Samaritan consonant corresponding to the Hebrew consonant *yodh*.[46] According to Pike, who draws from the Qabbalah, this consonant represents "the Created or Generative Agent, which, sent down into the circular space, thereinto immitted light, in the successive Divine Emanations."[47] This may be difficult to understand for those unfamiliar with Gnostic and occultic jargon. The basics of Qabbalistic philosophy as regards creation stem from the "Tree of Life." God is said to be Infinite Light[48] manifested through the different Sephiroth (spheres or emanations) of the Tree of Life. This is quite similar to the Gnostic idea of creation, which holds that the material universe came into existence through "aeons" or angelic intermediaries (emanations) which manifested themselves as a result of a divine "falling out" of the *plērōma.*[49]

The Pythagorean Connection

For this degree, the Lodge is lighted by twenty-seven lights—three groups of nine, forming a triple triangle (the triple triangle, forming the nine-sided star, hangs over the presiding officer and is also an emblem on the Apron).[50] The numbers twenty-seven and three also carry significance. Hutchens explains that "the number 27 was peculiarly significant to the ancient Pythagorean[51] numerologists, as were all multiples of nine . . . 27 was deemed particularly significant since it was the cube of three, the Pythagorean number of Deity."[52]

The early church theologian and philosopher Justin Martyr considered Pythagoras's teachings heresy: "If you desire to see a clearer proof of the opinion of Pythagoras concerning one God, hear his own opinion, for he spoke as follows: 'God is one; and He Himself does not, as some suppose, exist outside the world, but in it.'"[53] Pythagoras considered the universe divine and the human soul a fragment of the divine. Man therefore should seek purification of the soul to prepare it for its return to the Universal Soul, or Deity, of which the soul of man is a part.[54]

The Zohar Connection

The number twenty-seven also plays a significant role in *The Zohar*. The tetragrammaton consists of the Hebrew consonants *YHV* (the "supernal letters" in *The Zohar*). *The Zohar* tells of the mystical significance of the three consonants (the *H* being repeated), which contain three "orders" each, for a total of nine. These in turn each have three suborders, bringing the total number to twenty-seven. The mystical significance of all this is to understand the all-inclusive Generative Principle called God, which is made up of both male and female principles: "For when the world was created it was the supernal letters that brought into being all the works of the lower world, literally after their own pattern." The connection with Scottish Rite Freemasonry's emphasis on the *ineffable name* now surfaces, for we read, "Hence, whoever has a knowledge of them and is observant of them is beloved both on high and below."[55] The symbolism of the letter *yodh* given earlier by Pike,[56] and the over-all flavor of Qabbalistic philosophy throughout the ritual clearly suggest a Qabbalistic significance for the number twenty-seven as it pertains to this degree.

The Scottish Rite ritualistic scheme blends multiple religious systems in its search for "Truth." Here the Mason who claims to be a Christian must not only deal with this unbiblical syncretism, which he actively participates in, or at the least associates with, but he must also face the Scottish Rite's claim to point him to the "Truth," even though his Lord and Savior says that He is the truth (John 14:6). And though Jesus is the Light of the World (John 1:4–5, 9; esp. John 8:12), we read in ritual,

> You still advance toward the *Light,* toward that star,[57] blazing in the distance, which is an emblem of the Divine *Truth,* given by God to the first men, and preserved amid all the vicissitudes of ages in the traditions and teachings of Masonry, in all the sanctuaries of initiation in the world. How far you will advance depends upon yourself alone. Here, as everywhere in the world, darkness struggles with light, and clouds and shadows intervene between you and the *Truth.* When you shall have become imbued with the morality of Masonry, with which you are, and for some time will be, exclusively occupied— when you shall have learned to practice all the virtues which it inculcates—when they have become familiar to you as your household gods—then you will be prepared to receive its lofty philosophical instruction, and to scale the heights upon whose summit Light and Truth sit enthroned.[58]

The Ninth and Tenth Degrees

The ninth and tenth degrees are called the *Elu of the Nine* and the *Elu of the Fifteen,* respectively. These degrees are mentioned in order to note that, in the *Scottish Rite* Blue Lodge degree of Master Mason, the three murderers of Hiram are *not* found or sentenced; this occurs in the ninth and tenth degrees. Thus the Apron for the tenth degree is decorated with three severed heads dripping with blood and resting atop a gate.[59]

The Thirteenth Degree: Royal Arch of Solomon[60]

The thirteenth degree is also known as *The Royal Arch of Enoch,* which is quite significant in light of our observation at the beginning of this chapter. The legend of Enoch is central to understanding this degree. According to Masonic tradition, Enoch "dreamed that the Deity appeared to him in visible shape, and said to him, 'Enoch, thou hast longed to know my *true Name.* Arise, and follow me, and thou shalt learn it.'"[61] Enoch was then transported to a mountain, where, upon the clouds, he saw the name, the pronunciation of which was then whispered in his ear. As the dream continued, he was ordered not to pronounce the true name to anyone. He then descended into the earth through nine subterranean apartments with arched ceilings. In the last arched apartment (thus the title "Royal Arch of Solomon") he saw engraved upon a triangular plate of gold the ineffable name just as he had seen it on the mountain. That is when he awoke.[62] Taking his dream seriously, Enoch proceeded to the mountain he had dreamed of, excavated nine apartments, and built arches around them. In the lowest arched apartment he engraved the ineffable name upon a gold triangular plate, placed it in a cube of agate, and placed the cube upon a pedestal of white alabaster.[63]

Since the world was wicked and was about to be destroyed by a flood (not the flood of Noah's time), Enoch was responsible for preserving the ineffable name, though he told no one at that time. When Enoch's generation was destroyed by the flood, no one knew the true name until God made it known to Moses in Exodus 3:14–15.[64] The engraved name itself was not found until Solomon erected a building for administrating public justice, whereupon his workmen, who erected the building on the Enochian site, stumbled upon the ninth arch containing the ineffable name.[65]

Ritual

As the ritual continues to be acted out, the Mason playing King Solomon declares, "We may now make the Word [ineffable name] known to those whose eminent merits shall entitle them to receive it . . . for it is *the true word of a Mason,* and the True Name of the Great Architect of the Universe."[66] He then bestows upon the three workmen who discovered the vault the title of "Masons of the Ninth or Royal Arch," and makes it a degree in Masonry.[67] Afterward Solomon establishes the degree of Grand, Elect, Perfect and Sublime Mason (or Perfect Elu),[68] and he, one other king and the three workmen are "then rewarded by receiving the true pronunciation and explanation of the Sacred Name, and learning the true nature and attributes of the Deity."[69]

Again, Scottish Rite Freemasonry shares with the Qabbalah this yearning for knowledge of the true name of Deity.[70] Since the Qabbalah teaches that the true name was known to certain chosen ones who received the keys to esoteric knowledge, it is no surprise that the Scottish Rite *Liturgy* explains that the Hebrews' and other religions' "superstitious notions in regard to the efficacy of the Word, and the prohibition against pronouncing it, could, being errors, have formed no part of the pure primitive religion, or of the esoteric doctrine taught by Moses, and the full knowledge of which was confined to the initiates."[71] The *Liturgy* later states that this superstitious fear and the loss of the True Word represent ignorance of the true nature and attributes of God.[72] Scottish Rite Freemasonry, through a correct understanding of its degrees, offers the initiate[73] the key to truly comprehending the sacred name of Deity.

Continuing this theme of a select few who understood the true name and nature of Deity, the *Liturgy* relates that, even amidst this general ignorance alluded to above, "Among *all* the ancient nations there was one faith and one idea of Deity for the enlightened, intelligent and educated, and another for the common people."[74] Whether through Zoroaster, Menu, Confucius, Socrates, or Jesus, this "true understanding" was only communicated to a few favored people, especially to the initiates of the Greater Mysteries in Egypt, India, Persia, Phoenicia, Samothrace, and Greece.[75] In short,

> The Supreme, Self-existent, Eternal, All-wise, All-powerful, Infinitely Good, Pitying, Beneficent and Merciful Creator and Preserver of the Universe was the same, by whatever name he was called, to the intellectual and enlightened men of all nations. The name was nothing, if not a symbol and representative hieroglyph of his nature and attributes. The name AL represented his remoteness *above* men, his *inaccessibility;* BAL and BALA, his *might;* ALOHIM, his various *potencies;* IHUH, *existence* and the *generation* of things. . . . As MOLOCH or MALEK he was but an omnipotent *monarch,* a tremendous and irresponsible *Will;* as ADONAI, only an arbitrary LORD and *Master;* as AL *Shadai, potent* and a destroyer.[76]

In keeping with this eclectic spirit, after the Sacred Word *YHVH* is communicated only by its consonants,[77] the ritual alludes to nine names of Deity, corresponding to Enoch's nine vaults and arches. These different names of "the one true God" are synonyms of the ineffable name and are taken from Egypt, Phoenicia, India, Assyria, and the Old Testament.[78] One of these names is the Hindu *Aum* or *Om.*[79]

The *Liturgy* admits that this degree and others have connections with the Qabbalah. "There are profounder meanings concealed in the symbols of this degree, connected with the philosophical system of the Hebrew Kaba- lists, which you will learn hereafter, if you should be so fortunate as to ad- vance. They are unfolded in the higher degrees."[80] Though the divine name may be made known to the Mason in the fourteenth degree,[81] that of Grand, Elect, Perfect and Sublime Mason (or Perfect Elu), one of these "profounder meanings" occurs in the twenty-eighth degree (Knight of the Sun). Accord- ing to Pike, "Yod is Hakemah[82] [Wisdom], and He Binah [Understanding]; Vav [or Waw] is Tephareth[83] [Beauty], and the last He, Malkuth [Kingdom]."[84] Similarly, *The Zohar* communicates the Qabbalistic doctrine that "the *Yod* stands for *Hokhmah* the Father, and the first *Hé* for *Binah,* the Mother. The *Vau,* having the numerical value of six, symbolizes the 'six ends', the grades of six days, and more particularly *Tifereth,* the center of this group. The sec- ond *Hé* naturally symbolizes *Malkuth.*"[85] The similarity between Masonic ritual and the Qabbalah is unquestionable.

The Fourteenth Degree: Perfect Elu

The fourteenth degree is the last degree in the Lodge of Perfection. It is also known as Grand, Elect, Perfect and Sublime Mason. Appropriately so, "The Lodge is styled the 'Secret Vault.'"[86] This alludes to the ninth arch of Enoch, which contains the cubical stone on which the gold triangular plate inscribed with the ineffable name is laid. "On the upper face are the ineffable names in Phoenician and Sanscrit characters . . . and around the plate are nine words in several different languages."[87]

Have We Found It?

The search for the true name appears to be coming to its climax as we read,

> *Qu:* What does the Triangle represent?
> *Ans:* It contains the Ineffable Name, and represents the Great Cre- ator of the Universe; in comparison with whom all men are so infi- nitely small and powerless, that the difference between the highest and the lowest is insignificant.
> *Qu:* What are you, my Brother?
> *Ans:* I *am* your Brother; a Gr[and], El[ect], Perf[ect] and Sub[lime] Mason; who have [*sic*] undergone all the tests and trials, and ob- tained the reward of my labors.

Qu: What is that reward?

Ans: The knowledge of the True God; a faint but true appreciation of His nature and infinite attributes; a confidence in His wisdom and Justice, His benevolence and love for His feeble creatures; securing me against scepticism and despair.

Qu: Have you the True Word of a Gr., El., Perf. and Sublime Mason?

Ans: I have.

Qu: What is it?

Ans: That knowledge and confidence; of which the visible word is but a symbol.[88]

The true *pronunciation* of the Sacred Word, however, still remains unknown to the candidate. The ritual continues as the candidate is led into the Lodge Room, again representing the ninth secret vault of Enoch. As he enters the Lodge Room, the candidate is asked to give a series of three passwords. One of these passwords is "Marah-maur-abrek" and is said to mean, "The Vault, the Place of Light! Bow ye the head."[89] After a long series of questions to test the authenticity of his Masonry, he is asked,

Qu: Are you a Royal Arch Mason . . . ?

Ans: I have descended through the nine arches into the subterranean vault, and seen the luminous pedestal, the cube of agate, and THE GREAT WORD, . . .

Qu: Can you pronounce the Sacred Word?

Ans: I cannot. I have come hither in hopes to obtain that secret.[90]

Another series of test questions follows, after which the candidate kneels at the altar to take his obligation. He rises and is led to a table of bread and wine ("the table of the Bread of the Presence"[91]), where he and the brethren partake of the elements as a pledge of brotherhood.[92]

Shortly thereafter the Thrice Puissant (or Venerable Master, representing King Solomon) states, "GRAND SACRED WORD: . . . *YHVH*.[93] The true pronunciation of which word I give you in a whisper, in which way only I can communicate it to you, or you to any other person [#&%&]."[94] This is decoded to spell "IHUH."[95] This may simply be seen as another way to transliterate the tetragrammaton, *YHVH*, as Pike shows in *Morals and Dogma*.[96] Consequently the *Liturgy* reports that in the East of the Lodge Room appear two interlaced triangles "with the Phoenician letters IHU,[97] at the points, and those of Sanscrit in the center."[98]

What is the purpose of all this? Simply that, in the true pronunciation and symbolism of the ineffable name of Deity lies a correct though finite understanding of the nature of God and His attributes. As seen earlier in the question-and-answer dialogue from *The Magnum Opus,* the reward of the Mason's labors is the knowledge of the true God and a faint but true appreciation of His nature and infinite attributes, etc. The *Liturgy* echoes this.

> His [a Grand, Elect, Perfect and Sublime Mason's] reward is the knowledge of the True God; a faint but true appreciation of his nature and infinite attributes; a confidence in his wisdom and justice; an implicit trust in his beneficence and love for his creatures, securing him against skepticism and despair . . . and he works by the Light of Truth, which emanates from him whose Holy Name glitters upon the triangular plate of gold, and lights the Lodge.[99]

This Masonic doctrine is strikingly similar to the Qabbalah. In Qabbalistic philosophy the *apprehension* and *comprehension* of the divine name are most cherished gifts: "Hence, whoever has a knowledge of them [the letters *YHV*] and is observant of them is beloved both on high and below . . . [and] happy is his portion in this world and in the world to come."[100]

We should not suppose that because the divine name used by Scottish Rite Freemasonry is taken from the Bible, it is therefore Christian. Though the divine name *YHVH* appears in the ritual, one must investigate the *content* that is being poured into the divine name. That is to say, is the *teaching* about the God of the divine name biblical? The Scottish Rite's fourteenth degree teaches a mixture of the following. (1) Even if one knows the true name and what it symbolizes, one's understanding of God is still finite and limited; though degrees 4–14 are styled the Lodge of Perfection, our conceptions of Deity are still confined to the finite mind. (2) God is the Great Unknowable. (3) Man, in his different cultures, has different conceptions of the Deity. (4) Yet there were some from all ancient cultures who knew the true God to the best of their finite faith and reason; no matter what the name or designation may have been, they saw behind the veil and caught a glimpse of the true God. (5) The Mason can be in the line of these ancient sages if he understands the meaning of the lesson of the fourteenth degree. These points are now illustrated in the following excerpt from the *Liturgy:*

> We are all of us, though not all equally, mistaken. The cherished dogmas of each of us are not, as we fondly suppose, the pure truth of

God; but simply our own special form of error, our guesses at truth, the refracted and fragmentary rays of light that have fallen upon our own minds. Our little systems have their day, and cease to be; they are but broken lights of God; and he is more than they. Perfect truth is not attainable anywhere. We style this degree that of Perfection; and yet what it teaches is imperfect and defective. Yet we are not to relax in the pursuit of truth . . . and thus Masonry is a continual struggle toward the light. . . .

That which is most injurious is to entertain unworthy conceptions of the nature and attributes of God; and it is this that Masonry symbolizes by ignorance of the True Word. The true word of a Mason is, not the entire, perfect, absolute truth in regard to God; but the highest and noblest conception of him that our minds are capable of forming; and this *word* is ineffable, because one man cannot communicate to another his own conception of Deity; since every man's conception of God must be proportioned to his mental cultivation, and intellectual powers, and moral excellence. God is, as man conceives him, the reflected image of the man himself.[101]

Masonry, around whose altars the Christian, the Hebrew, the Moslem, the Brahmin, the followers of Confucius and Zoroaster can assemble as brethren and unite to the one God who is above *all* the Baalim, must needs leave it to each of its initiates to look for the foundation of his faith and hope to the written scriptures of his own religion.[102]

This seems like a strange, if not confusing, mixture. God is infinitely beyond our comprehension, and yet Masonry claims to provide the ultimate conception of Him. Men have different conceptions of the Deity, and yet Masonry provides the altar around which these all may unite as brethren of the one God. Men may look to their own sacred texts for the foundation of their faith, and yet Masonry harnesses all these texts into one mass. Finally, no one can communicate to another his own conception of the Deity, and yet the ineffable name and its true pronunciation have been given to Scottish Rite Masons who attain the fourteenth degree.

We must also remember that in the previous degree the *Liturgy* stated that

there was one faith and one idea of Deity for the enlightened, intelligent and educated, and another for the common people. . . . It is certain that *they* [the enlightened] possessed a knowledge of the true nature and attributes of God; as the same class of men did among the other nations—Zoroaster, Menu, Confucius, Socrates and Plato.[103]

What is implied here is that the Scottish Rite's *YHVH* was known by all the above-mentioned teachers and any other great teacher of religion, who in turn taught it to the select few who were worthy to receive it.

YHVH *a Canopy Designation*

In light of the following prayer it is reasonable to assume that the *YHVH* of the Scottish Rite subsumes all the differing individual conceptions of Deity that its initiates may have. He is reverenced, subsuming all these different ideas of Deity under Himself. Here men of differing faiths may be led in prayer to the one true God discovered in the thirteenth and fourteenth degrees. Notice that one God is petitioned on behalf of all Masons assembled, evidencing the belief that the brethren can "unite to the one God who is above all the Baalim" ("Baalim" meaning the many nations' *conceptions* of God).

> Direct us, O Supreme Ruler of the Universe! keep us from falling into the pits which our enemies dig for us! Animate us with thy divine spirit! . . . Strengthen us with thy holy power; and, that we may add to thy glory, help us to perform our Masonic duties, and to practice all Masonic virtues! Amen![104]

Biblical Response

The foundation of our biblical response is the person of Jesus Christ; specifically, the claims of Christ Himself and the claims made about Him.

In the fourth degree the candidate is restored to light and is told, "You have yet many steps to ascend before you can reach the heights on which Truth sits enthroned." The meaning of this statement must be obtained in the context of the thirteenth and fourteenth degrees. "Light" then means the first rays of understanding of the nature of God and His attributes. When the Mason begins to comprehend this, he is on his way toward the enlightenment and reward so cherished in Qabbalistic philosophy.[105] This we take to mean "the *heights* on which Truth sits enthroned."

Both the Christian Mason and the Mason wanting to provide an apologetic for the Craft must recognize the problems that arise when the words "light" and "truth" are used in a context devoid of the biblical Christ. Christ must be the material of worship, truth, and light. Moreover, no one can obtain truth and light apart from Him. Yet, the Scottish Rite teaches that one may indeed do so apart from Christ. Though it does not exclude Christ *per se,* it states to non-Christians that they can find truth and light without turning to Christ.

In a true theological framework, Christ not only points to the light; He is the light (John 8:12; 9:5). Christ not only points to the truth; He is the truth (John 14:6). When one has faith (trust) in Christ, one does not have many steps to ascend before "Truth" is attained; through Christ, who is the truth, one knows the truth, and the truth sets one free (John 8:32). Moreover, salvation (from the just penalty of hell by faith in the atonement of Christ—see Acts 4:12; Eph. 2:8–9; Gal. 3:13–14; Col. 1:19–20) does *not* await those who emulate the virtues[106] and follow the example of Hiram Abif.

The Mason who claims Christ as Savior and Lord must come to grips with the contradiction between ritual and Christian theology concerning his being told that he is "restored to light" (meaning that he was not in the light before the degree) and with the statement that he has yet many steps to ascend before he can reach the heights on which truth sits enthroned (meaning that he does not yet know the truth). And the Masonic apologist must respond to this dilemma, not by skirting the issue, but by directly dealing with the biblical passages offered above.

Another issue is the problem of religious syncretism. Religious syncretism is the attempt to bring irreconcilable or opposing religious beliefs about God, faith, salvation, and humanity into a unified whole characterized by worship and ritual. Freemasonry is clearly syncretistic. Is the meshing of Christianity with different religions and religious philosophies biblical? We have seen how Freemasonry combines the divine name *YHVH*[107] with the philosophies of the Qabbalah and other non-Christian religions, the mention of King Solomon's Temple and Moses, and the quotation from the *Liturgy* in the fourteenth degree ("Masonry, around whose altars the Christian, the Hebrew, the Moslem . . ."). Even Masonic Scholar Henry Wilson Coil admits that Scottish Rite ritual is syncretistic (see chap. 5).

Masonic apologist Christopher Haffner, in his book *Workman Unashamed: The Testimony of a Christian Freemason,* devotes a whole chapter to syncretism in the effort to defend the Lodge's use of it.[108] Haffner calls the Old Testament's condemnation of syncretism "almost neurotic,"[109] citing examples from Ezra 9–10; Ezekiel 47; Exodus 25–27, 31; and 2 Chronicles 28. He observes that in Ezra 9 the repentant people of Israel dismiss the foreign women taken as wives, for it has led them to practice the abominable ways of the Canaanites, the Hittites, and the Amorites. Yet in Ezekiel 47:22

allotment is made for "aliens [foreigners] who stay in your midst." Haffner sees this as almost neurotic, concluding that, "far from there being a continual and absolute demand for purity, syncretism—symbolized by marriage—was always present in Israel as a tension."[110]

There are problems with Haffner's apologetic. First, he does not define *syncretism.* The term itself can be ambiguous. Second, the weight of Haffner's argument rests upon a survey of the supposed contradiction between the Ezra and Ezekiel passages regarding residing with foreigners. In the Ezra passage the foreign women are banished (10:1–3). In the Ezekiel passage foreigners are not banished but accepted (47:21–23). Are these passages truly contradictory?

Haffner confuses the two contexts of Ezra and Ezekiel. It is true that Yahweh commanded His covenant people not to intermarry (see Deut. 7:1–4), but this command was given to guard the Israelites from the trap of following foreign gods.[111] This command is quite typical in a theocracy. In the Ezra passage the condemnation was directed at the syncretism resulting from intermarriage (see 9:1–2)! In the Ezekiel passage the Israelites were fulfilling the Mosaic Law by loving the alien, allowing her or him to reside in their midst (cf. Lev. 19:34). Yet in Leviticus, the Israelites, *or any of the aliens residing with them,* who gave offerings to the god Molech were to be stoned to death (20:2; see also vv. 6, 23, 26–27). Here as well *syncretism* would be condemned. Haffner rightly notes how the Israelites banished the foreign wives, but then he quotes from the Ezekiel passage where foreigners were allowed to reside in the midst of the Israelites. This gives the impression that the two passages contradict each other when in reality they do not. Moreover, by focusing his argument on the supposed contradiction between Ezra and Ezekiel as regards banishing foreigners versus accepting them, Haffner takes his readers' attention away from the real focus—syncretism. Yahweh always condemned syncretism. In the Ezra passage it was an actual problem. In the Ezekiel passage it was a potential problem, but it would have been condemned had it occurred. *This* is the issue, though Haffner never addresses it head-on.

Haffner is simply wrong when he states that, "far from there being a continual and absolute demand for purity, syncretism—symbolized by marriage—was always present in Israel as a tension." But Yahweh *is* consistent in demanding from His covenant people absolute purity in their worship of Him. Haffner's reasoning is also flawed. He assumes that because there was a tension present among the Israelites, there was therefore no absolute demand for purity. There most certainly *was* an absolute demand for purity (no syncretism) on Yahweh's part, *and* a tension on Israel's part. The two did in fact coexist!

Haffner makes another argument that needs to be examined. From Exodus 25:10–27:21 and 31:1–11 he postulates that "practical examples of syncretism can be seen in the worship of the Jews, as expressed in its setting."[112] The key phrase here is "as expressed in its setting."

Haffner should realize, as any observer of Israelite worship would realize, that the *worship itself,* as regards the *object* of the Israelites' worship, is not syncretistic. Though Haffner is quite correct when he mentions examples of syncretism in the sense of the tabernacle's resembling the temple of the sun-god in Egypt (Ex. 25–27), his argument is both careless and simplistic. First, he fails to mention that the style of the tabernacle resembled that of the temple in Egypt because the tripartite structure of the Egyptian temple was a fairly standard design for temple architecture in the ancient Near East.[113] Second, similarity in design does not necessarily connote similarity in worship. Even if the *trappings* of worship—iconography, architecture, the concept of sacrifice, ritualistic procedure—were similar, it does not necessarily follow that the object of worship was the same.

Archaeology offers significant evidence regarding the uniqueness of Israel's object of worship. To date, all excavation shows no material evidence of a male icon in the religion of ancient Israel. Whereas the cultures of Mesopotamia, Egypt, Canaan, and Philistia abounded with statues, frescoes, seals, and engravings that portrayed multiple male deities, in Israel there is a complete lack of such evidence. Thus, Haffner's argument seems to offer a Masonic apologetic, but it crumbles under close scrutiny.[114]

The Scottish Rite attempt to make *YHVH* the one true God known by the many names of Egyptian, Assyrian, Phoenician, and Indian deities (see the section under the thirteenth degree) simply does not square with the biblical record. First, the law laid down by Yahweh through Moses clearly stipulated that Israel was not to worship the gods of the surrounding nations. They were to have nothing to do with them (Ex. 20:3–5; 23:13, 24, 32–33; Num. 25:1–4; Deut. 5:7; 6:14; 7:16; 8:19; 13:1–5). Second, the prophets of the God of Israel, upon Israel's constant religious syncretism brought about by their whoring after other gods, continually warned the people of the judgment of Yahweh that would come upon them because of their religious syncretism (for example, see Josh. 23:6–7, 15–16; Jer. 1:13–16; 5:19; 7:1–15, 18; Masons should especially read Josh. 24:14–16, 23–24; Jer. 43:11–13; 44:8). Note the distinction between Yahweh and the gods of other nations—and this is a distinction *as regards both the identity and the object of worship.* From the biblical point of view, these gods are *not* Yahweh. Moreover, the gods of the surrounding nations do not point to *YHVH* in some veiled manner that can only be known by the "sages." The

Israelites were to worship Yahweh and Him alone, without yoking Him to other gods.

In the fourteenth degree we are told that the Christian, the Moslem, the Brahmin, the Hebrew, etc., can all assemble as brethren around the altar of Masonry and "unite to the one God who is above all the Baalim." From the biblical perspective the God of the Bible (the true and living God) will not be the God to whom they are uniting. Again, our reason is that Jesus is not the ground of this claim made by ritual. Simply put, how can this Masonic claim be true when Jesus said, "I am the way, the truth, and the life; no one can come to the Father except through me" (John 14:6)? Is the Moslem, the Jew, the Brahmin, or the follower of Confucius or Zoroaster putting his trust and faith in Jesus Christ? No. How, then, can he unite with the Christian under the one true God without Jesus as the material and ground of their "uniting"? To teach that this can occur apart from Christ flatly contradicts the biblical claim of the sole and exclusive mediatorship of Christ between humanity and the Father (1 Tim. 2:5). In light of this, the Masonic/Qabbalistic emphasis on the necessity of the true pronunciation of the sacred name of God in order to understand His nature and attributes is worthless, for it is in the face of Christ that one sees the glory of God (2 Cor. 4:6), and it is through faith in Christ that one knows and sees the Father (John 14:6, 7, 9, 21).

Conclusion

In my study of the ritual of the Lodge of Perfection, I am, as a Christian researcher, both fascinated and grieved: fascinated because of the elaborate meshing of different religions and their doctrines around a central nonhistorical legend; grieved because to believe such things places one outside Christ and His church. Perhaps you share my fascination and/or grief. If so, you should find the following chapters most interesting.

Notes

1. Hutchens mentions that "the biblical account of the story of Hiram is occasionally at variance with the legend as told in Masonic instruction" (Rex R. Hutchens, *A Bridge to Light* [Washington, D.C.: The Supreme Council, 33rd, Ancient and Accepted Scottish Rite of Freemasonry, Southern Jurisdiction, United States of America, 1988], 10).
2. Ibid., 9. Hutchens defines "ineffable" as "something which should not be spoken."
3. Ibid., 10–11.

4. For an account of the legend of Enoch, see Thomas Smith Webb, *The Freemason's Monitor* (Printed for Henry Cushing and Thomas Smith Webb, Providence, 1805), 275–76.
5. Pronounced as *Yodh Hey Vav* [or *Waw*] *Hey*. *YHVH* is pronounced "Yahweh" and is rendered by translators as "Lord" in modern Bibles.
6. The popular transliteration *Sepher Ha Zohar* means "The Book of Splendour."
7. See Harry Sperling and Maurice Simon, *The Zohar,* 5 vols., 2d ed. (London and New York: The Soncino Press, 1984), 2:111.
8. See *Liturgy,* pt. 2, p. 187.
9. Hutchens, *A Bridge to Light,* 12.
10. *Liturgy,* pt. 2, p. 11.
11. *The Magnum Opus,* iv…7. Cf. also *Liturgy,* pt. 2, p. 18.
12. Hutchens, *A Bridge to Light,* 15. This observation is based on ritual; cf. *Liturgy,* pt. 2, p. 16.
13. Ibid., 15.
14. Ibid.
15. See Albert Mackey, *Mackey's Revised Encyclopedia of Freemasonry,* 2 vols. (Richmond: Macoy Publishing and Masonic Supply Co., 1966), 2:1139.
16. Albert Pike, *The Book of the Words* (Kila, Mont.: Kessinger Publishing Co., reprint, n.d.), 92.
17. These and the following brackets are not mine.
18. *Liturgy,* pt. 2, p. 18; cf. *The Magnum Opus,* iv…7.
19. Pike's emphasis obviously refers to the first letter of the Hebrew tetragrammaton (meaning literally "four letters"), *YHVH,* which plays a most central part in Qabbalistic philosophy (see all through *The Zohar*).
20. *Liturgy,* pt. 2, p. 19; cf. *The Magnum Opus,* iv…7 . In *Morals and Dogma,* Pike meshes the Hebrew tetragrammaton, *YHWH,* into the Qabbalistic "Tree of Life" (p. 798; see also Hutchens, *A Bridge to Light,* 15). Also, what Pike states about the letter *yodh* has Qabbalistic overtones (see his observation concerning the Hebrew consonant *yodh* in this chapter under the eighth degree).
21. *The Magnum Opus,* iv…3.
22. Ibid., 5.
23. This is the Master representing King Solomon.
24. *The Magnum Opus,* iv…6.
25. Ibid.; cf. *Liturgy,* pt. 2, p. 16; and Hutchens, *A Bridge to Light,* 9.
26. *Liturgy,* pt. 2, p. 17. Qabbalistic lore as recorded in *The Zohar* implies that Enoch and other ancients (some patriarchs, such as Moses) possessed the true knowledge of the divine name. Masonic tradition, drawing from Qabbalism, states the same (see Webb, *The Freemason's Monitor,* 275ff.). In addition, *The Zohar,* 2:112, (and thus Masonic tradition) teaches that Solomon's Temple was to be the place where the divine presence could be called down. The Bible teaches none of this.
27. Ibid.; cf. *The Magnum Opus,* iv…6.

28. Hutchens, *A Bridge to Light,* 17–18.
29. See Robin Lane Fox, *Pagans and Christians* (San Francisco: Harper & Row, 1986), 171, 186.
30. Pike, *The Magnum Opus,* iv…7.
31. Hutchens, *A Bridge to Light,* 18.
32. *Liturgy,* pt. 2, pp. 47–48.
33. These could represent the first and last consonants as well, but see *The Magnum Opus,* vi…6.
34. See ibid.
35. This is one of the alternate ways in which Pike refers to Hiram. The alliance mentioned is that between King Solomon and Hiram *king of Tyre* (see 2 Chron. 2), who is different from Hiram Abif.
36. *Liturgy,* pt. 2, pp. 47–48. See also *The Magnum Opus,* vi…6, for essentially the same wording.
37. *The Book of the Words,* 93. This represents the Hebrew consonants *yodh* and *waw*.
38. See *The Magnum Opus,* 9.
39. *The Book of the Words,* 93. See also *The Zohar,* 1:10–13.
40. The Hebrew Pike uses is *alep̄, bet, resh* (pronounced *aleph, bait, raysh*), his transliteration being slightly different than that used today.
41. *The Book of the Words,* 96.
42. In the introduction to this book, *Intendent* rather than *Intendant* is used. That is because of the different sources cited, which use different spellings.
43. That is, history according to Masonic tradition. It should not be confused with actual history. Hutchens admits this and makes the differentiation between actual historical fact and "Masonic Tradition" (*A Bridge to Light,* 10).
44. *The Magnum Opus,* viii…6.
45. *Liturgy,* pt. 2, pp. 72–73. See Hutchens, *A Bridge to Light,* 48. I maintain that the majority of Masons are not *true* Masons, but are Masons in title alone. They simply do not understand the esotericism of this system, which, according to many Masonic scholars, is what makes a Mason in the true sense of the word. The *Legenda* states, "In our time, moreover, a great number of men who believe themselves Free Masons, are ignorant of the meaning of their Rites, and have lost the keys of their Mysteries. They do not even any longer comprehend their symbolic pictures, and as little understand the hieroglyphical signs with which the hangings of their Lodges are decorated. . . . They can be read by the aid of the Kabalistic clues" (4–14, p. 15).
46. Pike provides a chart at the end of *The Book of the Words* to show this correspondence.
47. *The Book of the Words,* 100. See also p. 99.
48. Transliterated by occultists in various ways: *Aur ha Ensoph, Ain Soph Aur,* etc.
49. *Plērōma* is the Greek word meaning "fullness" and is the Gnostic designation for the Deity. The Gnostic idea of the creation of the material realm given here

is a general view. There are, of course, different nuances represented by different ancient Gnostic schools of thought. For an in-depth discussion, consult Kurt Rudolph, *Gnosis: The Nature and History of Gnosticism* (San Francisco: Harper & Row, 1987).

50. *Liturgy,* pt. 2, p. 67; *The Magnum Opus,* viii...1.
51. Pythagoras was a sixth-century B.C. Greek philosopher. Central to his philosophical system was a view of God and the relationship of man to the universe. The Pythagoreans worshiped the god Apollo, and believed that Pythagoras was an incarnation of Apollo (see Paul Edwards, ed., *The Encyclopedia of Philosophy,* 8 vols. [New York: Macmillan, 1967], 7:37–39).
52. Hutchens, *A Bridge to Light,* 49. Numbers played a large part in Pythagoreanism. See Edwards, *The Encyclopedia of Philosophy,* 7:38–39, for a discussion of numbers.
53. Alexander Roberts and James Donaldson, eds., *The Ante-Nicene Fathers,* 9 vols. (Grand Rapids: Eerdmans, 1977), 1:281.
54. Edwards, *The Encyclopedia of Philosophy,* 7:38.
55. *The Zohar,* 2:110–11.
56. See also A. E. Waite, *The Holy Kabbalah* (Secaucus, N.J.: Citadel Press, n.d.), 207: "On the YOD are all things based." Also, *The Zohar,* 1:68–69.
57. See the symbolism of the nine-pointed star, already discussed.
58. *Liturgy,* pt. 2, p. 73; cf. *The Magnum Opus,* viii...6; and *Morals and Dogma,* 136.
59. Hutchens, *A Bridge to Light,* 65. The replica of the Apron for the tenth degree appears in the *Liturgy,* pt. 2, p. 94, as well as in *A Bridge to Light,* 62.
60. Formerly titled *Knights of the Ninth Arch* and *Knights of the Royal Arch of Solomon.*
61. *Liturgy,* pt. 2, p. 149. This and much of the following from the *Liturgy* may also be found in *The Magnum Opus,* xiii...7ff., and in *Morals and Dogma,* 204–17.
62. Ibid.
63. Ibid.
64. *Liturgy,* pt. 2, p. 151.
65. Ibid., 153.
66. Ibid., 156.
67. Ibid.
68. This is the fourteenth degree and will be examined next.
69. *Liturgy,* pt. 2, 157.
70. One cannot read *The Zohar* without concluding that a central concern is the knowledge of the sacred name of Deity: "Whoever has a knowledge of them [the letters of the tetragrammaton] is beloved both on high and below" (2:111).
71. *Liturgy,* pt. 2, p. 160.
72. Ibid., 161.
73. Again, by "initiate" the *Liturgy* does not mean any man who flippantly receives the degrees, but the man who carefully and studiously examines the essential core of the degrees, and the wealth of hidden knowledge contained therein.

74. *Liturgy,* pt. 2, p. 162.
75. Ibid., 163.
76. Ibid., 163–64. *Al* is the Hebrew for "over," *Bala* the Sanskrit for "strength," *Melek* the Hebrew for "king."
77. The pronunciation is not given as yet. See n. 81.
78. *The Magnum Opus,* xiii…6.
79. Ibid.
80. *Liturgy,* pt. 2, p. 166.
81. The ritual contained in *The Magnum Opus* reads, "*Qu[estion]:* What saw you upon that plate [the triangular plate of gold]? *Ans[wer]:* The mysterious and Ineffable Name of the Gr[eat] Architect of the Universe. *Qu:* What is that Name? *Ans:* I know its letters. None but the Grand, Elect, Ancient, Perfect and Sublime Masons know its true pronunciation" (xiii…2–3).
82. Or *chokmah.*
83. Or *tifereth.*
84. *Morals and Dogm*a, 758. In this quotation *"Yod"* equals the first consonant (*Y*) in the tetragrammaton, *"He"* the second (*H*), and *"Vav"* the third (*W*). See also Hutchens, *A Bridge to Light,* 91.
85. *The Zohar,* 5:406.
86. *Liturgy,* pt. 2, p. 173.
87. Ibid., 174. In *The Magnum Opus,* Pike specifically states that these "are the nine names of Deity in different languages, as given in the Royal Arch degree" (xiv…1).
88. *The Magnum Opus,* xiv… 3–4.
89. *The Book of the Words,* 127. According to Pike there is a better interpretation of this password, though he is not sure what it may be. This Hebrew phrase, however, properly transliterated as *mearah maor abrek,* is correctly translated by Pike, as any standard Hebrew lexicon will show. In *The Book of the Words,* Pike refers to other rituals that have the translation as "God be praised. We have found it!" (p. 119). This is contained in a rare manuscript of the twenty-five degrees of the Scottish Rite of Stephen Morin titled *The Francken Manuscript, 1783* (Kila, Mont.: Kessinger Publishing Co., n.d.), 155.
90. *The Magnum Opus,* xiv…6.
91. *Liturgy,* pt. 2, p. 176. Hutchens states, "In an act reminiscent of the ancient Hebrew, Indian and Persian sacrifice of bread and wine, the brethren partake of the bread and wine from the Table of the Bread of the Presence. The Bread itself, according to Mackey, is a symbol of 'the eternal life by which we are brought into the presence of God and know Him' ([*Encyclopedia*] Vol. 2, p. 934); the wine represents 'the inward refreshment of a good conscience . . . [and] should remind us of the eternal refreshments which the good are to receive in the future life for the faithful performance of duty in the present' (Vol. 2, p. 1110). The ceremonial sharing of bread and wine are a symbol of the perfection of the candidate, of his bond with the Masonic fraternity and of the secrecy demanded from the Perfect Elu" (*A Bridge to Light,* 102).

92. *Liturgy,* pt. 2, p. 185; cf. *The Magnum Opus,* xiv…7.

93. Here the actual Hebrew consonants appear.

94. *The Magnum Opus,* xiv…10. The strange signs in brackets actually appear in the ritual, with the exception that I have substituted # and %, for lack of the signs used by Pike. The two occurrences of "&" are the same as used by Pike.

95. *The Magnum Opus,* 13.

96. See pp. 697–98.

97. The fourth consonant, a repeated *H*, does not have to be repeated if the point is to give the three consonants which make up the divine name.

98. *Liturgy,* pt. 2, pp. 173–74.

99. Ibid., 198. For further elaboration, see *Morals and Dogma,* 700.

100. *The Zohar,* 2:111.

101. Though true of some, this is not true of the Christian. Biblical revelation describes and defines God. Moreover, God made humanity in *His* image (Gen. 1:26–27).

102. *Liturgy,* pt. 2, pp. 201–2; cf. *Morals and Dogma,* 223, 226.

103. Ibid., 162–63.

104. *Liturgy,* pt. 2, p. 207.

105. "Hence, whoever has a knowledge of them [the Hebrew, *YHVH*] and is observant of them is beloved both on high and below" (*The Zohar,* 2:111).

106. "Virtues" most likely means the Four Cardinal Virtues (Temperance, Fortitude, Prudence, and Justice) mentioned in the Entered Apprentice degree.

107. By making the tetragrammaton a central focus of the Lodge of Perfection, the Scottish Rite enters into the arena of Christian theology.

108. Christopher Haffner, *Workman Unashamed: The Testimony of a Christian Freemason* (London: Lewis Masonic, 1989), 198–205.

109. Ibid., 199.

110. Ibid.

111. Apparently, however, intermarriage was permissible, since Moses married a Midianite and Boaz married Ruth the Moabite. In these two instances, however, the spouses of Moses and Boaz clearly followed Yahweh. (In Ruth's case, see Ruth 1:16–17, and bear in mind that the Moabite deity was Molech!)

112. Haffner, *Workman Unashamed,* 199.

113. See Amihai Mazar, *Archaeology of the Land of the Bible* (New York: Doubleday, 1990), 212.

114. Haffner argues that "syncretism in architecture and theology are different things, but is not the culture of any age a single whole?" This is too simplistic a question, suggesting that if the answer is yes, it then must mean that the theology of the culture of any age is therefore the same. And what does Haffner mean by "culture"? He is vague here. Does he mean to lump the Israelites, the Egyptians, and other surrounding nations into one culture? Or does he mean "the same basic geographical region"? Overall I find Haffner's arguments (here and in other places) naive and misleading. I welcome Mr. Haffner to debate my criticisms.

CHAPTER 7

THE CHAPTER OF ROSE CROIX: BLENDING CHRISTIANITY WITH OTHER RELIGIONS

"Whatever the truth of history, the contributions to the symbolism of Freemasonry by the religions, philosophies, mythologies and occult mysteries of the past lie upon its surface for all to see."
—*Rex R. Hutchens,* A Bridge to Light

It should now be evident that since the fourth degree we have been engaged in a story line. The "WORD," once engraved and preserved by Enoch, was found by Hiram, only to be lost at his death. King Solomon's workmen found it again and the king preserved it, but it was lost again when the Temple was destroyed. It was then that the Sacred Word became preserved through oral tradition. Our story line continues in the Scottish Rite's *Chapter of the Rose Croix.*

The chapter consists of four degrees. They are *Knight of the East* (fifteen), *Prince of Jerusalem* (sixteen), *Knight of the East and West* (seventeen), and *Knight Rose Croix* (eighteen). This degree system is a mixture of Pythagoreanism, Qabbalism, ancient Hebrew history, Christianity, and other religions of the world.[1] The time period is late sixth century B.C. to late first century A.D., "from the destruction of King Solomon's Temple in 588 B.C. through the

158

writing of the Book of Revelation[2] in approximately 100 A.D."[3] During this time Zerubbabel built the second Temple (535 B.C.), though another destruction occurred in 70 A.D. during the siege of Titus.[4] According to Hutchens,

> The 15th and 16th Degrees of the Chapter illustrate the renewal of virtue which brought the Hebrews back to Jerusalem to rebuild the city and House of the Lord. They anticipate the coming of the Messiah in the 17th degree which expounds the messianic doctrine of love. The importance of this doctrine is taught in the 18th degree.[5]

The Fifteenth Degree: Knight of the East

The fifteenth degree mixes biblical history (the Old Testament book of Ezra) with fiction and features Zerubbabel (played by the candidate)—a Perfect Elu or fourteenth-degree Mason and thus a possessor of the knowledge of the divine name of God[6]—approaching Cyrus, King of Persia, and asking him for permission to rebuild the Temple. Cyrus, an initiate in the mysteries of Mithra,[7] permits the rebuilding. Masonic tradition informs us that as the Hebrews slowly returned west to Jerusalem, a few initiates met in secret to practice the ceremonies of Masonry.[8]

> They explored the ruins [of the destroyed Temple of King Solomon[9]] until they discovered the entrance to the Secret Vault, entering which they reached the vault, and found the Cubical Stone, and the fragments of the plate, from which the Sacred Word had been erased. . . . Finding the plate broken up, and no trace of letters upon it, they melted it down, and broke to pieces the cubical stone and pedestal, whose fragments they buried deep in the earth, that no trace of their Mysteries might remain. Thenceforward the WORD was transmitted orally.[10]

This is how the Sacred Word is communicated today in Scottish Rite Freemasonry. The allegorical events depicted in this degree are what constitute the goal of Freemasonry, which is to spiritually erect the Temple today in the hearts of Freemasons.[11]

The Sixteenth Degree: Prince of Jerusalem

The legend and history continue in the sixteenth degree. Efforts to rebuild the Temple were thwarted by the Samaritans and other adversaries, as well as by the lack of support from Cyrus because of his preoccupation with wars.[12] During the reign of Cyrus's successor, Darius, the Temple was finished and dedicated in 516 B.C.[13]

This degree covers a wide span of time. It relates that (1) the holy city Jerusalem was overtaken by Ptolemy Soter (320 B.C.) and Antiochus (170 B.C.); (2) the Maccabean government began (166 B.C.); (3) Judas Hyrcanus claimed the title of King of the Jews (107 B.C.); (4) the city was laid under siege again, this time by Roman legions commanded by Pompeius (63 B.C.); (5) King Herod then rebuilt the Temple in 18 B.C.; (6) Titus burned the Temple (A.D. 70); (7) after this a mass dispersion of Jews took place (early first century A.D.). At this point Masonic tradition (or legend) comes into play, as we are told that a few initiates remained to preserve the secrets of the ancient mysteries regarding the Craft.[14] Dates are also given for similar losses of the Phoenicians. They, being dispersed to different countries such as Ireland and several nations of Europe, practiced the same mysteries as did these Hebrew initiates.[15]

Masonic legend then continues concerning the spread of the order during the Middle Ages.[16]

> We no longer expect to rebuild the Temple at Jerusalem. The Holy House of the Temple is to us only a symbol. To us, the whole universe is God's Temple, and so is every upright heart. To establish all over the world the reign of Peace, Loving-kindness, and Toleration, is to build that Temple, most acceptable to God, in which Masonry is now engaged.[17]

This theology is reflected in the following prayer to God:

> We thank Thee, we praise Thee, we magnify Thee, for Thy great gift of Light, the Life of all the Universe; and we pray Thee to let also the Dawn of Masonry, the True Light, coeval with the world, shine again in the souls of men, teaching Love and Truth, Peace and Toleration! Put Thy Law in our consciences, and write it in our hearts; and be Thou our God, and let us be Thy People.[18]

Our saga continues with the seventeenth degree.

The Seventeenth Degree: Knight of the East and West

It would seem from Masonic ritual that the Mason reaches the summit when he learns the true pronunciation and understanding of the ineffable name of

Deity. In the seventeenth degree we find that this is not the case. The candidate is told,

> This [the seventeenth degree] is the first of the Philosophical degrees of the Ancient and Accepted Scottish Rite; and the beginning of a course of instruction which will fully unveil the heart and inner mysteries of Masonry. Do not despair because you have often seemed on the point of attaining the inmost light, and have as often been disappointed. In all time Truth has been hidden under symbols, and often under a succession of allegories; where veil after veil had to be penetrated, before the true Light was reached, and the essential Truth stood revealed.[19]

According to the *Liturgy*, "Bodies of this Degree are styled PRECEPTORIES; and each regularly consists of twenty-four members only,"[20] alluding to the twenty-four elders of Revelation 4:4.[21]

The Scene

The Lodge Room is adorned with eight columns, on which can be found seven Samaritan letters representing the initials of the last seven Sephiroth of the Qabbalistic Tree of Life.[22] These are named *Hesed* (mercy), *Geburah* (force or severity), *Tifereth* (beauty), *Nezah* (victory), *Hod* (glory), *Yesod* (foundation), and *Malkuth* (kingdom).[23] The Sephiroth, of which there are ten and which are all represented in this degree, are divine emanations from the Deity (the *En Sof*, the Limitless One) and the way by which the *En Sof* manifests Itself.[24] Creation as well is said to have come into being through emanations of the Deity.[25] The ten Sephiroth of the Qabbalistic Tree of Life are symbolized by the triangular Apron. Hutchens explains, "Its triangular shape is symbolic of the Deity in His first three emanations. In the center is a gold Tetractys[26] formed of ten Hebrew *yods*.[27] [See below.] They represent the ten Sephiroth (or manifestations of Deity) on the Tree of Life in the Kabalah."[28]

$$Y$$
$$Y \quad Y$$
$$Y \quad Y \quad Y$$
$$Y \quad Y \quad Y \quad Y$$

So it is in the *Liturgy* as well.[29]

Which Jesus?

Unlike the preceding degrees, the seventeenth degree of the Scottish Rite occupies much of its time with the book of Revelation and Jesus Christ. It therefore warrants our examination.

The seventeenth degree is called the Knight of the East and West because it draws from many religions from the East and West. It is in the Jewel of the degree that we encounter the syncretism of the Qabbalah and other religions with Christianity. The Jewel is a heptagonal medal with the engraved initials of the last seven Sephiroth on the outer edge of each side. In the center is a lamb lying on a book with seven seals, on which are engraved the same letters.[30] The Jewel is attached to two interlaced Cordons (decorated sashes), which are white and black and enclose the Hebrew letters *Y* and *H*.[31] These two colors symbolize "the dualism of Zoroaster and Manes, of the two Principles of good and evil."[32] The Jewel itself is half gold and half silver to represent "the sun and moon, themselves symbols to the ancients of Osiris and Isis, since gold is the metal which they appropriated to the sun, representative of the male or generative power, and silver was by them appropriated to the moon, representative of the female or productive power."[33]

"The tracing-board [a board or canvas upon which the emblems of the degree appear] of the degree is a heptagon," relates the *Liturgy,* and "in the center of the heptagon is the figure of a man in a long white robe, with a golden girdle around his waist, and long snow-white hair and beard; his right hand stretched out, and holding seven stars; his head encircled by an aureole, his eyes raying light, and in his mouth a two-edged sword."[34] This reference to Revelation 1:13–20 closes with the statement that around the "man"[35] stand seven golden candlesticks, representing the seven churches of Revelation 2 and 3.[36]

For the ritual ceremony the book with seven seals and a silver basin are placed upon the Masonic altar.[37] The Master of the Lodge represents John the Baptist, an Essene. The Essenes were a first-century (and onward) communal group of Jews who lived in Palestine near the Dead Sea during the ministry of Jesus. They lived in expectation of the coming rule of God characterized by the coming of the Messiah. They believed in the immortality of souls, ceremonies of purification, and members being bound by oaths.[38] Given these similar beliefs, some Masonic ritualists and scholars trace the beginnings of Freemasonry back to this communal group.[39]

In the seventeenth degree the candidate symbolically becomes an Essene.[40] The fabricated Masonic "tradition" of sects of initiates who survived the dispersion of the Jews and preserved through oral tradition the mysteries surrounding the tetragrammaton is the drama of this degree. The candidate is portrayed thus:

> A weary traveler, after crossing the desert, wanders on the shore of the Dead Sea in darkness, seeking for Light, desiring to know the Mysteries. He comes from the schools of philosophy and at the feet of the Pharisees and Kabalists, and is vouched for as a Prince of Jerusalem [sixteenth degree] and a patient and humble searcher after Truth.[41]

After a series of questions regarding the candidate's duties as a Mason, several verses from the book of Revelation are read (2:7, 11, 17, 26–28; 3:5, 12, 21, 19).[42] From these verses the Mason is taught that eternal life comes "to the one who overcomes." He then declares that he is in search of the "Light," but has not yet found it. He is told that "light comes from God" and that "we should implore His aid,"[43] and a prayer is offered.[44]

The Master (who plays John the Baptist) states,

> My Brother, the innocent and pure of heart alone can be admitted to our mysteries. (A brother brings a basin of pure water and a white towel, and places them on the table). In token of that innocence and purity, and as a pledge to us that your hands shall henceforward never be defiled by covetousness, unjust gain, tyranny, oppression, injustice, baseness or fraud, you will wash them in the pure water before you.[45]

After reading Ecclesiastes 9:5–6 and 12:1–2 and 6–7, the candidate professes faith in one God and in the immortality of the soul. He is then baptized with water poured over his head, symbolizing a consecration to the service of Truth.[46] The Master says,

> In imitation of our Ancient Masters, the Egyptians, and as a token and solemn pledge that you here, henceforth and forever, renounce all that is vicious, sordid and base, I pour upon thy head this pure water; and I devote and consecrate thee to the service of Truth, Justice, Virtue and Benevolence.[47]

The *Liturgy* begins with the following, most of which is also found in *The Magnum Opus* directly after the above:

> John the Baptist said to those whom he baptized: "One cometh hereafter who shall baptize you with the Holy Spirit and with fire. His fan

will be in his hand, and he will thoroughly sweep his threshing floor, and gather his wheat into his granary, and burn up the chaff with a devouring fire. His axe is prepared for the trees; and every tree that beareth not good fruit will be cut down and cast into the fire. . . . A symbol of that baptism, with the Spirit and with fire; purified by which, man becomes God's soldier to war against Fanaticism, Intolerance, Bigotry, Falsehood . . ."[48]

The Master then asks, "My Brethren, who among you is worthy to open the Book with the Seven Seals?"[49] When there is no reply, the Master turns to the candidate and asks if he is prepared to shed his blood in proof of his fidelity and courage.[50] The candidate answers in the affirmative. The bandage is removed from his eyes (symbolizing coming into the light), and he is led to the altar, where he is made to kneel, place his hands on the book with seven seals, and swear an obligation.[51] The Master anoints him with oil and says, "You are worthy to open the Book with seven seals."[52] The candidate then proceeds to open the Seven Seals while the corresponding catastrophic phenomena of Revelation are mentioned, with certain additions.[53] During this portion of the ritual, there is mention of those being saved by the blood of the Lamb, and that the kingdoms of this world will become kingdoms of God and His anointed and that He shall reign forever and ever.[54]

We should not interpret this last point in the biblical sense. Interestingly, in order to alleviate possible "misunderstanding" and "confusion" on the part of Christian Masons when they read that the candidate is worthy to open the Seven Seals (which is blasphemy, since only Christ is worthy of such a task), Hutchens states that "Pike relied on the teachings of many faiths in his reworking[55] of the Scottish Rite degrees and in this respect Christianity was not slighted."[56] Hutchens *implies* that the ritualistic system of the Scottish Rite is a homogenization of different religions.[57] But what we must understand is that all through the Old and New Testaments, God's covenant people were commanded not to mix their beliefs with other belief systems (Deut. 13:1–11, 13; Isa. 8:20; 2 Peter 2:1; 2 John 7–10).

This eclectic atmosphere exists both in the whole of the Scottish Rite degree system and in the seventeenth degree. Pike did not choose the Apocalypse, in his reworking of the degrees, because of a conviction that the Bible was God's only revelation to humanity. He included much of the world's religions and their holy books in the formation of ritual. In his monumental work *Morals and Dogma* Pike does not write about Jesus as being the unique[58] Son of God, or of His being the only way for humanity to be saved from the pains of hell. If he does so, it is primarily to *represent* what Christians have affirmed throughout the ages,[59] or to glean from the Bible the "similarities" he sees in other religions. Pike does this by redefining biblical terms to suit his own worldview. For example, he expends much energy relating to his readers the Gnostic/Qabbalistic theories of a heavenly emanation known as the Christ, Christos, Word, Thought, or Reason coming from the Unknowable.[60]

Pike concludes,

> This is the *real* idea of the Ancient Nations: GOD, the Almighty Father, and Source of All; His THOUGHT, *conceiving* the whole Universe, and *willing* its creation: His WORD, *uttering* that THOUGHT, and thus becoming the Creator or Demiourgos, in whom was Life and Light, and that Light the Life of the Universe. . . . Behold THE TRUE MASONIC TRINITY; the UNIVERSAL SOUL, the THOUGHT *in* the Soul, the WORD, or Thought expressed; the THREE IN ONE, of Trinitarian Ecossias [i.e., Scottish Trinitarian; see the twenty-sixth degree].[61]

Though Pike qualifies his conclusion by saying, "Here Masonry pauses, and leaves its Initiates to carry out and develop these great Truths in such manner as to each may seem most accordant with reason, philosophy, truth, and his religious faith,"[62] he nonetheless calls his own statements "great Truths." He then capsulizes the Christian doctrine of the Trinity and the "trinities" of other nations, "While all these faiths assert their claims to the exclusive possession of the Truth, Masonry inculcates its old doctrine, and no more: . . . That God is ONE; that HIS THOUGHT uttered in His WORD, created the Universe . . . ."[63] As I will show in the "Biblical Response" section, this is not the God of the Bible.

The Eighteenth Degree: Knight of the Rose Croix

In addition, Pike's view of Jesus is different from the biblical Jesus.[64] In *The Magnum Opus,* eighteenth degree, he accurately quotes John 1:1, which reads, "In the beginning was the Word, and the Word was with God, and the Word was God." He proceeds, however, to interpret the verse through his Qabbalistic/Gnostic grid.

> The first sentence [John 1:1], fully rendered into our language, would read thus: When the process of emanation, of creation or evolution

of existences inferior to the Supreme God began, the Word came into existence and was: and this Word was [*pros ton Theon*][65] *near to God*; i.e. the immediate or first emanation from God: and it was God Himself, developed or manifested in that particular mode, and in action.[66]

There is a built-in tension to the Scottish Rite's view of Jesus Christ.[67] On the one hand, the Rite is careful to state that it offers initiates no dogmatic view of Jesus, no view that would tend to separate one brother from another. For example, the following series of questions is put to candidates for the eighteenth degree:[68]

1st. What is your religious belief?

2d. Do you respect the character of every Reformer that has in the different periods of the world's history appeared on earth to teach men virtue and morality?

3d. Do you regard with toleration the religious opinions of other men?

4th. Are you willing to meet in the Masonic Temple, and to recognize as Brothers, all good Masons who believe in one God and in the Immortality of the Soul, whether they have received that belief from the teachings of Moses, of Zoroaster, of Buddha, of Mahomet, or of the founder of the Christian religion?

5th. Do you recognize the fact that all the emblems, forms and ceremonies of Masonry are symbolical of certain great primitive truths, which each one is at liberty to interpret in accordance with his own faith?

6th. Are you willing to unite in ceremonies which those of another faith may regard as peculiarly applicable to the events recorded in their own sacred books, they leaving to you the perfect right to apply the same ceremonies to your own, or give them a more general or more narrow interpretation as you may choose?[69]

Your answers are such as sound reason and an enlightened intellect require, and such as befit one who desires to become a Knight of the Rose Croix. These being your views, you may, without offence to your conscience, unite with us in a Degree which the Christian Knight sees manifest allusions to a Divine Redeemer, the Son of Deity, or even the Deity incarnate, who died to atone for the sins of part or the whole of mankind; in which the follower of Moses may see represented the career of a Messiah yet to come; while others, of other creeds, see symbolized only the general belief, embodied in the creeds of all nations, in a Saviour of the World, in anticipation of whose supposed advent many nations have rejoiced, and for whom many still continue to look.[70]

On the other hand, Pike states in the ritual that the interpretation of John 1:1 is "rendered into *our* language." And, concerning Jesus' death on the cross, he says, "Once again the old tragedy was enacted, and another type of the Principle of Good was murdered by Ignorance and Brutality,"[71] and "Those whom God has sent to regenerate Humanity, men, blinded by ignorance[72] and misled by craft, have put to death."[73]

Scottish Rite Freemasonry, in the acting out of its decision to be all things to all men regarding its view of Jesus, actually ends up with its own view after all! Jesus is "another type of the Principle of Good," one of many "whom God has sent to regenerate humanity." The Bible, however, teaches that Jesus is the *unique* Son of God (John 1:14, 18) come to take away the sins of the world (John 1:29; 1 John 2:2).

Another Gospel

What does the Scottish Rite mean by its "Gospel of Love"(see n. 72)? Is the atonement seen as a *sacrifice* for sins that we have committed and that place us at enmity with God, or as an *example* of a great reformer laying down his life to free the oppressed from the tyranny of societal and spiritual ignorance? The following quotation from the *Liturgy* reveals the answer:

> The doctrine of him who lost his life for having proclaimed that all men, children of a common Father, were Brethren, shines upon us from the awful night of the Past. . . . The doctrine of him who suffered an ignominious death for endeavoring to substitute Truth for Error, and Love for Hatred and Persecution, has gone round the world, and prevails against Ignorance and Superstition. . . . The doctrine of him who gave up his life to insure forever the liberty of the oppressed, the rights of the weak, and the overthrow of tyranny over mind and body, has become the supreme law of regenerated humanity.[74]

Throughout the rituals of the Scottish Rite there is no mention of *all* humanity's need for Christ's atonement. Nor does it correctly define the gospel—which the apostle Paul says consists of Christ's dying for our sins and His being buried, being raised on the third day, and appearing after His resurrection to others (1 Cor. 15:1–4). Rather than reflecting what the Scriptures teach, the Rite says that the "Gospel" is "the New Law, the Law of Love, which, by whomsoever proclaimed, was first written upon the pages of the great Book of Nature . . . that Law, which is the same in every country, and consistent with every religion."[75] Jesus' laying down of His life was an example of a great reformer sacrificing Himself for oppressed humanity, for the cause of the Fatherhood of God and the Brotherhood of Man.

Logically, the Scottish Rite's claim that they are without the dogmas that have marred sectarian religion is self-defeating. "Upon the highways of dogmatism we will not travel," says the Rite, but this is itself a dogmatic statement!

Biblical Response

Earlier in this chapter we noted the ritual's claim that "every upright heart" is "God's Temple" and the prayer for God to "Put Thy Law in our consciences, and write it in our hearts; and be Thou our God, and let us be Thy People." Thus, the Rite implies that this "Law" refers to practicing and furthering "Love, Truth, Peace and Toleration." In addition, every upright heart characterized by this law is God's temple.[76]

The prayer was an allusion to Jeremiah 31:33: "But this shall be the covenant that I will make with the house of Israel; After those days, saith the LORD, I will put my law in their inward parts, and write it in their hearts; and will be their God, and they shall be my people" (KJV). The issues concerning us here are: (1) what is the law, (2) how does one reap the blessing of the law being put within, and (3) to whom must we look for this blessing?

According to Scripture, "law" refers to the various regulations that Yahweh gave to His covenant people "in the day [period of time] that I took them by the hand to bring them out of the land of Egypt" (Jer. 31:32, KJV). The Israelites broke this covenant (v. 32). But the day would come when Yahweh would make another covenant. Rather than being engraved on stone, this covenant would be engraved upon the human heart, a characteristic of Yahweh's new covenant.

How one reaps the blessing of the new covenant, and to whom one must look for this blessing, must be answered by the New Testament (or new covenant). First, we must understand that the Old Testament law was not inferior in any way; Paul called it perfect, holy, and just (Rom. 7:12). But what the law could not do because of sin, God did by sending His Son Jesus Christ as an offering for sin (Rom. 8:3). Thus are the requirements of the law fulfilled for those who walk according to the Holy Spirit (Rom. 8:4). Therefore, there is no condemnation for those who are in Christ (Rom. 8:1).

Herein lies the rub: only those who are "in Christ" are free from the requirements of the law. The book of Hebrews concerns itself with the supremacy of Christ and the all-sufficiency of His sacrifice on the cross. Chapter 10 teaches that the law, with its yearly sacrifices for sins, served as a reminder that the blood of bulls and goats could not take away sin (vv. 1–4). But Christ could, and did! Christ, by His one offering, has perfected forever those who are being sanctified (v. 14). Therefore, the fulfillment of Jeremiah 31:33 (quoted in Heb. 10:16–17) occurs only through the blood of Christ (vv. 19–20).

Here again Scottish Rite ritual takes a biblical passage out of context, this time by not teaching that Christ is the only fulfillment of the Jeremiah passage alluded to in their prayer. If Christ's sacrifice is the only answer to sin, any other view or attempt to procure this promise of God to oneself apart from the saving grace of Christ is blasphemous.

Is every upright heart God's Temple, as the Scottish Rite would have us believe? Certainly not if "upright" is defined apart from Christ. What makes a heart upright? We must find the answer to that question in Jesus Christ, not in ourselves, not by our good deeds, and not in any other so-called Deity. In short, any system (such as the Scottish Rite) claiming that every upright heart is God's Temple, while at the same time allowing for the numerous deities and spiritual paths of its initiates for its fulfillment, is making an antibiblical claim. The view of Christ as God and Savior, the view of Christ as the One who makes the fulfillment of Jeremiah 31:33 possible, must be exclusive, not inclusive, if we are to give proper glory to God.

Toleration?

The Rite claims that religious toleration is a virtue. They cite examples of cruel religious *in*tolerance on the part of those claiming to be Christian. Who can approve of the Roman Catholic Church's torture by the men of the crusading order of Knights Templars in the fourteenth century? Human history abounds with such cruelties done in the name of God and religion. And Christendom is not the only religion guilty of such atrocities.

There is, however, another type of intolerance that the Rite condemns. Exclusive claims to truth, along with using exclusive claims to show that

others are wrong, are scorned by Masons. One need only read the February
and May 1993 issues of *The Scottish Rite Journal* to verify this. These two
issues were devoted exclusively to debating the Southern Baptist Convention's examination of Freemasonry. Following are some statements from these
issues regarding toleration, or the lack thereof:

> Freemasonry leaves each person to embrace the creed of his choice
> and teaches toleration.[77]

> I invite all Masons of all Blue Lodges and of all Appendant Bodies
> to join the Scottish Rite, Southern and Northern Masonic Jurisdic-
> tions, in opposing the religious extremism which today threatens not
> only Freemasonry but the most fundamental of American principles,
> freedom of conscience.[78]

> Political, social, or religious dictatorships or hierarchial structures
> cannot, in fact do not dare, tolerate differences of opinion. They can-
> not afford any dissension or freedom of thought. Under rule, Free-
> masonry and all like groups must be attacked or destroyed. Such
> systems may claim to be open-minded, but they depend on their con-
> stituents or followers to have minds closed to all but their own par-
> ticular "way" or doctrine. Freemasonry promotes freedom of thought
> and discussion.[79]

This is only a sampling of the general mind-set of Masons concerning
Freemasonry and Christianity. Such statements as the above are self-defeating and contradict statements found in Scottish Rite ritual. First, it is self-
defeating to speak out against religious intolerance and yet assert that
"Freemasonry leaves each person to embrace the creed of his choice and
teaches toleration." The author of this statement is actually declaring that he
is intolerant of intolerance! Almost immediately after stating that "Freemasonry teaches toleration," he says, "Today, however, *divisive* sectarianism is
gaining strength."[80] The fact that two whole issues of the *Scottish Rite Journal* were dedicated to speaking out against the intolerance of other religious
groups shows that the Scottish Rite is itself intolerant! Masonic statements of
this sort abound.

What if a man's creed teaches that his way of believing is the only way?
Would the Lodge let such a man join its ranks? Would it tolerate a candidate
who answered "no" to questions three and four above, concerning toleration
of other religions and brotherhood with those of other faiths? What if he was
not willing to see those who believe in one God and the immortality of the

soul as brothers? *The Magnum Opus* answers, "If these questions are all answered in the affirmative, the M[aster] of ceremonies proceeds. If any one is answered in the negative, he informs the candidate that it is not possible for him to receive this degree, and permits him to retire."[81] In the eighteenth degree this prayer is given: "Impart unto us the power of persuasion, that our words, always kind and gentle, may convince *misled* men of the excellence of the Truth."[82] I challenge Scottish Rite Masons to answer two questions: Why are they misled? What is the Truth?

A Gnostic Jesus

In the Scottish Rite, Jesus is called a "Demiourgos" (or "Demiurge," a demigod, a deity of lesser nature), inferior to the "Supreme God." He is also portrayed as "another type of the principle of good."[83] These statements flatly contradict the Bible, which teaches that Jesus is the *unique* Son of God, the only one of His kind, fully human and fully divine (John 1:14, 18).[84] The two heretical views of Jesus in the Scottish Rite are not new. They reflect the ancient Gnostic doctrine of the vile and base creation[85] coming into existence via a cosmic tragedy of a falling out of inferior aeons, gods, or emanations (the "Christ") from the Supreme God, who was called the *plērōma* (Greek, "fullness").[86] Because of this cosmogony the Gnostics saw the creator of the world of matter as inferior, a demigod.[87] With this framework imposed upon the biblical text, the Scottish Rite makes Jesus a demigod of inferior quality.

There is, however, no biblical evidence that Jesus is inferior in nature to the Father. The contrary is the case. Both the accounts written about Him and those quoting Him set forth that He is the Son of God, which, understood in the milieu of His day, make Him equal[88] to God (John 5:18). John, who relates explicitly the deity of Jesus in his gospel, asserts at the beginning and the end of his gospel that Jesus is God the Son (John 1:1; 20:28). Other texts speak of Jesus as the Creator of heaven and earth (Col. 1:16), and, contrary to Gnosticism, "in Him all the fulness [*plērōma*] of the Deity resides in bodily form" (Col. 2:9). Moreover, God called His creation *good* (Gen. 1: 31), contrary to the Gnostic belief that it is defiled.

Conclusion

The Jesus of the Scottish Rite is not the Jesus of the New Testament. Theirs is a counterfeit Jesus (see 2 Cor. 11:3–4). If the Rite would show Jesus to be the unique Son of God, God the Son, the Creator of heaven and earth, the only way for humanity to be saved, the One whose shed blood can cleanse of all sin, the One who was intolerant of false prophets and is coming to judge the living and the dead, the One in whom it is necessary to believe if one is to escape the penalty of hell, and the One who will separate the sheep from the goats by saying to those who use His name falsely, "I never knew you: depart from me, ye that work iniquity " (Matt. 7:23, KJV)—*then* it would be teaching of the real Jesus.

Notes

1. Rex R. Hutchens, *A Bridge to Light* (Washington, D.C.: The Supreme Council, 33rd, Ancient and Accepted Scottish Rite of Freemasonry, Southern Jurisdiction, United States of America, 1988), 111.
2. Hutchens states that "besides the conventional Christian interpretations, Pike believed this Book was both a demonstration of Persian influences on Christianity and an example of the Kabbalistic teachings found in the New Testament" (*A Bridge to Light*, 114). This was the prevailing view in Pike's time; he was, no doubt, influenced by the History of Religions school. For an excellent and scholarly refutation of this opinion, see Edwin M. Yamauchi, *Persia and the Bible* (Grand Rapids: Baker, 1990).
3. Hutchens, *A Bridge to Light*, 111.
4. Ibid., 111–12.
5. Ibid., 114.
6. See *The Magnum Opus*, xv...4; *A Bridge to Light*, 120; *Liturgy*, pt. 3, p. 17.
7. Hutchens, *A Bridge to Light*, 120.
8. *Liturgy*, pt. 3, p. 36.
9. In the fourteenth degree we are told that King Solomon constructed a place near the entrance of the Temple for the cubical stone and the triangular plate of gold with the ineffable name of Deity. See *A Bridge to Light*, 98.
10. *Liturgy*, pt. 3, p. 36. See also *The Magnum Opus*, xv...13.
11. *Liturgy*, pt. 3, p. 38.
12. *A Bridge to Light*, 126.
13. Ibid., 127.
14. *Liturgy*, pt. 3, pp. 76–77. See also *The Magnum Opus*, xvi...10.
15. *Liturgy*, pt. 3, p. 77.
16. Ibid., 78–80.
17. Ibid., 81.
18. Ibid., 57.
19. Ibid., 116.
20. Ibid., 95.
21. *A Bridge to Light*, 135.
22. *Liturgy*, pt. 3, p. 96; *A Bridge to Light*, 135. The first three Sephiroth —*Kether* (the crown), *Chokmah* (wisdom), and *Binah* (understanding)—and their begin-

ning consonants also decorate the Lodge Room. See the *Liturgy*, pt. 3, p. 96. In this note the transliteration of the *Liturgy* was used.

23. *The Zohar*, 1:xvii. The transliteration of *The Zohar* was used without the diacritical marks.

24. Ibid., 1:xvi–xvii.

25. Ibid. Though the Qabbalah shares with ancient Gnosticism this divine flowing forth of the Deity, and thereby a coming into existence of the material universe, it does not downgrade the material world to the extreme that ancient Gnostic systems did.

26. The Tetractys comes from Pythagorean symbolism. It represented the sacred number in which all numbers were contained (see Pike, *Morals and Dogma*, 88). Pike states that in the thirty-first degree the Tetractys represents the Deity (p. 826).

27. *Yod* is the first consonant of the divine name (the tetragrammaton).

28. *A Bridge to Light*, 133. This diagram, transliterated for the reader, appears on p. 132 of Hutchens's book, drawn on the Apron for the degree.

29. *Liturgy*, pt. 3, p. 115.

30. Ibid., 98; *A Bridge to Light*, 133.

31. *Liturgy*, pt. 3, p. 115; *A Bridge to Light*, 132.

32. *Liturgy*, pt. 3, p. 115; *A Bridge to Light*, 133. Zoroaster founded the religion known as Zoroastrianism; Manes founded Manicheanism.

33. *Liturgy*, pt. 3, p. 115; *A Bridge to Light*, 133.

34. *Liturgy*, pt. 3, p. 97. See also *The Magnum Opus*, xvii…1.

35. The biblical account in Rev. 1:13 speaks of "one like unto the Son of man" (KJV).

36. *Liturgy*, pt. 3, p. 97.

37. Ibid.; *The Magnum Opus*, xvii…4.

38. For an excellent summary of this community, see G. W. Buchanan, "Essenes," in *The International Standard Bible Encyclopedia*, ed. Geoffrey W. Bromiley, 4 vols. (Grand Rapids: Eerdmans, 1982), 2:147–55. It cannot be stated for certain that John was an Essene (2:1108ff.).

39. See *A Bridge to Light*, 135–36.

40. *A Bridge to Light*, 136.

41. *Liturgy*, pt. 3, p. 104; *The Magnum Opus*, xvii…5.

42. *Liturgy*, pt. 3, p. 105; *The Magnum Opus*, xvii…6.

43. *The Magnum Opus*, xvii…6.

44. *The Magnum Opus*, xvii…6; *Liturgy*, pt. 3, p. 106.

45. *The Magnum Opus*, xvii…7.

46. Ibid.

47. Ibid.

48. *Liturgy*, pt. 3, pp. 107–8; *The Magnum Opus*, xvii…7. Both works omit from the quote Jesus' immediate entrance (see Matt. 3:13–17).

49. *The Magnum Opus*, xvii…7.

50. Ibid., xvii…8; *Liturgy,* pt. 3, p. 108.
51. *The Magnum Opus,* xvii…8.
52. Ibid., xvii…9.
53. Ibid. See the *Liturgy,* pt. 3, pp. 109–15.
54. *The Magnum Opus,* xvii…10; *Liturgy,* pt. 3, p. 114.
55. Pike's "reworking" is *The Magnum Opus.*
56. *A Bridge to Light,* 136–37.
57. Hutchens explicitly says that "the symbolism is borrowed to teach different lessons from those taught in the book of Revelation. These lessons are not intended to replace those of any faith but are rather simple opportunities for further instruction on the importance of moral rectitude. For example, the book of seven seals used in the ceremony of the degree of Knight of the East and West is not intended to represent the Book of Seven Seals in the Apocalypse. Christ alone is worthy to open that Book but the book in the ceremony is opened by one of the candidates, who, with others is symbolically sent forth to war against evil" (p. 137).

    I am not convinced by Hutchens's argument. Why does he state that "here [in the seventeenth degree] the events in the drama and many of the words in the ritual are directly taken from the Revelation of God through Jesus Christ to St. John the Evangelist"? Why does he mention earlier that "on the altar is a book sealed with seven seals (Revelation 5:1)" (p. 135)? If the *book of seven seals* (Hutchens's use of upper- and lowercase letters is interesting. Pike uses uppercase letters to refer to the seals that the candidate opens [*The Magnum Opus,* xvii…9]) "is not intended to represent the Book of Seven Seals in the Apocalypse," why, then, does he cite Rev. 5:1? And why does he immediately follow with, "As the candidate opens the seven seals from the book one by one, the vivid imagery from the Book of Revelation is again included in the ritual in an abbreviated form. The opening of the seals ushers in the most dreadful disasters: four horsemen set off . . . the souls of the dead martyrs crying out for vengeance . . . a great earthquake. . . . The world is ravaged by hail and fire" (p. 137)? Moreover, even if one chooses to assume that Hutchens's argument is valid, Christians may rightly raise objection to someone's taking Scripture and using it in the way the Scottish Rite does, in a way that was not intended by the original author.
58. In John 1:14, 18 the Greek word *monogenēs* implies uniqueness. Thus Jesus is the unique Son of God. See Gerhard Kittel, ed., *Theological Dictionary of the New Testament,* 10 vols. (Grand Rapids: Eerdmans, 1967), 4:739–41. Several exegetes hold the same view. See, for example, Leon Morris, *The Gospel According to John,* The New International Commentary on the New Testament (Grand Rapids: Eerdmans, 1971), 105.
59. *Morals and Dogma,* 559. Some cite Pike's frequent allusions to Jesus in order to refute statements like mine. Quotations from *Morals and Dogma* such as "The agonies of the garden of Gethsemane and those of the Cross on Calvary

preceded the Resurrection and were the means of Redemption" (p. 307) are, however, interpreted in too simplistic a way by Masonic apologists. After all, the same can be said of Krishna (pp. 277, 603) and Hiram (p. 79; there spelled "Khurum").

60. Ibid., 559–68.
61. Ibid., 575. Hutchens conspicuously writes, "His WORD, uttering that THOUGHT, and thus becoming the Creator . . . in whom was Life and Light" (*A Bridge to Light,* 237). Notice the ellipsis (. . .). Could Hutchens have left out "or Demiourgos," which means "an inferior deity"? This certainly would have blasphemously referred to Jesus Christ. Theologically, even if it is left out, there is still a problem, for Jesus never "became" the Creator.
62. Ibid., 575–76.
63. Ibid., 576–77; *A Bridge to Light,* 237.
64. In 2 Cor. 11:4 the apostle Paul warns the church of someone coming and preaching a Jesus other than the Jesus he preached. In Paul's day, as well as in ours, the existence of counterfeit "Christs" threatened the unity and growth of the church.
65. Transliterated for the reader. Pike wrote this in Greek and the brackets are his.
66. *The Magnum opus,* xviii…15. See chap. 5, n. 11, for a brief summation of the Qabbalistic worldview.
67. *Christology* is the study of the person and work of Jesus Christ.
68. We cannot be entirely sure if these six questions exist in the current ritual, since they are from *The Magnum Opus.* Judging from the quotation from the *Liturgy* that follows these questions, either they are all in the current ritual or similar questions appear.
69. *The Magnum Opus,* xviii…5.
70. *Liturgy,* pt. 3, p. 157. See *The Magnum Opus,* xviii…5, which is essentially similar.
71. Ibid., 183. Here Jesus is seen as simply one of many exemplars of this "Principle of Good." See the quotation in chap. 8 from the source listed in n. 74.
72. In Scottish Rite philosophy this ignorance is symbolized by the loss of the True Word (or sacred name of God). The True Word represents a knowledge of the nature and attributes of God, one of these attributes being His love for all His creatures regardless of what religious persuasions they may represent. It is interesting that the eighteenth degree has as its story line the loss once again of the True Word, and spiritual intolerance resulting from that loss. Here Jesus comes as one of many other redeemers who brought the same message to humanity—the gospel of love.
73. *Liturgy,* pt. 3, p. 186.
74. Ibid., 189.
75. Ibid., 164.
76. See the quotations from notes 17 and 18.
77. Judge James B. Wilkinson, 33rd, "Extremism vs. Freedom: A Masonic Call to Action," *The Scottish Rite Journal* (February 1993): 9.

78. C. Fred Kleinknecht, 33rd, "Closing Ranks: The Buck Stops Here," *The Scottish Rite Journal* (May 1993): 4.

79. Forrest D. Haggard, 33rd, "Freemasonry and Religion Are Compatible," *The Scottish Rite Journal* (May 1993): 7–8.

80. Wilkinson, "Extremism vs. Freedom," 9, emphasis added.

81. *The Magnum Opus,* xviii...5.

82. *Liturgy,* pt. 3, p. 184, emphasis added.

83. See note 71. See also the quotation from the source in note 73.

84. See n. 58.

85. For example, "Just as all the useless afterbirth of one who bears a little child falls, likewise the matter which came into being from the shadow was cast aside" ("On the Origin of the World," in *The Nag Hammadi Library,* ed. James M. Robinson [San Francisco: Harper & Row, 1981], 163).

86. See Kurt Rudolph, *Gnosis: The Nature and History of Gnosticism* (San Francisco: Harper & Row, 1987), 53–94.

87. Ibid., 73.

88. In John 5:18 the word "equal" (Greek, *ison*) means equality in nature, rank, and authority. The context itself makes this clear: "He was calling God His own Father, making Himself equal to God." Equality is the thrust of the passage (witness the Son raising the dead and judging [5:21–22]; and that all might honor the Son in the same way as they honor the Father [John 5:23]). For his explanation of *ison,* see Joseph Henry Thayer, *A Greek-English Lexicon of the New Testament* (Grand Rapids: Zondervan, n.d.), 307.

CHAPTER 8

THE COUNCIL OF KADOSH:
MADE HOLY BY THE LODGE

"Freemasonry accepts good men who are found to be worthy,
regardless of their religious convictions, and strives to make better men
of them by emphasizing a firm belief in the Fatherhood of God, the
Brotherhood of Man, and the Immortality of the Soul."
—Grand Lodge of Massachusetts, Freemasonry: A Way of Life

Degrees nineteen through thirty make up the third body of degrees in Scottish Rite Freemasonry—the Council of Kadosh. It would take a whole book to treat all the degrees in this body, and so I have been selective, choosing those degrees which have more theological content.

Kadosh is a Hebrew word meaning "holy," "sanctified," or "set apart." Hutchens explains that the aim of Masonry is "to set apart from the rest of humanity those exemplary men who practice her noble virtues in the pursuit of truth."[1] In addition to exploring further the moral, political, and religious lessons of the Lodge of Perfection and the Chapter of Rose Croix, the Council examines world religions and seeks "to explain as clearly and as accurately as possible the nature of Deity and the relationship between Him and mankind."[2] Moreover,

The purely religious degrees are also referred to as the "Mystery Degrees." They comprise the 23rd through 26th. The 23rd degree is described by Pike as an illustration of the Lesser Mysteries;[3] that is, knowledge that all may know. The 24th degree teaches the mysteries of the Hebraic faith; the 25th, those of Islam; and finally, the 26th, those of Christianity. When these degrees are understood in this context, it is possible to see their essential unity—teaching that which is to be found in all faiths. Since no religious doctrine is given preference in Masonry, the Mystery Degrees should be viewed as a whole, each degree receiving equal attention. . . . The 28th degree is purely philosophical and the most mystical of all. The tenets of numerology,[4] astrology,[5] and alchemy[6] are explained.[7]

The remaining degrees of the Council of Kadosh (nineteenth through twenty-second, twenty-seventh, twenty-ninth, and thirtieth) combine "chivalric ideals, the practice of virtue and lessons on philosophy to remind us that Masonry involves the pursuit of knowledge and the practice of virtue."[8]

All this points to what seems to be the foremost object of Masonry—knowledge of the True Word and knowledge of God. The *Legenda* states that knowledge of the "True Word" and of God is of primary importance in the degrees.

Degrees, if worthy to be called such, are so many steps of the mystic ladder, by which we ascend to the knowledge of the TRUE WORD, to the Knowledge of GOD and of NATURE, which is His Revelation. They are, therefore, instructions, by symbols and their interpretations in political, philosophical and religious knowledge. If not this, they are nothing or merely vain and empty ceremonies.[9]

We now proceed to the nineteenth degree.

The Nineteenth Degree: Grand Pontiff

The degree of *Grand Pontiff*[10] presents as a decoration twelve columns around the Lodge room bearing the initials of the twelve tribes mentioned in Revelation 7:4–8 (cf. Gen. 49). Under these initials are the twelve zodiacal signs, and under these the twelve names of Deity.[11] Pike notes the similarities between the symbolism of the twelve tribes and that of astrology and ancient pagan gods and goddesses.

There is an astonishing coincidence between the characteristics assigned by Jacob to his sons, and those of the signs of the Zodiac, or the planets that have their domicile [residence] in those signs. . . . Sagittarius, chasing the Celestial Wolf, is an emblem of *Benjamin,* whom Jacob compares to a hunter: and in that constellation the Romans placed the domicile of Diana the huntress. Virgo, the domicile of Mercury, is borne on the flag of *Naphtali,* whose eloquence and agility Jacob magnifies, both of which are attributes of the Courier of the Gods.[12]

The ritual also contains symbols of the twelve tribes. Hope for peace, salvation, the search for light, and the restoration of spiritual sight is set forth. For example, the ninth column states that "peace shall be the Universal Law to all the children of a common Father."[13] The eighth column promises that, "when the Divine Light cometh, we shall see and know."[14] The fifth column reads, "Naphtali believes, hopes, waits and is patient. *Believes* that all death is new life. . . . *Hopes* for the time when this incessant flux and change shall cease, and the new Law of Love and Light rule in all spheres and over all existences; and *waits* with patience the fulfillment of the inviolable promises of God."[15]

The Play Begins, But Christ Is Missing

At one point in the ritual the candidate is seized by several brothers, who cover his head with a thick cloth and lead him to a dark room where he is left alone but is able to hear voices outside.[16] After five minutes in entire silence and solitude several brothers[17] begin to recite phrases which either allude to or are found in the book of Revelation. Below is a sampling:

> *1st Bro:* All who will not worship the Beast with seven heads and ten horns, and upon his horns ten crowns, and the mysterious name upon his forehead, shall be slain.[18] All men, the high and the low, the rich and the poor, freemen and slaves, shall receive upon their right hand, or on their forehead, his mark, his name, and the number of his name, which is six hundred threescore and six; or they shall neither buy nor sell; for his is power, dominion, and the authority of the great dragon. Man, helpless and in darkness, wilt thou receive his mark, that thou mayest emerge to light?

> *2nd Bro:* . . . If any man worship the Beast and his image, and receive his mark on his forehead or in his hand, he shall drink the wine of

God's indignation, and be banished from the presence of the Holy Angels and of the Word[19] that is the Redeemer.

3rd Bro: Have patience, oh! thou, who, though in darkness, art still our brother! Keep the commandments of God, and thy faith in His justice and infinite goodness! Blessed are the dead that die in the Lord.[20]

Immediately following this the brethren recite verses from Revelation 16:2–17, omitting some portions and adding others.[21] As the brethren continue to act out the ritual, note the interesting interpretation of "Babylon the Great" in the following:

1st Bro: The cities of the nations have fallen; and Intolerance, that Great Babylon,[22] is no more. The chains imposed by fraud upon the human mind, the manacles and fetters fastened by force upon Free Thought have fallen . . . and they shall no longer be drunk with the blood of the Saints and Martyrs of the Truth.

2nd Bro: Salvation, glory, honour and power to the Eternal God and Infinite Father. . . . Blessed are they that obey his law,[23] and trust in his goodness, that they might have right to the Tree of Life, and may enter in through the gates into the city.[24] Brother, who art in darkness, wilt thou obey that law, and trust in that Infinite Goodness, and be patient, though the appointed time may seem to draw no nearer during thy life, nor thy labors and exertions to produce any fruit?[25]

The candidate answers in the affirmative and is told, "Come, then, with us to the abode of Light!"[26] He is led out of confinement and into the Lodge, where Revelation 21 is recited—again with omissions and additions. First, verses 1–2 are quoted.[27] Then verses 3 and 4 are alluded to, "God" being substituted by "Father" and "He."[28] This is key to our discussion, for the Scottish Rite omits the allusion to Christ in verses 5–7. Ritual states, "He that sits upon the Throne saith: I make all things new. Write! for these words are true. To him that thirsts I give freely the waters of the Spring of Life. He that overcometh shall inherit all things. I will be his Father, and will love my child."[29]

Revelation 21:5–7 actually reads,

And he that sat upon the throne said, Behold, I make all things new. And he said unto me, Write: for these words are true and faithful. And he said unto me, It is done. *I am Alpha and Omega, the beginning and the end.* I will give unto him that is athirst of the fountain of the water of life freely. He that overcometh shall inherit all things; and I will be his God, and he shall be my son. (KJV, emphasis added)

It is true that in Revelation both the Father and Jesus Christ are said to have thrones (3:21). But John ascribes titles of deity (Alpha and Omega, the beginning and the end, the first and the last) to Jesus Christ (1:8,[30] 11,[31] 17; 2:8; 21:6; 22:13; cf. Isa. 44:6). Jesus is the Alpha and Omega (21:6), and it is He who is the "faithful and true witness" (3:14). Consequently, His words are "true and faithful" (21:5). Also, the Alpha and Omega says that it is He who gives from the fountain of the water of life (21:6). Jesus' words to the Samaritan woman exhorting her to come to Him for living water that will well up in springs of eternal life (John 4:7–14)—meaning the Holy Spirit (John 7:37–39)—are a definite cross-reference and thus more evidence that it is Jesus who is speaking in Revelation 21:6. Through selective, inaccurate, and out-of-context citing of the Scriptures, the Scottish Rite ritual takes passages that are intended to exalt and refer to Jesus Christ and makes them refer to the "common Father of all mankind."

The ritual includes other omissions as well. The following examples show how Scripture is manipulated in ritual. Omissions that point to Jesus and salvation are in italic type.

[RITUAL]: In the heavenly city there shall be no Temple: for the LORD GOD Almighty and the Redeemer[32] are its Temple.[33]

[SCRIPTURE]: And I saw no temple therein: for the Lord God Almighty and the *Lamb* are the temple of it (Rev. 21:22, KJV).

[RITUAL]: Nor sun nor moon shall be needed there: for the Very Light shall shine therein and give it light. In that Light shall all nations walk.[34]

[SCRIPTURE]: And the city had no need of the sun, neither of the moon, to shine in it: for the glory of God did lighten it, and *the Lamb is the light thereof.* And the nations of them *which are saved* shall walk in the light of it (Rev. 21:23–24, KJV).

In its grasp for nonsectarianism the Rite has once again eliminated Christ from the Bible passages it quotes or alludes to.

An Unholy Anointing

After the candidate goes to the "Holy Altar" and swears an obligation,[35] the Thrice Puissant says to him, "Malaki-Tsaduc,[36] King of Salem, whose name signifies The Just King,[37] was the priest of the Most High God. He met Abraham returning from the slaying of the Kings, and blessed him: and Abraham gave unto him the tenth of the spoils."[38] The Thrice Puissant then anoints the candidate's head with oil[39] and says, "Be thou a Priest forever, after the order of Malaki-Tsaduc."[40]

Biblical Response

Here again the Scottish Rite is guilty of blasphemy. It fails to recognize that the Melchizedek priesthood belongs *exclusively* to Jesus Christ. The epistle to the Hebrews was written mainly because Hebrew Christians were undergoing tremendous persecution. In order to give them hope, the writer begins with the teaching of the supremacy of Christ and His deity (1:3–14), and the finality of His revelation to us (1:2). He also establishes Christ's full humanity, and thus His being the faithful High Priest, able to make atonement for the sins of the people (2:14–17).[41] One of the main points of Hebrews is that Christ's sacrifice for sin is "once for all" (9:28; 10:10, 14). Consequently, there is no longer a need for the priesthood in the Old Testament sense, since Christ's flesh (figurative of His sacrifice) is now the veil that leads to the Holy of Holies (10:19–20).

Hebrews 7, which the Thrice Puissant quotes (vv. 1–2), teaches that Christ is a great high priest after the order of Melchizedek. Christ's priesthood is forever (v. 17), efficacious (v. 25), and perfect (v. 28); and, given the overall teaching of Hebrews, this priesthood belongs exclusively to Christ and is without a successor (v. 24).[42] Therefore, to even symbolically bestow the priesthood of Melchizedek upon another violates the biblical revelation that Jesus Christ alone holds this title. Given the fact that Hebrews sees this priesthood as having a saving effect upon the called of God, we are not dealing with mundane matters.

The Twentieth Degree: Master of the Symbolic Lodge

In the twentieth degree the tetragrammaton appears on the Apron in Phoenician characters, as well as the Hebrew word for "light."[43] The second password of the degree is "Yah-balin."[44] In Pike's *Book of the Words* it is spelled "Jubelum," and of it we are told,

This is probably Jabulum, incorrectly copied; which, as I have shown, meant "the product of, that which proceeded, issued or emanated from Om." If correctly written, it is compounded of . . . *Yu or Yah-u* . . . *Baal* or *Bal* or *Bel,* and *Om,* thus combining the names of the Hebrew, Phoenician and Hindu Deities, to indicate that they are in reality the same.[45]

At the end of the ritual for this degree, the candle of Truth is lit, and the Venerable Master says, "I bear the Light of Truth into the world, to overcome Falsehood and Error."[46]

We need to ask What is this "light" so symbolized in this degree? According to ritual, it is the "truth" that the Venerable Master bears to the world. Unfortunately, this light is simply symbolic of the recurring theme throughout the Scottish Rite ritualistic system: the true God is known by many names. But these names are not those which the Bible gives as titles for Yahweh ("LORD of Hosts," "LORD God," "Holy One of Israel"). Instead, the Rite offers as synonyms for Yahweh the names of Phoenician and Hindu deities. This is indeed an unholy alliance.

The Twenty-third Degree: Chief of the Tabernacle

The twenty-third degree is based on the Old Testament and is, therefore, quite Hebraic. As in the nineteenth degree, the twelve tribes are mentioned here along with Moses and Aaron. Being a "lesser mystery" degree, it conveys to the candidate that the "ONE" is the true and living God and that the deities of the nations are but different attributes of God.[47] The list includes Bel and Amun.[48] This is characteristic of Freemasonry's concept of the function of the ancient lesser mysteries, which sought to inculcate in the initiate's mind the teaching that all the different gods of the nations could be brought under the umbrella of the ONE.

In this degree the cross is used as "a symbol of the Universe of which God is the Soul; and it teaches thee how insignificant is man, and how continually he should humble himself in the presence of that Great Being who knows his inmost thoughts."[49] The degree also pictures Israel wandering in the wilderness. Consequently, the Lodge is set up like the tabernacle of Moses described in Exodus 26–36, complete with the Court of the Tabernacle, the Tabernacle, the Veil or Curtain, the Laver of Bronze, the Table of the Presence or Shewbread, and the Ark of the Covenant.[50] Again, the candidate is asked what he desires. He answers, "Light," and is pronounced "a Son of Light."[51] Before this he is sprinkled with the water of purification.[52]

Alluding to the Candelabrum, which decorates the Apron of this degree, Hutchens writes,

> The candelabrum symbolizes to us, as to the ancients, the seven planets: the sun, the moon, Mercury, Venus, Mars, Jupiter and Saturn. It also represents the seven archangels and seven of the ten manifestations of Deity; specifically, the seven Sephiroth [of the Qabbalistic Tree of Life] which follow Will, Wisdom and Understanding: Justice, Mercy, Beauty, Glory, Victory, Dominion and Kingdom.[53]

Thus, in this degree we find (1) the meshing of Old Testament events and theology with the occultic philosophy of the Qabbalah, (2) the candidate coming out of darkness and into light, and (3) repentance of sins and purity of heart without Christ as the direct cause.

The Twenty-fourth Degree: Prince of the Tabernacle

The twenty-fourth degree teaches "the mysteries of the Hebraic faith."[54] This, however, refers to the Qabbalah: "Thou desirest to know the Ancient Hebrew Mysteries. Thou seest above me the Mystic Triangle with the ancient Hebrew letter *Yud* in the centre. It is an emblem of the Deity, familiar to our masters, the Kabalists."[55] This degree presents a mixture of astrological signs; Egyptian, Mithraic, Dionysian, and Orphic Mysteries; and Hindu deities. For example,

> The three lights on the East, West and South of the Altar, represent the Summer Solstice and the Vernal and Autumnal equinoxes; the three persons of the Indian Godhead, the Creator,[56] Preserver[57] and Destroyer;[58] the three Egyptian Gods, Osiris, Isis and Horus: and, to us, the absolute Reason, the creative Power, and the Protecting Intelligence that constitute the Godhead.[59]

Ancient Gnosticism also influences the lessons of this degree.

> Masonry is the Gnosis. . . . What compels Masons to be secret is not fear of the Light; for Light is what they desire, seek for, and adore. But they fear Profaners.[60] . . . Moreover, at the present day, a great

number of those who think themselves Freemasons know not the meaning of the ceremonies, and have lost the keys of the mysteries. They do not even comprehend their symbolical charts, nor understand their hieroglyphical signs with which the walls and ceiling of their Lodges are ornamented. . . . We may read them with the aid of the Kabalistic keys.[61]

Consequently, a Gnostic interpretation of the soul of man is given.

The Soul is immortal. . . . The Soul, a spark of the Universal Soul, imprisoned in the body, becomes sordid with the body's imperfections; and must be purified before it can return and mingle again with the Universal Source. It is immortal, not of necessity, but unless God pleases, as it and all things emanated from Him, to absorb it again into Himself.[62]

After giving the Sacred Word, *YHVH,* the candidate is led to several stations in the Lodge room. At one point he is stopped at a station and has water poured over his head. He is then told, "I test thee with WATER, the second test. Let it ever remind thee that none but the pure of heart can be admitted to the Holy Tabernacle in the Heavens; where God, who is Infinite Purity, presides."[63] The degree features a lengthy lecture section in which many of the teachings of the ancient Mystery Religions are recounted. This is to teach the candidate that what he has gone through in the ritual is much like the ancient mysteries.[64]

Are the "pure of heart" and the soul's being "purified before it can return and mingle again with the Universal Source" subtle statements that can escape the unenlightened man who calls himself a Mason? According to Scottish Rite philosophy, *yes!* To the Adept (or enlightened man), the great teachings of the ancient mysteries are presented in this modern ritual. The hope is that he will quickly seize upon them, using the great teachings of Masonry pertaining to the Deity, to His revelation of the Great Book of Nature, and to the system of morality veiled in allegory and illustrated by symbols. In this (unbiblical) way he is thought to purify the soul.

The Twenty-fifth Degree: Knight of the Brazen Serpent

Hutchens notes that in the twenty-fifth degree, "some Islamic doctrine is presented through the re-creation of initiation into the elite group among the

Druse, a quasi-Islamic religious sect living in the Lebanon area . . . it is believed the Druse religious system is basically Islamic intermingled with Gnostic, Christian and Hebrew doctrine."[65]

The degree also includes, in its apparel and Lodge ornamentation, astrology and gods and goddesses from other religions. The Apron is white and edged with black and is spotted with silver and gold stars, representing the Pleiades, the Hyades, Orion, Capella, Perseus, Scorpio, and Ursa Major. It also contains the tetragrammaton in Phoenician characters.[66] In addition, "The Order is a crimson ribbon, on which are embroidered the words, one under the other, . . . OSIRIS . . . AHURA . . . OSARSIPH . . . MOSES."[67] On another ribbon appear the names "ISIS" and "CERES."[68]

The Cast of Characters in Ritual

Some of the officers of the Lodge represent an interesting blend of biblical persons with Egyptian gods: "The presiding officer represents Moses and Osiris. . . . The Senior Warden represents Joshua and Horus. . . . The Junior Warden represents Caleb, or Anubis."[69] During the opening ceremonies questions of whom these biblical characters represent are answered by giving the names of these gods and how they relate to different astrological signs.[70] For example, to the question "Whom do you, my Brother, represent here?"[71] the *Liturgy* answers: "Horus, the son of Isis and Osiris; before whom Tuphon, the malignant Serpent of the Northern Pole, flees aghast . . . and the dogs of Orion climb upward."[72] The Most Potent Leader (Presiding Officer) represents

> Osiris, King of the Starry influences of Light and Life; Ahura Mazda,[73] Great Principle of Light and Good; Moses, Atys, Adonis, Dionusos, Bacchus, Apollo;—all Personifications that in all ages have represented with most feeble expression the Divine Principle of Good, the Eternal, Infinite, Incomprehensible Self and Source of Light and Life.[74]

More Gnosis

In typical Gnostic fashion, this degree teaches the ascent of the soul through the spheres to the Great Source of Light.[75]

> *Qu:* What are our duties, as Knights of the Brazen Serpent? *Ans:* To purify the soul of its alloy of earthliness, that through the gate of

Capricorn and the seven spheres it may at length ascend to its eternal home beyond the Stars.[76]

Two ancient Gnostic theological ingredients are evident in this teaching: the imprisoned soul being purified and released from its earthly body, and the soul's ascent through heavenly spheres. These themes constantly emerge in ancient Gnostic writings.[77]

Another element of the ritual of the twenty-fifth degree is characteristic of ancient Gnosticism. It appears that the advancement toward light is achieved only by those whose intellects are capable of receiving it: "You desire to attain the Light. You can only advance *toward* its Source and Essence, which are of the Deity. So much of the Truth as it is given to mortals to know is within the reach of those alone whose intellects are unclouded by passion or excess."[78] The *pneumatikoi* (spiritual ones), as they were known in ancient Gnostic systems, were those whose knowledge rose above that of the *sarkikoi* (fleshly ones) to comprehend the Infinite One. These were the worthy who could then enjoy the release and ascent of their souls (in essence the same as, and consequently a spark of, the Infinite) to the place of the Infinite Source, thereby becoming one with the Infinite, their original abode.[79]

A Taste of Islam

The ceremony of the degree takes place in four apartments (sections), called House of the Earth, House of the Planets, House of the Sun and Moon, and House of the Light.[80] On the altar are placed the Bible, the Hebrew Pentateuch, and the Koran.[81] During the ceremony the candidate is asked to read from the Koran and in some places verses from the Koran are modified to reflect the universality of Freemasonry. For example, the *Kalimah* (lit. "the word") or testimony of faith (*shahādah*) of Islam is the first of the "Five Pillars" (or fundamentals) of Islam. It states that "there is no god but God (Allah) and that Mohammad is the messenger [Prophet] of God."[82] Hutchens says that the Masonic ritual has been modified to read, "There is no god but God; and the teachers of the Truth are His Prophets."[83] Aside from the fact that the Christian (as well as the orthodox Jew or Muslim) would find it blasphemous to place the Koran alongside the Bible, the Muslim would also find it blasphemous to change the first of the Five Pillars of Islam in any way, as Scottish Rite ritual has. As mentioned earlier, the Scottish Rite must not only face the fact that its ritual violates Christian doctrine, but it should also consider that its ritual would assuredly provoke the Muslim!

The candidate promises, in writing, to rid himself of one shortcoming in symbolic purification.[84] After he is led to the next apartment, he reads further from the Koran. Hutchens writes,

> He is instructed to be thankful to God, constant in prayer, penitent and humble, generous, merciful, and *Endeavor not to live for thyself alone, but so that when thou hast died there shall be some to stand up and say, "Dear God, it has been well for us that Thou didst let him live. He has not wished to find his way to heaven alone."*[85]

Enter the Druse

The candidate then receives a white turban, as "an emblem of purity of faith and a Knight of the Brazen Serpent."[86] He is instructed on the divine hierarchy of the Druse, which was a Gnostic-flavored cult of the eleventh century A.D.[87] Note the emanation-like theology, characteristic of ancient Gnosticism, in the following portrayal of the Druse's divine hierarchy:

> [The divine heirarchy is] represented by the five stars of different colors on the white disk suspended in the East [of the Lodge room]. The disk symbolizes Albar the Most High, or the Deity, who from His glorious light produced the universal Intelligence. From the light of Intelligence He produced the Soul; from the light of the Soul, the Word; from the light of the Word, the Preceding; from the light of the Preceding, the Following; and from the light of the Following, the Universe. The divine Soul is said to be the cause of the production of the universe and within man it is emotion, feeling, sympathy, justice, beneficence, the moral being of God, or simply, all that of the divine nature which is spoken of as the heart of man. . . . In the House of the Planets, the soul is the principle concern; we learn the soul of man is a part of the Divine.[88]

To summarize, the twenty-fifth degree impresses upon the initiate the obtaining of mercy and forgiveness (of sins) and explains some of the symbols of Masonry.[89] The various legends of the ancient mysteries' particular gods, goddesses, and heroes dying and coming back to life are recounted in this degree.[90] Of course, Hiram Abif is the Masonic variation of such a "universal legend."[91] Also, this degree syncretizes Old Testament narrative, Gnostic philosophy, the ancient Mystery Religions and their death-life myths, and astrology.

The Twenty-sixth Degree: Prince of Mercy

This degree is also known as *Scottish Trinitarian* (Trinitarian Ecossias).[92] For our purposes we will examine what the Scottish Rite ritual says the Trinity is, and how it views the Christian doctrine of the Trinity.

Trinity

The degree conveys to the initiate different concepts of "Trinity" in several religions. Here the candidate represents the ancient Christian "catechumen," one who went through various stages of discipleship before baptism into the community of faith.[93] But rather than undergoing careful scrutiny and discipleship in Christian doctrine for a few years, as the ancient Christians did, the Masonic candidate is instructed in the various concepts of "Trinity" in other religions. To the ancient Christian catechumen these conceptions would have been considered pagan in the truest sense. Nonetheless, in a theatrical-type set representing the catacombs of Rome (where Christians held secret meetings because of persecution) the Mason, representing a Christian catechumen, is taught,

> Thus said the Holy Books of Ancient India: There are three Supreme Gods, the three Forms and Aspects of the First, the Supreme, Single, Invisible GOD, Cause of all Phenomena, and the Soul of the World:[94] and these three, the Powers of *Creation, Preservation,* and *Destruction,*[95] distinct in persons, are but one God, the Triple Form of the Supreme, the Word AUM,[96] first utterance of the Eternal.[97]

> The Supreme GOD ALFADER, said our ancient Brethren, the Druids, is Eternal. . . . ODIN and FREA, His First-Created, and THOR, their son, are the Supreme Council and Trinity of the Gods.[98]

> AMUN-RE, said the Ancient Egyptians, the Uncreated, is the Supreme Triad, Father, Mother, and Son, from whom the long chain of Triads descends to the Incarnations in human form.[99]

Ritual then proceeds to quote from the first chapter of the gospel of John, coupled with the King James Version of 1 John 5:7: "There are Three that bear record in Heaven; The FATHER, the WORD, and the HOLY SPIRIT, and these Three are One."[100] The conclusion to all this is that in all ages the golden threads of Truth have gleamed in the woof of error. Fortunate the Mason who, by the Light of Wisdom, the true Masonic Light, second emanation from the Deity,[101] can discern the golden threads. . . . Thus in all ages the Word of God, his THOUGHT, not uttered in a voice audible to mortal ears,[102] has spoken in the Souls of Men, and taught them the great Truths of Reason, Philosophy and Religion.[103]

Hutchens reasons that "the trinity of Deity belongs to no single religion."[104]

The ritual affirms that the Mason is free to exercise his personal belief in any particular "Trinity" he chooses. He is told, "No one has the right to object, if the Christian Mason sees foreshadowed in Krishna and Sosiosch, in Mithra and Osiris, the Divine WORD that, as he believes, became man, and died upon the cross to redeem a fallen race." Conversely, "Nor can *he* object if others see in the WORD that was in the beginning with God, and which God was, only the LOGOS of Plato and Philo, and the Uttered THOUGHT or First Emanation of LIGHT." As a matter of fact, the Scottish Rite claims not to "undervalue the importance of any Truth" and not to dictate to the Muslim, the Christian, or the Hebrew what to believe, since "We utter no word that can be deemed irreverent by any one of any faith."[105] The ritual is then careful to state, "To every Mason there is a God. . . . How, or by what intermediates He creates and acts, and in what way He unfolds and manifests Himself, Masonry leaves to Creeds and Religions to inquire."[106]

Yet there is an element in ritual and in related writings that is puzzling. Why, after all this caution, do we find a *creed* in Scottish Rite Freemasonry? First, the *Liturgy* relates to us "the Masonic Trinity, Three Potencies of one Essence";[107] indeed, the colors of the degree—green, red, and white—"symbolize the Masonic Trinity."[108] Second, *The Magnum Opus* states,

God, the unknown FATHER . . . , known to us only by His Attributes;[109] the ABSOLUTE I AM: . . . The THOUGHT of God . . . ; and the WORD . . . , Manifestation and Expression of the Thought; . . . Behold THE TRUE MASONIC TRINITY: the UNIVERSAL SOUL; the THOUGHT *in* the Soul, the WORD, or Thought expressed; the THREE IN ONE, of a Trinitarian Ecossias.[110]

Third, Hutchens reproduces the last part of the preceding quotation under the heading "The Creed of Masonry."[111] These are only some of the possible examples of how Scottish Rite Freemasonry talks out of both sides of its mouth.

A Masonic Creed and Doctrine

The Mason may object that I have left out a portion of ritual that clarifies the "Masonic Trinity." *The Magnum Opus* states, "Here Masonry pauses, and leaves its initiates to carry out and develop *these great Truths* in such a manner as to each may seem most accordant with reason, philosophy, truth and his religious faith."[112] It then goes on to list how each man of a differing faith would view his "Trinity."

The problem, however, still exists. After this listing we find the following in *The Magnum Opus, A Bridge to Light,* and *Morals and Dogma:*

> While all these faiths assert their claims to the exclusive possession of the Truth, Masonry inculcates its old doctrine, and no more. . . . That God is ONE; that His THOUGHT, uttered in His WORD, created the Universe, and preserves it by those Eternal Laws, which are the expression of that Thought.[113]

Whether the Scottish Rite admits to it or not, this is a creed[114] and a doctrine.

This phenomenon is mentioned with regard to T.G.A.O.T.U. in the Blue Lodge degrees. A canopy creed or doctrine is set up by the Rite whereby T.G.A.O.T.U. can subsume any Scottish Rite Freemason's idea of "Trinity." This is evidenced by a preceding quotation, stating, "Masonry . . . leaves its initiates to carry out and develop these great Truths in such a manner as to each may seem most accordant with . . . his religious faith." This canopy creed must be viewed in the context of prayers offered in the ritual. For example,

> Infinitely Illustrious and Supreme Father. . . . Who directest the ineffable harmonies that are the law of the boundless Universe! Universal Parent of eternally successive being; . . . Author of Life, and Soul of all that moves. . . . Fill our souls with love for Thee! Save us from persecutors; teach us and all our Brethren to be tolerant of error, the common lot of man; and send our life a happy, blameless end![115]

Who is being prayed to? In context we must conclude that it is the One, God, the Unknown Father, the absolute I Am, spoken of in the previous quotations.

And from this God flow the emanations called "THOUGHT" and "WORD"—thus the Masonic Trinity. It is also important to note that in the prayer above, this God is addressed on behalf of all the Masons present. Clearly this "Supreme Father" serves as a designation for all Masons, and yet they may read their own particular gods into it.

In typical Masonic, esoteric fashion, the *Liturgy* leaves us with the following, suggesting a paradox surrounding the Masonic creed regarding its "Trinity":

> Perhaps you suspect that there is still remaining behind an inner meaning of the word "TRINITY," connecting itself with your title of Scottish Trinitarian. It may be so. Masonry discloses its secrets cautiously, and never makes the whole truth known at once. Listen to the language of one of her Adepts, and interpret it for yourself.[116]

More About the Scottish Rite's Jesus

Some other features of the twenty-sixth degree include mention of Jesus Christ. In ritual, "parallels are drawn between the slaying of Hiram and the death of Jesus."[117] Masonry

> sees in Moses, the Lawgiver of the Jews, in Confucius and Zoroaster, in Jesus of Nazareth, and in the Arabian Iconoclast, Great Teachers of Morality, and Eminent Reformers, if no more: and allows every brother of the Order to assign to each such higher and even Divine Character as his Creed and Truth require.[118]

Thus Jesus is seen as one of many "great reformers." We also find in ritual a perversion of John 17:3. Scripture records Jesus' praying to the Father, "This is life eternal, that they might know thee the only true God, and Jesus Christ, whom thou hast sent" (KJV). Ritual states, however, "This is Life Eternal, to know the only TRUE GOD, and the WORD that did create the Universe, in Whom is Light, and that Light the Life of men."[119]

When two different people use the same terms, that does not guarantee the same *definitions* of those terms. What does the ritual mean by the "WORD"? Speaking of John 1:1, "In the beginning was the Word, and the Word was with God, and the Word was God" (KJV), ritual states that the Word was the "first emanation from God" and came into existence "when the process of emanation, of creation or evolution of existences *inferior* to the Supreme God began."[120] Any student of ancient Gnosticism (a heretical religious system vigorously opposed by the early Christian church[121]) will notice the similarities between this ancient system and the concepts just cited from ritual, namely, a Supreme God (Greek, *plērōma*) giving rise to the inferior material creation (Greek, *kenōma*) through various emanations that were also deemed inferior to the Supreme. Thus, the Masonic definition of "WORD" is alien to the biblical understanding of the Word, who was eternally God, the second person of the Trinity, and not an inferior "emanation."[122]

Should You Be Baptized?

This degree includes "baptizing" the candidate. Hutchens mentions that this is one of several "final symbolic actions" serving as "marks, or tokens, of the solemn covenants entered into by the newly raised Prince of Mercy with the Masonic fraternity, the Deity and Truth."[123] The water, says Hutchens, "is poured on the candidate's head as a symbol of the soul's purification."[124] No doubt he draws his statements from ritual.

> *Qu:* What are the symbols of the purification necessary to make us perfect Masons? *Ans:* Lavation with pure water, or baptism; because to cleanse the body is emblematical of purifying the soul.[125]

Should You Partake?

Exactly what does Hutchens mean by "the soul's purification"? This highly theological and religious phrase ought to concern us. The symbol that follows this gives us a clue:

> [*Qu:*] What is to us the chief symbol of man's ultimate regeneration? [*Ans:*] The fraternal supper, of bread which nourishes, and of wine which refreshes and exhilarates; symbolical of the time which is to come, when all mankind shall be one great harmonious brotherhood; and teaching us these great lessons,—that as matter changes ever, but no single atom is annihilated, it is not rational to suppose that the far nobler soul does not continue to exist beyond the grave.[126]

The Magnum Opus furnishes more information: "The bread and wine teach us that our Mortal Body is no more We than the house in which we live, or the garments that we wear; but the Soul is I, the ONE, identical, unchangeable, immortal emanation from the Deity, to return to God and be happy forever."[127] Once again Gnostic-type language is employed, and the soul is seen as an emanation from the Deity (and thus no different in essence!), which ultimately returns *back* to the Deity. If the Gnostic framework is maintained, and there is no reason why it should not be, the purifying of the soul means the shedding of the base material body and the release of the soul toward its original divine abode.

This certainly is not the biblical meaning of the bread and wine used in the Christian sacrament. Rather, Jesus said that the elements represent[128] *His* body broken for his followers, and *His* shed blood on the cross for their sins (Matt. 26:26–29; Mark 14:22–25; Luke 22:17–20).

In spite of the biblical evidence and the Scottish Rite's use of bread and wine, Hutchens assures us that "these symbols of faith and virtue are not an irreverent imitation of the rites of any church but are a mark of the covenant among the brethren and with God."[129] But given the Masonic meaning of the bread and wine, the fact that the Bible portrays the elements as pointing to God's unique Son, and that Masons who claim to be Christians partake of this symbol, Christians must see it as "an irreverent imitation" and a blasphemous portrayal of what is sacred to the Christian church.

More importantly, shouldn't the Scottish Rite be concerned about whether or not this offends *God?* Since the Last Supper, which Jesus shared with His disciples, pointed to the greatest and most exclusive redemptive act in history, and to the Father's love for sinful humanity, no *other* "symbols" of bread and wine representing "a covenant with God" can be pleasing in His sight. This is because a covenant with God cannot be made on any other basis than that of the sacrifice of Christ on the cross (Heb. 9:11–15).[130]

We might also ask the Masonic apologist this question: Why does a group that claims to be *just* a fraternal order use symbols that point to a "covenant with God"? Adding fuel to the fire is this statement in the *Liturgy* regarding "the Bread of Life": "Faith in God's Word,[131] and a sincere reliance upon His loving-kindness, are the true bread of life."[132] This simply does not square with the biblical account, in which Jesus calls himself "the bread of life" (John 6:35, 48). Moreover, considering the claims of the Bible concerning His uniqueness (John 1:14, 18) and the fact that He is "the true vine" (John 15:1), we have no other choice than to affirm that He is therefore the *true* bread of life.

To conclude, although this degree often alludes to "the Christian faith" and "Jesus Christ," and although it is supposed to teach the mysteries of Christianity,[133] it actually teaches heresy.

The Twenty-eighth Degree:
Knight of the Sun, or Prince Adept

The twenty-eighth degree is a mixture of Qabbalah, Alchemy (Hermeticism),[134] and Astrology. Hutchens states that Qabbalistic philosophy concerns itself with "the search for knowledge of the Divine and of the soul."[135] Qabbalah purports to be a "spiritual" interpretation of the first five books of the Old Testament and teaches that "there were ten emanations [Sephiroth] which revealed the attributes of Deity manifested in the world."[136] Alchemy was the science of transmuting metals into gold or silver. This was called "operative alchemy." The spiritual version, "speculative alchemy," comprised "mystics who declared that alchemy was not the science of making gold but a spiritual science of regeneration and a sacred art devoted to interpreting the mysteries of God and life."[137] Hutchens writes that "when we speak of alchemy in Masonry our reference is to the second group."[138] Astrology is in part the ancient spiritual and physical "science" of telling one's destiny by the positions of certain heavenly bodies.

The Central Theme

The degree spends a great deal of time on this central theme: long ago God revealed the simple, undefiled true religion to certain cultures, which, in time, perverted this true revelation by forming symbols and representations of the truth. As a result these cultures came to worship the symbols or representations rather than the One, the true and living God.[139] In spite of this perversion over time, however, there were groups that served as treasuries of this great and primitive truth. Masonry sees these as the ancient mysteries. They used symbolism in its true sense—to transfer a knowledge of the divine to persons worthy and capable of receiving it.[140] Ritual states,

> In the Mysteries, wherever they were practised, was taught that truth of the primitive revelation, the existence of One Great Being, infinite and pervading the Universe, who was there worshipped without superstition; and his marvellous [*sic*] nature, essence and attributes taught to the Initiates; while the vulgar attributed his works to Secondary Gods, personified, and isolated from Him in fabulous independence.[141]

Ritual then makes a bold claim: "There is but one true Religion, but one legitimate Doctrine and Creed, as there is but one God, one Reason,[142] one

Universe."[143] Not long after this the ritual sets forth a prayer, which begins, "Our Father, the One GOD!"[144] We should not be surprised then to read that

> Masonry, when properly expounded, is at once the interpretation of the great book of nature,[145] the recital of physical and astronomical phenomena, the purest philosophy, and the place of deposit, where, as in a Treasury, are kept in safety all the great truths of the primitive revelation, that form the basis of all religions.[146]

Nature is considered "the primary, consistent, and certain revelation or unveiling of God."[147]

Just as the Qabbalah saw in its mysteries the one God being the *Ain Soph* (or *En Sof*), Scottish Rite Masonry, which is Qabbalistic[148] and a successor to the ancient mysteries,[149] states at the end of the twenty-eighth degree, "We conclude with that which has always been, and we believe always will be the Masonic idea of the Supreme Being: We call Him the Grand Architect of the Universe, considering that Universe as His most magnificent temple and perfect work of architecture."[150] This, along with the dogma of the immortality of the soul, is the great primitive truth that the Scottish Rite says was taught in its purest and simplest form in the beginning.

More Qabbalah, Alchemy, and Astrology

The ritual is enacted with the presiding officer representing "Father Adam" or "Adam Kadmon."[151] Seven other officers are styled "the Seven Malakoth."[152] The candidate is blindfolded, again to symbolize his being in darkness and in search of light. He is asked, "Are you prepared to receive instruction with humility, to allow your prejudices and wrong opinions to be overcome by reason, and to listen with reverence to the lessons of the ancient Sages?"[153] The candidate is cautioned to keep an open mind and then instructed on Qabbalistic and Hermetic philosophical ideas.[154] He is then instructed in the theme of the degree, with the seven Malakoth representing different planets and metals.[155] Thus, through the seven Malakoth, planets and metals, the Qabbalistic, Alchemistic, and Astrological underpinnings of the degree are set.

In Qabbalah, the Adam Kadmon (the primordial, or heavenly, man) is described as a ray of light coming from the *Ain Soph*. In turn the Sephiroth emanated from the Adam Kadmon. This is the opinion of some Qabbalistic adherents,[156] and it may be the reason why the presiding officer is seated in the East, which is a source of light.[157] The Scottish Rite's "Lecture of Father Adam" similarly states,

"HE [said the Hindus], whose nature is beyond the reach of our intellect, whose essence is not cognizable by our Senses, who is indiscernible but eternal, He, the All-pervading Spirit, whom even the mind cannot grasp, to frame of Him an idea or conception, *even He rayed Himself forth"* . . . [This] "One Existence" of the Hindus is the AINSOPH,[158] the endless, unlimited, nameless Deity. . . . The primitive Light of the Deity, who is nothing, filled all space. It is space itself. All creation has progressively emanated or flowed out from the Divine Light. The Infinite Ainsoph manifested himself, in the beginning, in one first Principle or Cause, the Deity containing the Universe, the SON of GOD, the universal from which manifoldness was to flow, the Macrocosm or Macroprosopos, to whom the Kabalists assigned a human figure, as the Holy Writings gave them the right to do, and called him Adam Kadmon, the Prototype of aggregate humanity.[159]

Not only is Hindu philosophy singled out. Conceptions of the Deity from different nations and cultures are elaborated upon, with the underlying teaching that these are shadows pointing to this great Qabbalistic doctrine.[160]

We must not see in the Adam Kadmon the Adam of the Garden. Rather, Qabbalistic philosophy sees in the latter a counterpart of the Divine Emanation, which is the former.[161] Thus, because Qabbalah teaches "as above, so below"[162] (and so does this degree[163]), man is seen in this sense (not the biblical sense[164]) and in this Masonic degree as "a shadow of the Divine."[165] This phraseology comes dangerously close to the aim of Qabbalah, which is "the restoration of the divine man in the medium of mortal man."[166]

To conclude, in the examination of this degree we find the claim that Freemasonry has preserved the great primitive revelation of God to humanity. Though shadows of this truth can be found in all religions, there were (and are) a select few who preserved the pure and undefiled tenets of God's truth. The ancient mysteries, taking men of differing faiths and conceptions of Deity and showing them that the true God was beyond what their creeds and belief systems had established, showed that the true God is unknowable, and that men's ideas of God are but shadows. This the Qabbalah did, though it saw this Great Unknowable to be the "Ain Soph." With this great philosophy the ancient mysteries had a rallying point, a firm theology upon which to rest, though they may have named the Great Unknowable differently. Scottish Rite Freemasonry is in the theological-philosophical lineage of the ancient mysteries and the Qabbalah, taking the deities of its initiates and teaching these initiates that their gods are but shadows of the Supreme, the Grand Architect of the Universe.[167] With the proverbial blindfold of ignorance removed, the candidate of the twenty-eighth degree is led to this light of "Truth" and becomes a Knight of the Sun, or Prince Adept.

The Thirtieth Degree: Knight Kadosh

The thirtieth degree, that of Knight Kadosh (which means "Holy Knight"), features ritualistic acts in four "apartments."[168] Jacques De Molay, the last Grand Master of the crusading order of Knights Templar, is the historical figure associated with this degree.[169] King Philip IV of France and Pope Clement V charged De Molay with heresy and put him to death in the fourteenth century.

A Morbid Decor

In the ritual for this degree, the first apartment is decorated with black and contains a tomb with three human skulls.[170] "Upon the [skull] on the left is the triple crown of the Pope, and on the one on the right a regal crown."[171] These represent Pope Clement (and other unholy, ambitious religious leaders) and King Philip (and other tyrannical kings).[172] The middle skull is supposedly that of Jacques De Molay and signifies immortality.[173] The three skulls represent the history of the human race, which is colored by repeated tragedies of the murders of righteous reformers or heroes by those who have misused power.[174] De Molay is thus a type of the Masonic hero Hiram Abif, and the three ruffians who murdered Hiram represent the evil persecutions of the righteous by religious and political tyrants throughout history. The Knight Kadosh is to pursue and conquer such types for the good of the human race. The candidate is taught this in the second apartment.[175]

An End-Time Hope

At the west end of the first apartment appear the words "HE WHO SHALL OVERCOME THE DREAD OF DEATH SHALL ASCEND ABOVE THE TERRESTRIAL SPHERE, AND BE ENTITLED TO INITIATION INTO THE GREATER MYSTERIES."[176] This degree, like its predecessors, features a mixture of Qabbalah, Astrology, and New Testament teaching.[177] The following prayer recalls some of what we have already observed, and adds the elements of worship and eschatology:[178]

Thou Eternal, Uncreated, Illimitable Being, of Infinite Beneficence and Love, that wast originally All in All, and at whose Thought the Universe flashed into being, coeval with Thee as Thy Thoughts were, and the great spheres began their eternal noiseless revolutions! From the depths of our hearts we adore Thee, we worship Thee, we offer Thee sincere and grateful homage. Enable us to imitate and emulate the virtues of all[179] who have lost their lives in endeavoring to serve and elevate Humanity! May he who here for the first time kneels with us, doing homage to Thee and honor to the illustrious memory of our murdered Grand Master, ever revere his name and memory, prove himself his true disciple, and emulate his virtues and magnanimity! . . . Aid us to punish and avenge the wrongs done to our predecessors and to Humanity, in such a way as may be consistent with Thy Law, and with our duty as good and true Masons. Aid us to subjugate and overcome Error, Intolerance, Oppression, and Bigotry! and may the day soon dawn when all the Earth shall be one Holy Land, and all mankind one great Lodge of Brethren.[180]

With all that we have learned of the Council of Kadosh, Scottish Rite degree system thus far, we cannot help but agree with following assessment:

The Blue Degrees are but the outer court or portico of the Temple. Part of the symbols are explained there to the Initiate, but he is intentionally misled by false interpretations. It is not intended that he shall understand them; but it is intended that he shall imagine he understands them. Their true explication is reserved for the Adepts, the Princes of Masonry. . . . It is well enough for the mass of those called Masons, to imagine that all is contained in the Blue Degrees; and whoso attempts to undeceive them will labor in vain, and without any true reward violate his obligations as an Adept.[181]

This degree system ingeniously imparts esoteric knowledge in a way that makes it almost impossible to understand the Blue degrees apart from it. Though the knowledge gained is unbiblical, and, from a Christian perspective, spiritually dangerous, it seems nonetheless reserved for the "Adepts" of Freemasonry. Those who are *merely* Blue Lodge Masons should think twice before calling themselves Masons in the true sense of the word: they have not had the opportunity to explore the Scottish Rite's "light" shed on the Blue degrees.

Biblical Response

Those who *are* merely Blue Lodge Masons but also claim Christ as their Lord and Savior should, if they have not already been convinced of the Blue Lodge's spiritual incompatibility with Christianity, think twice before entering the Scottish Rite degree system. Its blend of Gnostic and Qabbalistic philosophy subtly perverts and undermines the historical Christian gospel.

The degrees in the Council of Kadosh present the candidate with several themes in the study of comparative religion. One theme is that of the Trinity, treated in the twenty-sixth degree. This degree tries to show that the concept belongs to no one religion;[182] we find a trinity of gods mentioned in Indian, Scandinavian, and Egyptian religion, and there is also the Christian doctrine of the Trinity.[183] In addition, the degree sets forth "the Masonic Trinity, Three Potencies of one Essence,"[184] and "THE TRUE MASONIC TRINITY; the UNIVERSAL SOUL, the THOUGHT in the Soul, the WORD, or Thought expressed; the THREE IN ONE, of a Trinitarian Ecossias [Scottish Trinitarian]."[185]

What does the Scottish Rite imply in all this? On the one hand, it asserts that many cultures and belief systems had "rays" of the truth, gleams of light that shone through the darkness of error. We found this theme in other degrees, with the added idea here that the truth was hidden or marred by representations that came to be worshiped themselves (the deities of many nations are but attributes of the true God). True Adepts saw behind these mere representations the One Absolute Deity, the I AM, the true God who was "above all the Baalim."[186] Fortunate, then, is the Mason who can now discern these golden threads (this is one reason for the teaching of different "trinities" in the degree) as his ancient brethren did.[187]

The Scottish Rite says that there are rays of truth in the many ancient conceptions of God, and yet it offers the "True Masonic Trinity," "the real idea of the Ancient Nations."[188] The Universal Soul, the Thought, and the Word constitute the Three in One of a Scottish Trinitarian. We can only conclude that, in the Scottish Rite's opinion, this "Trinity" is the true Deity that lies behind all those conceptions—all the Baalim.

The bold dogmatic statements of the Lodge about its "Trinity" in the twenty-sixth degree must be challenged with a Christian explanation of the biblical Trinity. The word *Trinity* comes from *tri-unity,* which means three persons in unity, as the only true and living God. God exists as three distinct persons—Father, Son, and Holy Spirit ("person" meaning one who possesses intellect, will, and emotion). These three persons exist simultaneously and in perfect unity. The Christian doctrine of the Trinity states (1) that there is one God (Deut. 6:4; Isa. 43:10);[189] (2) that God is Father (2 Peter 1:17), Son (John 20:28), and Holy Spirit (Acts 5:3–4[190]);[191] and (3) that these three distinct persons are together the one God (Matt. 28:19; cf. Deut. 12:4–5).[192]

God is not the Universal Soul, Thought, and the Word, as the Lodge would have its initiates believe. The Masonic Trinity of the Scottish Rite may try to absorb all the ideas of triad or trinity of its Masonic initiates, but the biblical God may not be included in this blend, especially since the Bible teaches that Jesus Christ is to be worshiped as God.[193]

We have seen that the Scottish Rite teaches its dogma of the Masonic Trinity and its understanding of the soul of man. The "Universal Soul" is listed first. Each individual soul is an emanation from this Universal Soul (though it is trapped in a body). Ideally the individual soul, being in essence no different from the Universal Soul, will, if purified, return to the Universal Soul.

To reiterate, "Masonry is the Gnosis,"[194] and "The Soul is immortal . . . a spark of the Universal Soul, imprisoned in the body . . . and must be purified before it can return and mingle again with the Universal Source. . . . [The soul of man] is immortal . . . as it and all things emanated from Him, [only] to absorb it again into Himself."[195] This teaching is alien to biblical teaching. The Bible teaches that the first person of the Godhead is the Father; Jesus identifies Him as such. Rather than teaching that souls emanated from God, the Bible states that the first man, Adam, was *created* by a direct act of God, and that through the procreative process ordained by God, all who follow Adam and Eve are *created* body, soul, and/or spirit by God.[196] Rather than the *soul's* being purified, Scripture teaches that salvation involves the entire person, through faith in Jesus Christ. Rather than the soul's returning to "mingle again," or to "be absorbed into God," the Bible promises that the righteous will dwell in the presence of God, forever glorifying and worshiping Him with fellow believers.

Conclusion

The ritual of the Scottish Rite *is* dogmatic in its doctrines and related statements. It dogmatically states that it has no creed, save the belief in God and the immortality of the soul. Yet it also dogmatically defines God (the Masonic Trinity) and the soul ("the soul of man is a part of the Divine"[197]), as well as its source and ideal end. The Rite simply cannot escape the religious dogmatism it so vehemently vilifies unless it completely rids itself of all elements of religion. Such elements require that it be called a religion—an anti-Christian religion. We now move to our final portion of Scottish Rite ritual. The grand climax awaits us—the Holy Doctrine (or Secret Doctrine) of all ages is about to be revealed!

Notes

1. Rex R. Hutchens, *A Bridge to Light* (Washington, D.C.: The Supreme Council, 33rd, Ancient and Accepted Scottish Rite of Freemasonry, Southern Jurisdiction, United States of America, 1988), 157.
2. Ibid., 157–58.
3. See chap. 5, n. 7.
4. Numerology is an occult science of the mystical, though hidden, significance of numbers.
5. Astrology is an occult science based on the premise that one's destiny is ruled and can therefore be predicted by the alignment of heavenly bodies at the time of one's birth. Also, significant events can be predicted according to the alignment of heavenly bodies.
6. Alchemy involves the converting of base metals into gold and silver. This physical system can be spiritually interpreted. One may be spiritually transformed, coming into a "golden" knowledge of oneself by a gradual process of spiritual enlightenment. Depending on one's occult tradition, and thus his or her definition of God, this spiritual illumination may come in different ways. The *Philosopher's Stone*—in the physical science the foundation stone for the existence of all elements, and, in the metaphysical (spiritual) sense, the foundational knowledge of the oneness of life and creation—plays a central role in Alchemic philosophy.
7. *A Bridge to Light,* 158.
8. Ibid., 159.
9. *Legenda,* xix–xxx (Washington, D.C.: The Supreme Council of the Southern Jurisdiction, 1884), 5. Reprinted by Kessinger Publishing Co., Kila, Mont., n.d.
10. According to Hutchens, "pontiff means 'bridge builder'" (*A Bridge to Light,* 162).
11. *Legenda,* xix–xxx, p. 11.
12. *Morals and Dogma,* 461–62.
13. *The Magnum Opus,* xix…3; *Liturgy,* pt. 4, p. 14.
14. *The Magnum Opus,* xix…4; *Liturgy,* pt. 4, p. 15.
15. *The Magnum Opus,* xix…4; *Liturgy,* pt. 4, p. 16.
16. *The Magnum Opus,* xix…4.
17. It is not specified in the *Liturgy* that several brothers state the following, though the quotations taken from *The Magnum Opus* specify three brothers reciting.
18. Rev. 20:4 states that these shall reign with Christ a thousand years. Ritual does not mention this.

19. By "Word" the Scottish Rite does not mean Jesus Christ. Freemasonry would never state such a dogma. Pike intends more of a Gnostic/Qabbalistic type of "emanation" for the "Word." See his interpretation of John 1:1 under the eighteenth degree in chap. 7.

20. *The Magnum Opus,* xix…5; *Liturgy,* pt. 4, pp. 16–17.

21. *The Magnum Opus,* xix…5; *Liturgy,* pt. 4, pp. 17–18.

22. To interpret "Great Babylon" as "Intolerance" is an example of incompetent exegesis. The phrase should rightly be interpreted according to the Old Testament usage. Of course, the revelation of Yahweh to His prophets was anything *but* tolerant. All through the Old Testament we have the Lord admonishing His covenant people to turn from the detestable ways of the surrounding nations and not to yoke themselves in harlotry with other gods. False religion and ungodly power in this sense is the "Great Babylon" and is thus John's intent in Revelation. To my knowledge, no Bible commentary, lexicon, or theological dictionary suggests the Masonic interpretation even as an option. For a brief exposition of the word "Babylon," see Gerhard Kittel, ed., *Theological Dictionary of the New Testament,* 10 vols. (Grand Rapids: Eerdmans, 1967), 1:514–17.

23. This is most likely the "New Law of Love" mentioned in the ritual. It is the love shown by every great reformer willing to lay down his life for the common good and the destruction of intolerance. Rev. 22:14 actually reads, "Blessed *are* they that do his commandments" (KJV).

24. This quotation from Rev. 22:14 comes from Jesus, who is the Alpha and the Omega, the beginning and the end, the first and the last (v. 13). The exhortation to obey his commandments must be interpreted in light of the Old and New Testaments' witness, which clearly states that the ability to keep God's commandments comes from the ministry of the Holy Spirit, who is given to those who place their trust in the Jesus Christ of the Bible (Ezek. 36:26–27; John 8:24; Rom. 8:1–17; cf. LXX Deut. 32:39; Isa. 43:10).

25. *The Magnum Opus,* xix…5; *Liturgy,* pt. 4, pp. 18–19. The last sentence quoted is not contained in the *Liturgy,* though that does not necessarily mean it is missing from the ritual as practiced today.

26. *The Magnum Opus,* xix…6.

27. Ibid.; *Liturgy,* pt. 4, p. 19. Up to "heaven." "Prepared as a bride adorned for her husband" is left out.

28. Ibid.

29. *Liturgy,* pt. 4, p. 19; *The Magnum Opus,* xix…6.

30. Some believe that this refers to God the Father, though in light of the immediate context (1:7) and the fact that the Alpha and Omega is the One who is to come (1:8; cf. 22:12–13, 20), it clearly refers to Christ.

31. The KJV contains the allusion to Christ as the Alpha and Omega, the first and the last. Modern translations omit the phrase owing to evidence of textual variation found in extant manuscripts unearthed after the time of the King

James translation. These manuscripts are believed to be more reliable, and thus the omission.

32. Remember, by "Redeemer" Pike, and consequently ritual, does not mean the Lord Jesus Christ. Pike probably was referring to the Gnostic "Redeemer Christ." See n. 74.

33. *Liturgy,* pt. 4, p. 19; *The Magnum Opus,* xix…6.

34. Ibid.

35. *The Magnum Opus,* xix…6. See also the *Liturgy,* pt. 4, p. 20, where a drawing of an altar appears with a Hebrew inscription that means "the vows."

36. This is the biblical personage of Melchizedek, mentioned in Gen. 14:18 and Heb. 7:1–4. Melchizedek means "King of Righteousness" (Heb. 7:2). It may also be translated "my King is Righteous."

37. See the previous note.

38. *Liturgy,* pt. 4, p. 20. *The Magnum Opus,* xix…7.

39. *The Magnum Opus,* xix…7.

40. *Liturgy,* pt. 4, p. 20; *The Magnum Opus,* xix…7. One of the ornaments of this degree is a breastplate, obviously patterned after that of the high priest of Israel. It contains twelve different gems in a four-by-three matrix, each gem having the initials of twelve different names, or attributes, of Deity (see *A Bridge to Light,* 161).

41. The full deity and humanity of Christ is of great salvific importance. Because of His fully human nature He is able to redeem us in all our make-up as humans. In Heb. 2:17 the conjunction *hina* signals a purpose clause: He was made like His brethren in every respect [full humanity] *in order that* He might become a merciful and faithful high priest to God, and that He might make atonement for the sins of the people. Additionally, without His being fully God He would not be able to redeem humanity.

42. The Greek *aparabatos,* found nowhere else in the New Testament, is usually interpreted as "without successor." It could also mean "untransferable" or "inviolable." The context certainly favors all the above, given Christ's uniqueness as the Son of God (Greek, *monogenēs* in John 1:14, 18), the all-sufficiency of His sacrifice, and His supremacy.

43. *Liturgy,* pt. 4, p. 28; *The Magnum Opus,* xx…1; *A Bridge to Light,* 169. The Hebrew for "light" is *or.* Hutchens transliterates it *Aur.*

44. *The Magnum Opus,* xx…5, see p. 18.

45. Albert Pike, *The Book of the Words* (Kila, Mont.: Kessinger Publishing Co., n.d.), 151. Masonic researchers will recognize that this word is also a part of the seventh degree of the York Rite of Freemasonry, the Royal Arch degree, with the same meaning attached (with *om* being replaced with *on,* which refers to the Egyptian deity Osiris). See Malcom Duncan, *Duncan's Ritual of Freemasonry* (New York: Dick & Fitzgerald Publishers, n.d.), 223–25, and John Sheville and James Gould, *Guide to the Royal Arch Chapter* (Richmond: Macoy Publishing and Masonic Supply Co., 1981), 180. The *Autho-*

rized Chapter Guide to All Capitular Degrees for the Use of Royal Arch Masons (Grand Chapter of the State of New York, R.A.M., 1955), 152–63, relates the same esoteric lesson as has been discussed (the loss of the Sacred Word, the quoting of Ex. 6:3, the recovery of the Sacred Word, etc.). Furthermore, the Apron of the degree of the Royal Arch "is worn as a mark of distinction, separating us who know and worship the true Name from those who are ignorant of this august mystery" (*Authorized Chapter Guide,* State of New York, 157–58).

46. *The Magnum Opus,* xx…14. The *Liturgy* states, "The Master bears the Light of Truth into the World, to overcome Falsehood and Error" (pt. 4, p. 37). What "Truth" is alluded to here?

47. *Liturgy,* pt. 4, p. 77. See also *The Magnum Opus,* xxiii…9.

48. *The Magnum Opus,* xxiii…4.

49. Ibid.; *Liturgy,* pt. 4, p. 76.

50. *Liturgy,* pt. 4, pp. 64–70.

51. *The Magnum Opus,* xxiii…5; *Liturgy,* pt. 4, p. 78.

52. *The Magnum Opus,* xxiii…4. The candidate enters what is known as "the cell of probation and purification" and is then brought to Light. This occurs after his "having repented of his sins" (*A Bridge to Light,* 197).

53. *A Bridge to Light,* 193.

54. Ibid., 158.

55. *Liturgy,* pt. 4, p. 92.

56. Brahma. Throughout this book the proper sanskrit transliteration is not used.

57. Vishnu.

58. Shiva.

59. *The Magnum Opus,* xxiv…3. This "Godhead" of Reason, Power, and Intelligence is far removed from the tri-personal God of the Bible, who is Father, Son, and Holy Spirit.

60. Profaners are persons not worthy to receive the true light. In ancient Gnosticism they were the *Sarkikoi.* The Gnostics who were able to see spiritual truth were called the *Pneumatikoi.* In this degree the profane are symbolized by the rough ashlar and the enlightened by the perfect cube.

61. *Liturgy,* pt. 4, pp. 104–5.

62. Ibid., 103; *The Magnum Opus,* xxiv…8. See *A Bridge to Light,* 205. For a brief explanation of Qabbalistic philosophy, see chap. 5, n. 11.

63. *The Magnum Opus,* xxiv…4.

64. *The Magnum Opus,* xxiv…10–41. See *A Bridge to Light,* 206–10.

65. *A Bridge to Light,* 214.

66. Ibid., 213; *Liturgy,* pt. 4, p. 113; *The Magnum Opus,* xxv…2. The latter work replaces *Ursa Major* with *Bootes.* Also, the Phoenician script chosen by Pike fits best with the script of the Moabite Stone, Mesha Stelae of the ninth century B.C. However, the *vav* which Pike has chosen fits best with the Lachish Ostraca of the eighth century B.C., and even then it is a poor match (see James B. Prit-

chard, ed., *The Ancient Near East, Volume I: An Anthology of Texts and Pictures* [Princeton University Press, 1958], 315).

67. *Liturgy,* pt. 4, p. 112. The ellipses here appear in the original. See *A Bridge to Light,* 213.

68. *Liturgy,* pt. 4, p. 112; *A Bridge to Light,* 213.

69. *The Magnum Opus,* xxv...1. The *Liturgy,* pt. 4, pp. 111–12, does not list the gods after the biblical names.

70. *The Magnum Opus,* xxv...2–3.

71. Ibid., xxv...3.

72. *Liturgy,* pt. 4, p. 114. See also *The Magnum Opus,* xxv...3.

73. A god of a Persian religion called Zoroastrianism.

74. *Liturgy,* pt. 4, p. 114. *The Magnum Opus* leaves out Moses, considering Atys, Adonis, et al., "all Deities that in all ages have represented with most feeble expression the Divine Source of good, the Eternal, Infinite, Incomprehensible, *Father* of Light and Life" (xxv...3, emphasis added). Refer to the quotation in chap. 7 from the source listed in n. 73. Putting these statements together shows evidence that the Scottish Rite views Jesus as one of many personages representing this "Principle of Good."

75. See Kurt Rudolph, *Gnosis: The Nature and History of Gnosticism* (San Francisco: Harper & Row, 1987), 115, 117.

76. *The Magnum Opus,* xxv...3. For the answer portion, see the *Liturgy,* pt. 4, p. 115.

77. See James M. Robinson, ed., *The Nag Hammadi Library* (San Francisco: Harper & Row, 1981). Here, in *The Book of Thomas the Contender* (II.7.139:25–30), we read, "The Savior said, 'O blessed Thomas, of course this visible light shone on your behalf—not in order [that] you remain here, but rather that you come forth—and whenever all the elect abandon bestiality [animal existence, or the body] then this light will withdraw up to its essence, and its essence will welcome it since it is a good servant.'" These two themes mentioned may have some ring of Christian teaching, but the deemphasis of the physical body and the spherical ascent make this and the quotation from ritual distinctly Gnostic.

78. *Liturgy,* pt. 4, p. 116.

79. Rudolph, *Gnosis,* 57, 66–67, 116–17.

80. *A Bridge to Light,* 215.

81. Ibid., 216.

82. Cyril Glassé, *The Concise Encyclopedia of Islam* (San Francisco: HarperCollins, 1991), 132; see also p. 219.

83. *A Bridge to Light,* 216.

84. Ibid., 216–17.

85. Ibid., 217.

86. *A Bridge to Light,* 219.

87. The Druse are a heterodox sect that developed out of a segment of Islam but represent a quite different religion colored by Gnosticism. See Glassé, *Concise Encyclopedia of Islam,* 103.

88. *A Bridge to Light*, 219–20. For an in-depth treatment of the soul's origin and its descent from (and consequent ascent back to) heaven, see *Morals and Dogma*, 436–523.

89. *Morals and Dogma*, 435.

90. Ibid.

91. Ibid.

92. *Liturgy*, pt. 4, p. 127; *The Magnum Opus*, xxvi…1; *A Bridge to Light*, 228.

93. See Williston Walker et al., *The History of the Christian Church*, 4th ed. (New York: Macmillan, 1985), 107.

94. Undoubtedly this is Brahman.

95. These are, respectively, the deities Brahma, Vishnu, and Shiva. See *The Magnum Opus*, xxvi…23.

96. "Over the throne is a triple interlaced triangle . . . which in outline forms a nine-pointed star, in the center of which are the Sanskrit characters equivalent to A, U and M in the Roman alphabet" (*A Bridge to Light*, 229).

97. *Liturgy*, pt. 4, p. 130; *The Magnum Opus*, xxvi…4; see *A Bridge to Light*, 230.

98. *Liturgy*, pt. 4, p. 132; see *The Magnum Opus*, xvi…4; *A Bridge to Light*, 231.

99. *Liturgy*, pt. 4, p. 132; see *The Magnum Opus*, xxvi…5.

100. *Liturgy*, pt. 4, p. 132; see *The Magnum Opus*, xvi…6; *A Bridge to Light*, 231. The ritual substitutes "Spirit" for "Ghost." This verse is not included in modern translations because of a lack of evidence from manuscripts discovered after the KJV was translated.

101. The ritual's language here resembles more the Qabbalistic philosophy. "Wisdom" as an emanation from the Deity and its close relation to "Thought" identify it as such. See A. E. Waite, *The Holy Kabbalah* (Secaucus, N.J.: Citadel Press, n.d.), 204. Also, in the Qabbalistic Tree of Life, "Wisdom" can be taken to be the second emanation from the Deity.

102. This is far removed from the biblical record, which sees Jesus as the Word of God. God has *spoken* to us in these last days through Christ (Heb. 1:2) and *not*, as we shall see the ritual claim, "in the souls of men."

103. *Liturgy*, pt. 4, p. 133; *The Magnum Opus*, xxvi…6.

104. *A Bridge to Light*, 228.

105. *Liturgy*, pt. 4, p. 141; *The Magnum Opus*, xxvi…9.

106. Ibid.

107. Pt. 4, p. 144.

108. Ibid., 147; *A Bridge to Light*, 227; *The Magnum Opus*, xxvi…19.

109. This is heretical. The Father is known to us and by us through Jesus Christ (John 1:18, 14:9; 2 Cor. 4:4; Col. 1:15). Jesus is not an "attribute" of God; the Word, or Logos, is a *person* (John 1:1–3). As we shall see, this quotation proceeds implicitly to call the Word an *attribute* of the unknown God. Again, this philosophy is more in line with the Qabbalah. Here the *En Sof* (the Unknown God) is known through emanations or attributes, of which there are ten, as symbolized by the ten Sephiroth. See chap. 5, n. 11.

110. *The Magnum Opus,* xxvi...36; *Morals and Dogma,* 575.
111. *A Bridge to Light,* 237. Starting from "Behold THE TRUE MASONIC TRIN-ITY . . ."
112. Xxvi...36, emphasis added.
113. Respectively, xxvi...36; p. 237; and 576–77.
114. From the Latin *credo,* "I believe."
115. *Liturgy,* pt. 4, pp. 133–34; see *The Magnum Opus,* xxvi...7.
116. *Liturgy,* pt. 4, p. 147.
117. *A Bridge to Light,* 231.
118. *The Magnum Opus,* xxvi...10; *Morals and Dogma,* 525.
119. *Liturgy,* pt. 4, p. 141; *The Magnum Opus,* xvi...9.
120. *The Magnum Opus,* xviii...15, emphasis added. See n. 66 of chap. 7 and the section on the eighteenth degree for the full quotation.
121. The ritual attempts to show how ancient Gnosticism and early Christianity are compatible, citing examples from such early church fathers as Tertullian and Irenaeus to show that these theologians agreed with Gnosticism (*The Magnum Opus,* xxvi...20–21). In reality, these two Fathers wrote polemically *against* the Gnostics! Tertullian, in his *Against Marcion* and *Against the Valentinians,* and Irenaeus, in his monumental work *Against Heresies,* pull no punches in their condemnation of Gnostic heretical systems.
122. The Scottish Rite, through the influence of Pike, presents the very kind of proto-Gnostic theology that plagued (in its incipient form) the first-century church. Proto-Gnosticism posed a threat to the church at Colossae, prompting the apostle Paul to write of the supremacy of Christ, who is "the fullness [!] of the Godhead bodily" (Col. 2:9). Further, the exegesis of Col. 1:15ff. shows Jesus to be not one of those supposed Aeons or Emanations from God that the heretics claimed helped "create" the world, but the Creator of *them* (Col. 1:15–16)!
123. *A Bridge to Light,* 232. This serves to buttress the thesis of a "canopy" designation. Hutchens does not say "his [the candidate's] deity," but "the Deity."
124. Ibid.
125. *The Magnum Opus,* xxvi...17.
126. Ibid.; *Liturgy,* pt. 4, p. 145.
127. Xxvi...18. Along these lines of ancient Gnosticism, where in its various religious structures the material world and evil were seen either as illusory or a secondary reality not to be trusted, Hutchens makes an intriguing comment. Speaking of "the nine Great Truths of Masonry" that summarize the twenty-third through twenty-sixth degrees, he writes, "Evil is merely apparent, all is in reality good and perfect" (*A Bridge to Light,* 235–36).
128. It is hoped that those Christians with alternative interpretations of the elements will not be offended at my use of "represent." The issue at stake here is whether or not the sacrament of communion is viewed in a Christocentric context.
129. *A Bridge to Light,* 233.
130. We cannot read Hebrews without concluding that Christ is the all-sufficient

sacrifice for sin and the exclusive Mediator of the new covenant of reconciliation to God. To teach about a covenant between God and man that does not involve Christ as the center of the covenant is evidence of biblical ignorance.

131. We must take this to mean any holy book that the candidate places his faith in. The reader is referred back to the books laid upon the Masonic altar in the twenty-fifth degree.

132. Pt. 4, p. 146; *The Magnum Opus,* xxvi…18.

133. See *A Bridge to Light,* 158.

134. See chap. 5, nn. 11 and 12, and this chapter, n. 6.

135. *A Bridge to Light,* 249.

136. Ibid.

137. Ibid., 250.

138. Ibid.

139. See *A Bridge to Light,* 248–49; *Liturgy,* pt. 4, pp. 194–95, 198; *Morals and Dogma,* 583, 598–99, 610–11; *The Magnum Opus,* xxviii…8–25, esp. 16, 28–29.

140. *A Bridge to Light,* 248–49.

141. *The Magnum Opus,* xxviii…28–29.

142. By this term is meant the "Logos" in the Qabbalistic, and thus Masonic, sense (examined earlier). Contained in the same paragraph is this: "The Divine Light, that out-shining of the Supreme REASON or WORD of the Deity, 'which lighteth every man that cometh into the world,' has not been altogether wanting to the devout of any creed" (*Liturgy,* pt. 4, p. 188).

143. *Liturgy,* pt. 4, p. 188.

144. Ibid., 190; *The Magnum Opus,* xxviii…3.

145. The Christian should be aware of this seemingly harmless phrase, which a Mason may use to diffuse an argument. What this phrase really means is that nature points to this God of primitive religion. Scottish Rite Freemasonry also points to Him. That nature points to God is, of course, biblical (Rom. 1:18–20). The question is, *which* God does nature point to?

146. *The Magnum Opus,* xxviii…29.

147. *Liturgy,* pt. 4, p. 189. This is antithetical to Christian doctrine. Though nature reveals the eternal power and divine nature of God (Rom. 1:18–20), it is not sufficient for salvation (Rom. 1:16). Also, the biblical witness is replete with the teaching that in Jesus Christ we have the fullest revelation of God to humanity.

148. *The Magnum Opus,* xxviii… 30. See *A Bridge to Light,* 250–51, and especially the *Liturgy,* pt. 4, pp. 194–95.

149. *The Magnum Opus,* xxviii…29.

150. Ibid., xxviii…42.

151. *Liturgy,* pt. 4, p. 181.

152. Ibid., 182. *Malakoth* means "Kings, Envoys, Angels."

153. Ibid., 185.

154. *A Bridge to Light,* 258.
155. Ibid., 256.
156. Charles Poncé, *Kabbalah: An Introduction and Illumination for the World To-day* (Wheaton, Ill.: The Theosophical Publishing House, 1986), 80, 134.
157. See *A Bridge to Light,* 257.
158. Of course, there is no evidence of the *Ain Soph* in any of the standard Hindu philosophies. Ritual is simply trying to establish its premise that all the world's religions show a coloring of Masonry's one essential doctrinal theme.
159. *Liturgy,* pt. 4, pp. 196–97.
160. Ibid., 197–99.
161. Poncé, *Kabbalah,* p. 140.
162. Ibid., 142.
163. See *A Bridge to Light,* 248, 253.
164. That human beings have been created in the image of God (Gen. 1:26–27) means that God has given to His creatures attributes of Himself that are *communicable,* not *incommunicable.* Communicable attributes are those which are found in infinite measure in God, but can be found in finite measure in God's creatures, such as love. Incommunicable attributes are those found only in God, such as omnipresence. For a further expansion of these, and for a discussion on other classifications of attributes, see Millard J. Erickson, *Christian Theology* (Grand Rapids: Baker, 1985), 266–67.
165. *A Bridge to Light,* 257.
166. Poncé, *Kabbalah,* p. 140.
167. From *The Magnum Opus,* xxviii...30: "The Kabbalistic doctrine was long the religion of the Sage and the Savant; because, like Free Masonry it incessantly tends toward spiritual perfection, and the fusion of the creeds and Nationalities of Mankind."
168. *Liturgy,* pt. 4, p. 225; *A Bridge to Light,* 283.
169. *A Bridge to Light,* 282. Some Freemasons trace the origins of their Craft to the Knights Templar, who, as Masonic historians tell us, went underground during Philip's and the pope's persecution of the Order. See John Robinson's *Born In Blood: The Lost Secrets of Freemasonry* (New York: M. Evans & Co., 1989) for an extensive treatment of this theory of origin. See also the *Liturgy,* pt. 4, pp. 255–91.
170. *Liturgy,* pt. 4, p. 225; *A Bridge to Light,* 283.
171. *Liturgy,* pt. 4, p. 226.
172. *A Bridge to Light,* 283.
173. Ibid.
174. See ibid.
175. See ibid.
176. *Liturgy,* pt. 4, p. 226.
177. See the *Liturgy,* pt. 4, pp. 243, 250.
178. The study of the last days, or end times.

179. This includes Jesus Christ. The reader should note that Jesus is quoted in the ritual of this degree. The *Liturgy,* pt. 4, p. 243, quotes portions of Luke 10:25–28.
180. *Liturgy,* pt. 4, pp. 253–54.
181. *Liturgy,* pt. 4, pp. 260–61; *Morals and Dogma,* 819.
182. *A Bridge to Light,* 228.
183. The Scottish Rite claims that the Christian doctrine of the Trinity is just one of many triad-type or trinity-type doctrines of multiple nations and cultures. We are forced to agree here. However, we must be careful not to draw fallacious conclusions from that observation. Though the Scottish Rite has not, to my knowledge, drawn these conclusions, I want to address them, lest the reader draw them. The truth of the above claim does not necessarily mean that (1) all the different cultures that had triads therefore possessed the truth regarding who or what God is; (2) the triads of other nations are monotheistic, as the biblical doctrine of the Trinity is; (3) the triads of these nations influenced the biblical writers in any way (one must do historical study to see *when* and *where,* for example, the Hindu Trimurti of Brahma, Vishnu, and Shiva, three gods or forms of the one divine essence of Brahman, arose); or (4) the Christian doctrine of the Trinity is therefore false or just as true and valid as any other three-in-one concept.

Regarding 1 above, my response is grounded in the unique disclosure of God in the person of Jesus Christ. If a belief system does not include the biblical Christ revealing the Father, then it must be rejected outright. Regarding 2, of all the world's great religions, Judaism, Islam, and Christianity are truly monotheistic; they affirm the existence of only one personal God. Of these three, Christianity alone affirms one God who is three persons. The Egyptian, Hindu, and Scandinavian religious frameworks mentioned in the twenty-sixth degree are not monotheistic (the Egyptian and Scandinavian are polytheistic; the Hindu, polytheistic/pantheistic). Number 3 is self-explanatory. Regarding our observation, the Hindu Trimurti of Brahma, Vishnu, and Shiva arose somewhere during the post-Vedic era (600 B.C.–A.D. 200). Exactly where it arose is questionable. Moreover, many other examples of triads surface in Hindu literature, though not of Brahma, Vishnu, and Shiva. For example, Arthur A. Macdonell, in his *A History of Sanskrit Literature,* mentions the Rigvedic triad of Sun, Wind, and Fire, and the triad Sun, Indra, and Fire ([New York and London: D. Appleton and Co., 1929], 95). The *Maitrayana-Brahmana-Upanishad,* VI Prapathaka, 5, lists other triads. For this, see *Sacred Books of the East,* ed. F. Max Müller, 50 vols. (Delhi: Motilal Banarsidass Publishers, 1989), 15:308. There is no evidence, however, that the Trimurtis of Hinduism influenced the New Testament writers. The conclusion in 4 is fallacious because the fact that there are many triadic concepts does not necessarily mean they are all false. Nor does it imply that they are all valid or ontologically true. After all, no scientist would say that, on the basis of there being many concepts of why electricity works, all of them are false, or all theories of why electricity works are equally valid or true. The empirical evidence of Jesus Christ's existence and claims must serve as the launching pad for the Christian (after the evidence for the reliability, historicity, and authenticity of the New Testament documents has been satis-factorily established). If Christ is who He said He is, what He claimed about Himself, and if the New Testament writers are correct, then any "trinity" or "triad" without Christ is not ultimately true.

184. *Liturgy,* pt. 4, p. 144.

185. *The Magnum Opus,* xxvi…36; *A Bridge to Light,* 237.

186. *Liturgy,* pt. 2, 4–14, p. 202.

187. See the *Liturgy,* pt. 4, p. 133.

188. See *A Bridge to Light,* 237; *Morals and Dogma,* 575.

189. Although there are so-called gods (1 Cor. 8:5) and idols of various sorts, there is only one God by nature (see Gal. 4:8).

190. I recognize that the thrust of the verse is to communicate judgment upon Ana-nias and Sapphira. Nonetheless, a diagram of the two verses brings out the synonymous parallel of these two phrases: "lying to the Holy Spirit" (v. 3) and "lying to God" (v. 4).

191. In other words, what we have thus far is the fact that there is one God. Yet, we find in the New Testament that the Father is called God (2 Peter 1:17), the Son is called God (John 20:28), and the Holy Spirit is equated with God (Acts 5:3–4). Somehow the three persons are the one God. And this list of verses is far from exhaustive! The Father is repeatedly called God, just as the Son is. The case, however, is not as clear-cut with the Holy Spirit. Here we must rely on the scriptural witness of divine attributes being ascribed to Him (for *Him,* see John 16:13, where, in defiance of the rules of Greek, the masculine pronoun *ekeinos* ["He"] is used to refer to the neuter noun *pneuma* [Spirit]). For example, He is eternal (Heb. 9:14), omnipresent (Ps. 139:7–10), and omni-scient (1 Cor. 2:11).

192. In Matthew the instruction is to baptize "in the name of the Father, and of the Son, and of the Holy Spirit." The cross-reference to Deuteronomy is to clarify the meaning of "name," where the Lord's people were told to seek Him at the place where He would choose to establish His *name* for His dwelling. "Name" means divine presence and authority, which sheds light on the Matthew text. The command for the disciples is to baptize in the name (authority; notice the singular *name*) of the three persons of the Trinity. The three persons are then listed, each with the definite article "the" preceding the noun, and separated by "and" (Greek, *kai*), signifying three distinct nouns (persons).

193. Perhaps the reason why we have in the Masonic Trinity such impersonal terms as Universal Soul, Thought, and the Word, is that, by virtue of their imperson-ality (and thus ambiguity), anything may be read into them. To use "the Word" instead of Jesus lends the possibility that any great example of the "Principle of Good" (Zoroaster, Buddha, Krishna, Confucius, etc.) can be read into the term

(see *Liturgy,* pt. 4, p. 141; *The Magnum Opus,* xxvi…9). See the quotations from these sources listed in nn. 107 and 110.

194. *Liturgy,* pt. 4, p. 104.

195. Ibid., 103. See also *The Magnum Opus,* xxiv…8; *A Bridge to Light,* 205.

196. The "and/or" is so written to accommodate both the trichotomistic and dichotomistic views.

197. *A Bridge to Light,* 220.

CHAPTER 9

THE CONSISTORY: THE HOLY DOCTRINE AND THE ROYAL SECRET

*"A persistent tradition affirms that throughout the ages, and in every land,
behind the system of faith accepted by the masses an inner and deeper
doctrine has been held and taught by those able to grasp it."*
—*Joseph Fort Newton,* The Builders

Degrees thirty-one and thirty-two make up the fourth body of Scottish Rite
degrees, which is called the "Consistory." According to Hutchens, the thirty-
first degree "teaches us that the path to immortality is more than the mere
outward appearance of piety," while the thirty-second degree reviews the
three previous bodies of the Scottish Rite and teaches that the ancient roots of
"Masonic Truth" lie in the East. In addition, symbols of the previous degrees
"are given broader and deeper meaning."[1]

The Thirty-first Degree: Inspector Inquisitor

The thirty-first degree, or Inspector Inquisitor,[2] emphasizes the ancient Egyptian notion of the afterlife and draws from the teachings of the Egyptian *Book*

214

of the Dead.[3] Hutchens notes that some have attempted to trace the origins of the Craft to ancient Egyptian religion, though evidence is lacking, and that "our concern here is a path to immortality which the Egyptians elaborated and illustrated in their writings in a dramatic fashion."[4] This explains why the second section of the degree "takes place in a re-creation of the Court of the Dead in Egyptian mythology, a place where judgment is rendered on the worthiness of a recently deceased man to enter into the kingdom of the gods."[5]

The Council of the Gods

In "the Hall of Justice" of the Lodge are twelve Egyptian deities, some of which have to do with judgment of the dead, justice, truth, and souls. They are Osiris, Atum, Ma, Thoth, Anubis, Horus, Isis, Nephthys, Kebhsenuf, Tuamutef, Hapi, and Amset.[6] Hutchens writes, "The candidate is brought into the Court of the Dead to be judged for actions while living and to determine if he deserves to dwell among the gods."[7] The candidate then pleads his case before the gods (played by other Masons), claiming that he has led a virtuous life. Though the gods find this to be so, outward virtues are insufficient for acquiring entrance into the abode of the gods. The gods ask the candidate more questions, this time about his morality, religious piety, honesty, and selfishness (or lack of it). Finally, the council of the deities vote, some affirmatively and some negatively, as to the candidate's worthiness to dwell with the gods. The final decision rests with Osiris; since he once was a man, he is therefore better able to empathize with human fallibility. His judgment is that the candidate is worthy of admittance.[8]

The gist of this lesson is that men may obey laws, practice charity, and attend church because it is convenient or beneficial for them to be seen by others, and yet these outward manifestations are really worthless. Rather,

> His adherence to the laws of his society are from the respect he has for their moral worth, his charity is painful to himself and his religion is scrupulously private. Such men are striving toward perfection, being the best that they can be, ever seeking better ways to serve their families, their nation and their fellow man. Such are truly the souls worthy to dwell in the Realm of Light.[9]

In keeping with the thesis that all religions are shadows of the one great primitive religion originally given to humanity by God—this religion being preserved throughout history by the Adepts—we find that the Egyptian deities represented in this degree are the result of man's search for truth, though they represent and point to the great "GOD" behind all religions. Thus, "The Hall of Justice" teaches "the lesson of self-judgment, examining not only our actions but our motives, too."[10]

Clothed in White

Next, the candidate, donning a white robe, is led into a strongly lit room called the "Hall of Equity," which represents his admittance "into the Realm of Light where he will have rest and peace."[11] "The duty of this degree," says Hutchens, "is the judgment of each man by himself," as well as "to *inquire* into . . . the favor or displeasure of our Father who is in Heaven."[12] To this end, Blue Lodge symbols—namely, the Square, Compass, Plumb, and Level—teach the candidate correct outward actions and inward moral convictions.[13]

The Thirty-second Degree: Master of the Royal Secret [14]

Hutchens states that the thirty-second degree "unifies into a single coherent doctrine all of the duties and lessons of the preceding degrees. In it we continue our journey eastward in search of the Holy Doctrine of which the Royal Secret is the foundation." The thesis of one great primitive religion surfaces again, and this religion presents the "Holy [or Secret] Doctrine." The "basic truths known by the ancient sages" and the transfer of them to "the future concealed in allegory and symbolism and revealing them only to worthy men" are important objects of the degree. One of the duties Hutchens lists is that "a Soldier of the True Religion [one who holds to the Holy Doctrine, soon to be defined] combats spiritual tyranny [intolerance, loathed by Masons, as shown in the preceding degrees] with reason and truth."[15]

Preliminaries to the Holy Doctrine and the Royal Secret

The degree focuses on the ancient Aryan religion, which Pike considered to be the earliest religion. (Pike theorized that the Aryans were Freemasonry's spiritual ancestors, possessing the Holy Doctrine.[16]) Hutchens describes the Aryans as "a prehistoric tribe of central Asia which settled both Iran and northern India."[17] As a result, the doctrines of the Persians and the Hindus form a large part of the teachings of this degree, and the foundation for exploring the lessons of the degree (though both Persian and Hindu teachings stem from the Aryans).[18] For example, "The altar cover is purple with Sanskrit letters in gold—the letters of the mystic Hindu mantra AUM."[19] Pike taught that this word was brought about by the first initials of three Hindu deities—Agni, Usha, and Mitra.[20] Also, "In the East is a chair reached by ascending seven steps separated into groups of three and four. These numbers are symbolic of many meanings in this degree: . . . the seven stars of the constellation Ursa Major which became the *Amesha Spenta* or 'Bounteous Immortal Ones' of the Persian creed."[21] In turn, the Qabbalists saw in the symbolism of seven the emanations of Deity termed the Sephiroth.[22] Hutchens stresses that "these concepts are here to remind us of the universality of the great religious truths of man."[23]

As we see with the mention of the Qabbalah, this degree does not limit itself to Hindu and Persian creeds. In the west end of the Lodge room are triple interlaced triangles of white, red, and blue, and a five-pointed star of triangles, and these contain hidden meanings. According to Hutchens, "The triple interlaced triangles simply represent that trinitarian concept so common in the world's major faiths."[24] Regarding the colors, "For a Master of the Royal Secret red denotes the material aspect of man. . . . Blue denotes the spiritual aspect of man . . . beckoning man's eyes and thoughts heavenward toward that divine source. . . . White represents the soul itself, reflecting the purity of its original state and demanding of us the highest standards of conduct."[25]

As for the "Holy (or Secret) Doctrine" and the "Royal Secret," some introductory comments are necessary. First, we must remember that Freemasonry deals with the attainment of esoteric "knowledge." That is to say, the truth of the degrees' meanings is hidden even to those who call themselves Masons. The majority of men are not really Masons in the sense that Pike and Scottish Rite ritual mean. The true Mason is one who searches out the hidden truths embedded in the degrees, and studies to unlock the trunk of spiritual treasure so that he may discover and covet the wisdom of the ancient sages, themselves having preserved that one great primitive religion revealed by God to the first man.[26] Second, all through this ritualistic system Freemasonry teaches that all the world's religions are but pointers to the first revealed primitive truth. They contain only some truth, because of the thousands of years of man's overlaying with human concepts nature's revealing of the one supreme God. These finite concepts of Deity corrupt one's idea of the true Deity. As Hutchens asserts, "To be a Soldier of the True Religion is to recognize the corruption of the true religion given to man."[27] Third, in spite of God's true identity being hidden, throughout history there have been those who preserved the true name of Deity, those who saw the common threads of all the religions and looked behind the finitude of humanity's descriptions to encounter the One.

According to the *Readings,* XXXII, "The Sages of all the ancient races had a Secret and Holy Doctrine which was not made known to the People at large."[28] In keeping with our third observation above, "When [People] worshiped the Star, the Sages adored that which manifested itself as the Star. When these worshiped the Fire and Light, the Sages worshiped the Invisible Principle from which the Light flowed out."[29] This doctrine was, according to Pike and, consequently, the Scottish Rite ritualistic lessons, that of the Qabbalah.[30] This philosophy stressed that the Generative Principle (God) extended itself by its thought, and thus, by emanations, the universe flowed or came into being. According to the *Readings,* "The Kabalistic doctrine of creation by generation not only finds its warrant in the language of the Hebrew books [the Old Testament], but evidently obtained among all the ancient nations."[31]

This doctrine teaches that the Infinite is really "Unknowable." Indeed, "Man can have no knowledge or conception of the Infinite Deity. To him the Very Infinite God is as though He were not. We can only say of Him, 'HE IS.'"[32] Ritual and other writings by Pike call this Deity the Qabbalistic *Ain Soph* or *En Sof.* This was the Deity behind all the nations' fallen-short conceptions of God: "Yet was this Unknown Father, Ainsoph, never unmanifested, never inactive, never uncreating. . . . So manifested, or rather self-determined, He was Brahma-Maya and YHVH."[33] In another statement in the *Readings,* we find that "He impersonated Himself as Brahma, the Divine Generator, Who, the YHVH of the Hebrews. . . ."[34] That these are only "notions" of the true God is quite evident.[35] In yet another place we read, "Man must have his household Gods; and it is Christ and the Virgin Mary whom the mass of Catholics worship, as other sects adore Jesus alone and not the Father. Even the Holy Ghost, which is but a name and a myth to the multitude, is worshiped, upon some vague notion that it is possessed of human sympathies. The God of the Hebrews dwelt in the little cubical Holy of Holies of the Temple, on the Mercy-Seat, between the winged bulls called Karobim."[36]

The Holy or Secret Doctrine

Up until the thirty-second degree, Scottish Rite ritual only hints at the Secret Doctrine. Now in this degree it is spelled out for the initiate. That Holy Doctrine seems to be this: God, the Unknowable, the Being (Greek, *to on*) or *Ain Soph,*[37] exists, though veiled behind man's differing ideas of what the Deity is, and can be specially apprehended by the Adepts who have penetrated the veil. Let the reader remember that one of these "ideas" is Yahweh. We have seen in previous degrees that the Scottish Rite is both Gnostic and Qabbalistic, but here it is clearly revealed. Lest Masons argue that the Unknown *is known* in ritual and symbolized by the Hebrew tetragrammaton, the following is cited:

> The Ineffable Name [in past degrees revealed as *YHVH*], the Kabalists said, is not the Name of the VERY Deity, AINSOPH, the MOST HIDDEN; but only of Him Manifested and Self-limited as Creator or Source of the Universe. . . . The Secret Doctrine was substantially the same everywhere; and the Secret Word was the Symbol of the Secret Doctrine; and if any such Word was known to the Sages of the different Nations, it could not have been a Hebrew word; for the Hebrews were, compared to the great Nations, only a Tribe of little importance.[38]

There does, however, seem to be more to the Holy or Secret Doctrine—the immortality of the soul. According to the *Readings,* "The Secret Doctrine everywhere taught that the soul could by heroic effort, patient endurance, and the practice of the virtues, be enlightened and invigorated, and made to resemble God, whose image it is, so as at last to unite again with Him of whom it is an Emanation."[39] This Gnostic notion of an emanation (the soul) returning to its source (God, from whom all have emanated) comes about by "purification" through the practice of "the virtues." (These are most probably "The Four Cardinal Virtues" Temperance, Fortitude, Prudence, and Justice, and those truly commendable virtues, Brotherly Love, Relief, and Truth, mentioned in the first degree of Blue Lodge.) Thus, "From Him all has emanated. From Him all Souls go forth, and to Him, when purified, they return."[40] It seems that "this is the 'Light,' in search of which the Mason journeys. . . . To this end he is taught to practice the principle virtues, by which the body is kept pure and the spirit strengthened and enlightened, and to climb the three, five and seven steps that ascend toward the skies."[41] (These steps are found in the symbolism of the Blue Lodge's Fellow Craft degree.)

Thus, there seems to be a connection between the Secret Doctrine and the first three degrees. Some Masonic authors and Grand Lodges allude to this Secret Doctrine within the general context of Freemasonry.[42] It therefore seems quite probable that the Scottish Rite puts flesh on the bones of the first three degrees of Blue Lodge Freemasonry. This is, of course, only a possibility, since the Secret Doctrine lies buried beneath the symbolic teachings of the Blue Lodge, waiting for the Mason to discover it and join the company of the Sages (Adepts) throughout the ages.

The Royal Secret

So, what is "the Royal Secret"? First, it is the *foundation* of the Holy Doctrine, which we saw earlier. The Royal Secret is "Equilibrium," meaning "the harmony or balance which all of nature demonstrates to us and which is a guide for right living."[43] This equilibrium, or harmony, is also seen within the Deity: it is the balance between divine wisdom and divine power, divine justice and divine mercy, divine omnipotence and the free will of man; between good and evil in the world; and, finally, "between the Spiritual and Divine and the Material and Human in man."[44]

Morals and Dogma, in true Gnostic fashion, states that "this Equilibrium teaches us, above all, to reverence ourselves as immortal souls, and to have respect and charity for others, who are even such as we are, partakers with us of the Divine Nature,[45] lighted by a ray of the Divine Intelligence, struggling, like us, toward the light."[46] Hutchens implicitly concurs, relating that Masons are to **"achieve equilibrium** in [their] lives and attitudes, always recognizing that within *all men* is a minute ray of that Divine Intellect which created the universe; remember that **in man is God,** and that **man is indestructible and immortal.** Such are the great lessons of Scottish Rite Freemasonry!"[47] "Such, my Brother, is the TRUE WORD of a Master Mason; such the true ROYAL SECRET, which makes possible, and shall at length make real, the HOLY EMPIRE of true Masonic Brotherhood."[48]

Biblical Response

Once again the Scottish Rite employs distinctly theological themes, especially in the areas of salvation, humanity, and the apprehension of God.

The Rite assumes that the soul of man emanates (in Gnostic fashion) from God and thus is pure in its original state.[49] Though trapped in a body, the soul is a spark of the Divine. "In man is God," says Hutchens. In the end, a Mason may be admitted to "the Realm of Light"[50] if he practices "the virtues," making him fit to serve his nation, family, and fellow man.[51]

The Bible nowhere teaches this emanational theology (see "Biblical Response," chap. 8). It nowhere teaches that God is, in this sense, universally in all humanity. Or that good works are the ticket to the "Realm of Light." In fact, the Bible teaches the opposite: humanity is sinful in the sense of not obeying the righteous, holy, and just laws of God (see 1 John 3:4; Rom. 3:23); in man's heart, and flowing out of it, are evil thoughts, murders, adultery, fornication, theft, and slander (see Matt. 15:19).

How, then, are we to escape the wrath of God that we all justly deserve? Not by works, so that we may boast (Eph. 2:9). Rather, we are saved by grace through faith (Eph. 2:8), and our faith must be in the only person able to save humanity—the unique Son of God, Jesus Christ (John 1:14, 18; 14:6; Acts 4:12).

From the biblical standpoint, the Holy or Secret Doctrine of the Scottish Rite holds no truth whatsoever. First, the Rite's definition of God as hidden from all except the Adepts is not biblical (see "Biblical Response," chap. 8). Second, to teach that God, though in one sense unknowable, can be known apart from Jesus Christ, contradicts the biblical revelation.[52] Third, if the Secret Doctrine is correct, then Christianity's God (the Hebrews' *YHVH*) is only one of several "pointers" to the Scottish Rite's "ONE TRUE GOD." Biblically, the Scottish Rite's position cannot be sustained. God, the true and living God of the Bible, sent His Son so that the Son may make the Father known to us (John 1:18; 14:9). Again, the point must be made that this claim of Christianity *excludes all other claims or ways of knowing God.*

Notes

1. Rex R. Hutchens, *A Bridge to Light* (Washington, D.C.: The Supreme Council, 33rd, Ancient and Accepted Scottish Rite of Freemasonry, Southern Jurisdiction, United States of America, 1988), 295.
2. Also called *Grand Inspector Inquisitor Commander. The Magnum Opus* calls it *Grand Enquiring Commander.*
3. *A Bridge to Light,* 298. Hutchens calls upon "Wallace-Budge" (*sic*—cf. the spelling below) and his translation of *The Book of the Dead.* See E. A. Wallis Budge, *The Book of the Dead* (Secaucus, N.J.: Citadel, 1960).
4. Ibid., 299.
5. Ibid.
6. Ibid., 300.
7. Ibid., 300–301.
8. Ibid., 301–2.
9. Ibid., 303.
10. Ibid., 305.
11. Ibid., 304.
12. Ibid., 305.
13. See ibid., 306–7.
14. Also called *Sublime Prince of the Royal Secret.* See *The Magnum Opus,* xxxii...1.
15. *A Bridge to Light,* 310.
16. Regarding the Aryans, Pike was greatly influenced by the great nineteenth-century oriental linguist Max Müller (although Müller did not hold Pike's Masonic conclusions). Pike's theory that the Aryans were the possessors of the

Holy Doctrine is at best stretched. Nonetheless, a knowledge of what Pike thought about the Aryans helps us understand his Masonic teaching regarding "knowledge of the TRUE GOD." Interested readers may consult Pike's *Lectures of the Arya; Indo-Iranian Deities and Worship as Contained in the Rig-Veda;* and *Irano-Aryan Faith and Doctrine as Contained in the Zend-Avesta.* All these are available from Kessinger Publishing, P.O. Box 160, Kila, MT 59920. For comments on the Pike-Aryan connection, see Robert A. Morey, *The Origins and Teachings of Freemasonry* (Southbridge, Mass.: Crowne Publications, 1990), 45–48; and Hutchens, *A Bridge to Light,* 311.

17. Ibid., 311. Hutchens does caution his readers that Pike derived his views from the great orientalist Max Müller, who, in the nineteenth century, fathered the study of comparative religion and linguistics. Hutchens notes that Müller's pioneering research, although of great worth, contained "many errors which must be forgiven such an important pioneer in a largely untried field."

18. Ibid., 311–13.

19. Ibid., 313.

20. Ibid. Pike also stated that the word "represented the three Powers combined in [the Hindu] Deity: Brahma, Vishnu, and Shiva; or the Creating, Preserving, and Destroying Powers" (*Morals and Dogma,* 620). For this explanation, see *A Bridge to Light,* 312. *The Encyclopedia of Eastern Philosophy and Religion* (Boston: Shambhala, 1989) states that AUM is "the most comprehensive and venerable symbol of spiritual knowledge in Hinduism . . . it is a manifestation of spiritual power . . . which betokens the presence of the absolute within maya [lit. "illusion"]" (p. 254).

21. *A Bridge to Light,* 314.

22. Ibid., 317.

23. Ibid., 316.

24. Ibid., 317.

25. Ibid., 317–18.

26. An example of this pertains to the "Sacred Word" revealed to the candidate for the Master Mason degree. Pike states, "There are perhaps a few *thinking* Masons to whom it has not seemed strange that the TRUE WORD, promised to every Master Mason, is not given to every one, but only a substitute, of no particular sanctity or significance; not an approximation to the lost Word, but a mere trivial ordinary Pass Word, not even alluding to the Deity" (Albert Pike, *Readings,* XXXII [Washington, D.C.: The Supreme Council of the Southern Jurisdiction], 51). A photographic reproduction of this work can be obtained by contacting Kessinger Publishing Co., Kila, MT 59920.

27. *A Bridge to Light,* 321.

28. *Readings,* XXXII, 117.

29. Ibid.

30. Ibid., 117–19.

31. Ibid., 119.

32. Ibid., 122. This idea is exactly like that of Qabbalistic philosophy: "What is within the Thought no one can conceive, much less can one know the *En Sof*" (*The Zohar,* 1:89). Yet this Deity can be "glimpsed" by and through creation (p. 122). "The first and foremost profound Secret of the Kabalah, the Gnosis, and the other ancient doctrines, was the Cosmogony or Creation" (p. 126). This relates back to the claim of Blue Lodge ritual that one sees God through "the Great Book of Nature." This claim, however, differs from ancient Gnosticism and some Qabbalistic opinions. Here the distaste for the material creation which so characterizes these two philosophies prohibits the speculation that nature reveals, even remotely, the God who is pure Spirit and beyond the touch of defiled matter.

33. Ibid., 131. Here and following the Hebrew consonants of the tetragrammaton have been transliterated for the reader.

34. Ibid., 122.

35. See ibid., 123. Pike taught that these notions of God, if misunderstood, can breed "multitudinous errors."

36. *Readings,* XXXII, p. 134.

37. Ibid., 118.

38. Ibid., 70–71. From *Morals and Dogma:* "I AM, God said to Moses, that which Is, Was and Shall forever Be. But the Very God, in His unmanifested Essence, conceived of as not yet having created and as Alone, has no Name. Such was the doctrine of all the ancient Sages, and it is so expressly declared in the Kabalah" (pp. 848–49).

39. Ibid., 129.

40. Ibid., 78.

41. Ibid., 130.

42. See George H. Steinmetz, *Freemasonry: Its Hidden Meaning* (Richmond: Macoy Publishing and Masonic Supply Co., 1976), 41–49; Manly P. Hall, *The Secret Teachings of All Ages* (Los Angeles: The Philosophical Research Society, Inc., 1988), xx; Joseph F. Newton, *The Builders* (Lexington, Mass.: The Supreme Council, 33rd, A.A.S.R., Northern Masonic Jurisdiction, 1973), 51–61; Henry Pirtle, arr. *Kentucky Monitor,* 13th ed. (Louisville, Ky.: The Standard Printing Co., 1946), xix. Other Grand Lodges do so by recommending Newton's *Builders* to the new Mason. Albert Mackey, in *Mackey's Revised Encyclopedia of Freemasonry,* 2 vols. (Richmond: Macoy Publishing and Masonic Supply Co., 1966), states that "Freemasonry alone has no secret doctrine" (2:920). Here the phrase seems ambiguous. By "secret doctrine" Mackey may simply mean "secret teachings" rather than a specific "Secret Doctrine."

43. *A Bridge to Light,* 323.

44. Ibid., 323–24. Cf. *Morals and Dogma,* 859–61, which Hutchens quotes.

45. Pike, and consequently the Scottish Rite, takes this phrase from 2 Peter 1:4 out of context, making no mention of Christ regarding it. But it is precisely Christ who must be the object of one's faith in order for that person to be a "partaker of

the Divine Nature." Simply read 2 Peter 1:1–3, especially verse one. This puts a limit on those who are partakers, in contrast to the Gnostic-type interpretation asserted by the Rite.

46. *Morals and Dogma,* 861. In the previous note mention is made of the Scottish Rite's taking the stance of Pike and his *Morals and Dogma.* This is because Hutchens also includes this quotation in *A Bridge to Light* (p. 325).

47. *A Bridge to Light,* 322. Italics are added for emphasis, but boldface is in the original. The symbolism of the Evergreen or Sprig of Acacia contained in the Master Mason degree is strikingly similar to what Hutchens says regarding the soul of man. Here man is indestructible and immortal; there the soul is that immortal spark in man that will survive the grave and never, never die.

48. Ibid., 325; *Morals and Dogma,* 861.

49. See *A Bridge to Light,* 317–18.

50. *A Bridge to Light,* 303.

51. Ibid.

52. Since the Rite admits men of all faiths who believe in *a* Supreme Being, and teaches what is documented here, we can come to no other conclusion.

CONCLUSION

Freemasonry is much more than a fraternal order. It is a religion—one that is diametrically opposed to Christianity. Several reasons have been offered here to demonstrate that Freemasonry is a religion. First, it possesses a dogma concerning God. The Masonic god, T.G.A.O.T.U., subsumes the various deities of its initiates. He is addressed, prayed to, and relied upon. Second, the Lodge possesses a dogma about the immortality of the soul and life after death. It defines the soul, and it promises in its burial and memorial services that the soul of a departed brother is in the presence of God, regardless of whether he believed in Buddha, Krishna, Jesus, Brahman, Allah, or Confucius. Third, its symbolism of the Apron, Common Gavel, Plumb Line, Rough and Perfect Ashlars, Three Steps, and Canopy of a Lodge has theological—specifically salvific—overtones. Though a Mason is free to believe in Jesus Christ as the foundation of this symbolic teaching, Christ is viewed as only one of many saviors or exemplars of the principle of good that initiates may choose. Fourth, the Scottish Rite homogenizes Christianity, Islam, Qabbalah, Hinduism, Zoroastrianism, and other religions into a religious ritualistic system that "gleans the truths" from all of these traditions, thereby restoring the "great primitive religion" originally given to all humanity. For these reasons and others, Freemasonry must be considered a religion. For these reasons also I cannot see how a man can be a Christian and an *informed* Mason at the same time.

We should distinguish, however, between whether a Christian *can* be a Mason and whether a Christian *should* be a Mason. Empirically we know that Christians *can* be Masons from the fact that some are. The second question is more pressing, the answer to which is no. No man who claims Christ as Lord should sit back quietly at Lodge meetings or align himself with the Lodge when it makes unbiblical promises, such as that a deceased brother is in the presence of God even if he died rejecting the biblical Christ. The theological teachings of Freemasonry and the exclusive claims of Jesus Christ cannot be mixed. They are mutually exclusive, as we have seen in this examination of Masonic teaching.

What, then, are we to do? The question has both personal and corporate implications; it requires a response from individual Masons as well as the church. Personally, no man claiming to be a follower of Christ should affiliate with the Lodge. Corporately, the church or denomination that confronts this issue faces a long, arduous, and painful task. *Long* because a thorough study of the subject of Freemasonry takes an incredible amount of time; *arduous* because its primary sources, especially the rituals, are not easy to obtain; and *painful* because some of those we love and care for will no doubt be angry at what they deem to be unjustifiable intolerance.

Freemasonry is by no means *the* cancer plaguing the Christian church, though it is one of several. For this reason it must be challenged with solid research and sound biblical doctrine. I respectfully urge those denominations which claim to follow Christ as sovereign Lord but have not taken a stand against Freemasonry to do so. Though some will inevitably hate them for taking a stand, it is far better to have God's favor than man's. It is always true that when the church presents the error of other religions and the truth of Christ, it loses some people. But if some leave the church and continue with the Lodge, it will be made plain that they were never actually in Christ.

It is the truth that sets us free. However, the truth also divides; and that truth is the vehicle by which God leads some to repentance and some to harden their hearts. Let us stand fast.

APPENDIX: AN APPROACH TO SHARING WITH MASONS

Having read this book, you might be wondering, "What now?" Here is an approach you can take in talking with a Mason who claims to be a Christian. (If he does not profess to being a Christian, it is suggested that you first present the gospel to him.)

1. *State the fundamental Masonic principle—that every candidate for Freemasonry must affirm belief in a Supreme Being.* Masons may be Unitarians, Muslims, Hindus, Jews, Buddhists, etc. Men of these faiths, however, do not believe in the Christ of the Bible.

2. *State the fundamental Christian principle regarding truth—that there is a distinction between "It is true for him" and "It is true for him."* The first is subjective; the second is objective. The distinction is between what he *thinks* is true versus what is *actually* true. Earlier in this book I described a person who believes with all his heart that the 1993 Cleveland Indians won the World Series. It is true *for him* (He *feels* that it is true.), but it is not *true* for him (*in reality*). We are concerned with this second category. The fundamental Christian principle is that a statement must be true in reality.

3. *Discuss some of the symbols of Freemasonry.* You might start with the symbolism of the Lambskin Apron. Note how the Lodge teaches that

the Lamb has in all ages been deemed an emblem of innocence. He, therefore, who wears the Lambskin as the badge of a Mason, is thereby continually reminded of that purity of life and conduct, which are so essentially necessary to his gaining admission into the Celestial Lodge above, where the Supreme Architect of the Universe presides.

Ask the Mason if the Lodge thus presents a framework in which the Unitarian, Muslim, or Hindu is *falsely* "reminded of that purity of life and conduct so essential to his gaining admission into the Celestial Lodge above." Stress that his answer needs to concern what is true *in reality*; though it may be true *for him,* it is not *true* for him (John 14:6). You might move on then to note the symbolic teachings of the Covering of a Lodge, the Common Gavel, the Three Steps, the Rough and Perfect Ashlars, etc.

4. *Note that the real issue becomes one of allegiance.* Does the professing Christian want to be a part of an organization that promotes spiritual brotherhood with Hindus, Muslims, and others?

SELECT BIBLIOGRAPHY

Rituals

Authorized Chapter Guide to All Capitular Degrees. New York: Grand Chapter of the State of New York, R.A.M., 1963.

California Cipher. Richmond: Allen Publishing Co., 1990.

The Ceremonies of Craft Masonry. New Brunswick: The Grand Lodge of New Brunswick, 1954.

The Complete Workings of Craft Freemasonry. London: Lewis Masonic, 1982.

Duncan, Malcom C. *Duncan's Masonic Ritual and Monitor*. Chicago: Charles T. Powner Co., 1974.

Emulation Ritual. London: Lewis Masonic, 1986.

The Irish Workings of Craft Masonry in the Three Symbolic Degrees. London: Lewis Masonic, 1957.

Minnesota Cipher. Minnesota Grand Lodge, n.d.

Missouri Cipher. Missouri: Grand Lodge, A.F. & A.M. of Missouri, 1993.

Morin, Stephen. *Francken Manuscript*. Kila, Mont.: Kessinger Publishing Co., n.d.

Official Cipher. Boston: Grand Lodge of Masons in Massachusetts, 1978.

Official Cipher. New Hampshire: Grand Lodge of New Hampshire, F. & A.M., 1975.

Official Cipher. Portland: Grand Lodge of Masons in Maine. Revised, 1963.

The Oxford Ritual of Craft Freemasonry. London: Lewis Masonic, 1988.

Pike, Albert. *The Magnum Opus*. Kila, Mont.: Kessinger Publishing Co., 1992.

The Revised Ritual of Craft Freemasonry. London: Lewis Masonic, n.d.

The Scottish Workings of Craft Masonry. London: Lewis Masonic, 1982.

The Standard Ceremonies of Craft Masonry as Taught in the Stability Lodge of Instruction (Sometimes Known as the "Muggeridge Working"). London: Lewis Masonic, n.d.

The Standard Work and Lectures of Ancient Craft Masonry. New York: The Grand Lodge of Free and Accepted Masons of the State of New York, 1964.

The Sussex Ritual of Craft Freemasonry. London: Lewis Masonic, 1989.

Valentia,Viscount. *Ritus Oxoniensis: Being the Ritual of Craft Freemasonry As Antiently Practised in the Province of Oxfordshire and Elsewhere*. London: Lewis Masonic, 1988.

Monitors

Abshire, Glen R., ed. *Murrow Masonic Monitor and Ceremonies*. Oklahoma: Ancient, Free and Accepted Masons of the State of Oklahoma, 1988.

Allen, R. L., et al. *Tennessee Craftsman* or *Masonic Textbook*. 13th ed. Tennessee: Most Worshipful Grand Lodge of the State of Tennessee, Board of Custodians, 1959.

Bahnson, Charles F. *North Carolina Lodge Manual*. Raleigh: The Grand Lodge of North Carolina, 1991.

Blue Lodge Text-Book. Official Publication of the Grand Lodge of Mississippi, Free and Accepted Masons, 1978.

Bullock, Harris, Earl D. Harris, and James E. Moseley. *Masonic Manual of the Grand Lodge of Georgia*. Georgia: Grand Lodge of Georgia, Free and Accepted Masons, 1983.

Chappell, Will C., David Van Strien, and R. W. Herbert E. Kimball. *Burial Service for the Use of the Lodges Under the Jurisdiction of the Grand Lodge, F. and A.M. of New Hampshire*. New Hampshire: Grand Lodge of New Hampshire, 1956.

The Colorado Craftsman or *Masonic Monitor*. Revised. Colorado: The M.W. Grand Lodge A.F. & A.M. of Colorado, 1985.

Dove, John. *Virginia Text Book*. Highland Springs: Masonic Home Press, 1944.

The Florida Masonic Monitor. Florida: The Grand Lodge, F. & A.M. of Florida, 1992.

Huckaby, G. C., comp. *The Louisiana Monitor*. Walker, La.: Lavergne's River Parish Press, 1988.

Long, Odell S., comp. *Masonic Text Book*. West Virginia: The Most Worshipful Grand Lodge of A.F. & A.M. of the State of West Virginia, 1919.

Mackey, Albert G., ed. *The Ahiman Rezon* or *Book of Constitutions of the Grand Lodge of Ancient Free and Accepted Masons of South Carolina*. 17th ed. Revised by Frank O. Hart. Columbia: R. L. Bryan Co., 1947.

The Maine Masonic Text Book. Maine Printing Exchange, Inc., 1992.

A Manual for the Use of the Lodges. Trenton, N.J.: MacCrellish & Quigley Co., 1919.

Manual of Miami Valley Lodge no. 660. Dayton, Ohio: Free and Accepted Masons, n.d.

Masonic Trestle-Board. Boston: Grand Lodge of Massachusetts, A.F. & A.M., 1979.

Michigan Masonic Ceremonies. Michigan: The Grand Lodge of Free and Accepted Masons of Michigan under the direction of Lou B. Winsor, 1911.

Monitor for the Use of the Symbolic Lodges of Ancient, Free and Accepted Masons Under the Jurisdiction of The Grand Lodge, A.F. and A.M. of North Dakota. Grafton, N.Dak.: The Record Printers, 1965.

Monitor of the Lodge. Waco: Waco Printing Co., 1992.

Official Iowa Monitor. Iowa: Most Worshipful Grand Lodge of Iowa of Ancient Free and Accepted Mason, 1991.

Official Monitor and Ceremonies. New Mexico: The Grand Lodge of New Mexico, 1992.

Pike, Albert. *Liturgy of the Ancient and Accepted Scottish Rite of Freemasonry for the Southern Jurisdiction of the United States,* part 2, 4–14, 1962. (Obtained from the Scottish Rite, Southern Jurisdiction of Washington, D.C.)

———. *Liturgy of the Ancient and Accepted Scottish Rite of Freemasonry for the Southern Jurisdiction of the United States of America*, part 3, 15–18, 1982. (Obtained from the Scottish Rite, Southern Jurisdiction of Washington, D.C.)

———. *Liturgy of the Ancient and Accepted Scottish Rite of Freemasonry for the Southern Jurisdiction of the United States*, part 4, 19–30, 1944. (Obtained from the Scottish Rite, Southern Jurisdiction of Washington, D.C.)

Pirtle, Henry, arr. *Kentucky Monitor*. 13th ed. Louisville: The Standard Printing Co., 1946.

Reed, Thomas Milburne, comp. *Washington Monitor and Freemason's Guide to the Symbolic Degrees.* Revised. Washington: The Grand Lodge of Washington, 1983.

Standard Manual. Oregon: Grand Lodge of Ancient Free and Accepted Masons of Oregon, 1991.

Taylor, Laurence R., comp. *Indiana Monitor and Freemason's Guide.* Indiana: Most Worshipful Grand Lodge of Free and Accepted Masons of the State of Indiana, 1975.

Thummel, George H., Robert E. French, and Francis E. White, comps. *Monitor and Ceremonies.* Omaha: Grand Lodge of Nebraska, 1923.

Webb, Thomas S. *The Freemason's Monitor* or *Illustrations of Masonry.* Providence: Henry Cushing and Thomas S. Webb, 1805.

Other Masonic Sources

Baynard, Samuel H. *History of the Supreme Council, 33rd, A.A.S.R., Northern Masonic Jurisdiction, USA.* 2 vols. Williamsport, Pa.: Grit Publishing Co., 1938.

Cerza, Alphonse. *Let There Be Light: A Study in Anti-Masonry.* Silver Spring, Md.: The Masonic Service Association, 1983.

———. *A Masonic Reader's Guide.* Missouri: Missouri Lodge of Research, 1980.

Claudy, Carl H. *Foreign Countries.* Richmond, Va.: Macoy Publishing and Masonic Supply Co., 1971.

———. *Introduction to Freemasonry.* 1 vol. Washington, D.C: The Temple Publishers, 1959.

Coil, Henry Wilson. *Coil's Masonic Encyclopedia.* New York: Macoy Publishing and Masonic Supply Co., 1961.

———. *Conversations on Freemasonry.* Richmond: Macoy Publishing and Masonic Supply Co., n.d.

deHoyos, Art, and S. Brent Morris. *Is It True What They Say About Freemasonry?* Silver Spring, Md.: Masonic Service Association, 1994.

Gould, Robert F. *The History of Freemasonry.* 4 vols. New York: John C. Yorston & Co., n.d.

Haffner, Christopher. *Workman Unashamed: The Testimony of a Christian Freemason.* London: Lewis Masonic, 1989.

Haggard, Forrest D. *The Clergy and the Craft.* Missouri: Missouri Lodge of Research, 1970.

Hall, Manly P. *The Secret Teachings of All Ages: An Encyclopedic Outline of*

Masonic, Hermetic, Qabbalistic and Rosicrucian Symbolical Philosophy. Los Angeles: The Philosophical Research Society, 1988.

Hammond, William E. *What Masonry Means.* Richmond: Macoy Publishing and Masonic Supply Co., 1975.

Henderson, Kent. *Masonic World Guide.* London: Lewis Masonic, 1984.

Hutchens, Rex R. *A Bridge to Light.* Washington, D.C.: The Supreme Council, 33rd, Ancient and Accepted Scottish Rite of Freemasonry, Southern Jurisdiction, USA, 1988.

Legenda of the Lodge of Perfection. Southern Jurisdiction, USA, 1956.

Little Masonic Library. 5 vols. Richmond: Macoy Publishing and Masonic Supply Co., 1977.

Lodge Plan for Masonic Education: Mentor's Guide. Alberta: The Grand Lodge of Alberta, A.F. & A.M., 1993.

Mackey, Albert G. *The History of Freemasonry.* 7 vols. New York: The Masonic History Co., 1906.

———. *Mackey's Revised Encyclopedia of Freemasonry.* 3 vols. Richmond: Macoy Publishing and Masonic Supply Co., 1966.

———. *The Symbolism of Freemasonry.* Chicago: Charles T. Powner Co., 1975.

Macoy, Robert. *A Dictionary of Freemasonry.* New York: Bell Publishing Co., 1989.

Newton, Joseph Fort. *The Builders.* Lexington, Mass.: The Supreme Council, 33rd, A.A.S.R., Northern Masonic Jurisdiction, USA, 1973.

Perkins, Lynn F. *Masonry in the New Age.* Lakemont, Ga.: CSA Press, 1971.

———. *The Meaning of Masonry.* Lakemont, Ga.: CSA Press, 1971.

Pike, Albert. *The Book of the Words.* Kila, Mont.: Kessinger Publishing Co., reprint, n.d.

———. *Legenda and Readings of the Ancient and Accepted Scottish Rite of Freemasonry for the Southern Jurisdiction of the United States.* Kila, Mont.: Kessinger Publishing Co., reprint, n.d.

———. *Morals and Dogma.* Charleston, S.C.: The Supreme Council of the Southern Jurisdiction, A.A.S.R., USA, 1906.

Roberts, Allen E. *The Craft and Its Symbols: Opening the Door to Masonic Symbolism.* Richmond: Macoy Publishing and Masonic Supply Co., 1974.

Robinson, John J. *Born in Blood: The Lost Secrets of Freemasonry.* New York: M. Evans, 1989.

———. *A Pilgrim's Path.* New York: M. Evans and Co., 1993.

Sheville, John, and James L. Gould. *Guide to the Royal Arch Chapter.* Richmond: Macoy Publishing and Masonic Supply Co., 1981.

Steinmetz, George H. *Freemasonry: Its Hidden Meaning.* Richmond: Macoy Publishing and Masonic Supply Co., 1976.

Street, Oliver Day. *Symbolism of the Three Degrees.* 3 vols. Washington, D.C.: The Masonic Service Association, 1924.

Thorn, Richard P. *The Boy Who Cried Wolf.* New York: M. Evans and Co., 1994.

Tresner, Jim. *The Conscience and the Craft: Questions on Religion and Freemasonry.* New Mexico: Masonic Grand Lodge of New Mexico, 1992.

Waite, Arthur Edward. *A New Encyclopedia of Freemasonry.* New York: Crown Publishers, 1970.

Wilmshurst, W. L. *The Meaning of Masonry.* New York: Bell Publishing Co., 1980.

Non-Masonic Sources

Angus, Samuel. *The Mystery-Religions.* New York: Dover Publications, 1975.

Ankerberg, John, and John Weldon. *The Secret Teachings of the Masonic Lodge.* Chicago: Moody Press, 1990.

Bauer, Walter, William F. Arndt, and F. Wilbur Gingrich. *A Greek-English Lexicon of the New Testament and Other Early Christian Literature.* Chicago: University of Chicago Press, 1979.

Botterweck, G. Johannes, and Helmer Ringgren. *Theological Dictionary of the Old Testament.* 6 vols. Grand Rapids: Eerdmans, 1974.

Bromiley, Geoffrey W., ed. *The International Standard Bible Encyclopedia.* 4 vols. Grand Rapids: Eerdmans, 1979.

Brown, Francis, S. R. Driver, and Charles A. Briggs. *The New Brown-Driver-Briggs-Gesenius Hebrew and English Lexicon.* Peabody, Mass.: Hendrickson, 1979.

Budge, E. A. Wallis. *The Book of the Dead.* Secaucus, N.J.: University Books, 1960.

———. *Egyptian Religion.* New York: Citadel Press, 1987.

———. *Osiris & the Egyptian Resurrection.* 2 vols. New York: Dover, 1973.

Burkert, Walter. *Ancient Mystery Cults.* Cambridge, Mass.: Harvard University Press, 1987.

Clymer, R. Swinburne. *The Mysteries of Osiris* or *Ancient Egyptian Initiation.* Quakertown, Pa.: The Philosophical Publishing Co., 1951.

Cumont, Franz. *The Mysteries of Mithra.* New York: Dover Publications, 1956.

Edwards, Paul. *The Encyclopedia of Philosophy.* 8 vols. New York: Macmillan, 1967.

Erickson, Millard J. *Christian Theology.* Grand Rapids: Baker, 1985.

Ferm, Virgilius. *Encyclopedia of Religion.* New York: The Philosophical Library, 1945.

Finegan, Jack. *Myth and Mystery: An Introduction to the Pagan Religions of the Biblical World.* Grand Rapids: Baker, 1989.

Fox, Robin Lane. *Pagans and Christians.* San Francisco: Harper & Row, 1986.

Glassé, Cyril. *The Concise Encyclopedia of Islam.* New York: HarperCollins, 1989.

Harris, Jack. *Freemasonry: The Invisible Cult in Our Midst.* Towson, Md.: Jack Harris, 1983.

Harris, R. Laird, Gleason L. Archer, and Bruce K. Waltke. *Theological Wordbook of the Old Testament.* 2 vols. Chicago: Moody Press, 1980.

Holly, James L. *The Southern Baptist Convention and Freemasonry.* Beaumont, Tex.: Mission and Ministry to Men, n.d.

Kittel, Gerhard, ed. *Theological Dictionary of the New Testament.* 10 vols. Grand Rapids: Eerdmans, 1964.

Mazar, Amihai. *Archaeology of the Land of the Bible.* New York: Doubleday, 1990.

Morey, Robert A. *The Origins and Teachings of Freemasonry.* Southbridge, Mass.: Crowne Publications, 1990.

Müller, F. Max. *Sacred Books of the East.* 50 vols. Delhi: Motilal Banarsidass, 1988.

Poncé, Charles. *Kabbalah: An Introduction and Illumination for the World Today.* Wheaton, Ill.: The Theosophical Publishing House, 1973.

Pritchard, James B. *The Ancient Near East, Volume I: An Anthology of Texts and Pictures.* Princeton, N.J.: Princeton University Press, 1958.

Rehmus, E. E. *The Magician's Dictionary.* Los Angeles: Feral House, 1990.

Roberts, Alexander, and James Donaldson, eds. *The Ante-Nicene Fathers.* 9 vols. Grand Rapids: Eerdmans, 1977.

Robinson, James M., ed. *The Nag Hammadi Library.* San Francisco: Harper & Row, 1978.

Ronayne, Edmond. *Ronayne's Hand-Book of Freemasonry.* Chicago: Ezra A. Cook Publications, 1985.

Rudolph, Kurt. *Gnosis: The Nature and History of Gnosticism.* San Francisco: Harper & Row, 1987.

Schuhmacher, Stephan, and Gert Woerner, eds. *The Encyclopedia of Eastern Philosophy and Religion.* Boston: Shambhala, 1989.

Southern Baptist Convention, Home Mission Board. *A Study of Freemasonry*. Atlanta: Home Mission Board, 1993.

Sperling, Harry, and Maurice Simon. *The Zohar*. 5 vols. London: The Soncino Press, 1984.

Tsoukalas, Steven. *Freemasonry: Is It a Cult?* Exeter, N.H.: Sound Doctrine Ministries, 1989.

Waite, A. E. *The Holy Kabbalah*. Secaucus, N.J.: University Books, n.d.

Walker, Williston, et al. *A History of the Christian Church*. New York: Charles Scribner's Sons, 1985.

Wilson, Andrew, ed. *World Scripture*. New York: Paragon, 1991.

Yamauchi, Edwin M. *Persia and the Bible*. Grand Rapids: Baker, 1990.

INDEX